MONEY MONSTERS

WinklerMedia Publishing Group, Baltimore, MD

MONEY MONSTERS

Why the Big Banks Should Be Broken Up Before They Destroy the Global Financial System

By

Paul Marano

Contents

PART ONE

GENESIS

Chapter One

Cigar smoke wafted down the hallway in my direction. I enjoyed a good *puro* once in a while myself, but Sandy Weill kept those smelly Te-Amos burning throughout much of the day—even when he could have afforded the more upscale and aromatic Davidoffs—sending billowing blue smoke down the corridor in all directions, depending on which way the air currents were blowing. Between cigars, he bummed cigarettes from my immediate boss, Dave Dworsky, who occupied the office between Sandy and me at One Penn Plaza in New York City, when Sandy visited the branch from his downtown headquarters.

I worked as a stockbroker (um, a *customer's man*) at Shearson, following a four-year stint at Merrill Lynch. A fellow named Fred Friedman had hired me there after a comic-opera episode in my life, the aftermath of which had left me broke and in marital distress. It struck me one morning that what I needed most was money—cold, hard cash—so why not go where the money was? Without dwelling too much on the absurdity of what I was about to do, I sprung from bed one cold, sunny day in mid-November, put on the only suit I owned along with a white shirt and maroon tie, and took the train into Manhattan. I wasn't even aware of where I was going during the train ride into the city, but as I got off in Grand Central, my pace quickened, my confidence picked up, and I listened to an inner voice direct me downtown to Thirty-fourth Street, then due west across town to a Merrill Lynch office I knew about near Penn Station. I knew about the office because a good friend of mine owned the Blarney Stone across the street, and that was where he maintained his account.

"Good morning," I said to the receptionist. "I'm here to see the branch manager."

"May I tell him what this is about, sir?"

"Tell him it concerns a very large account." I knew that would at least get me into his office for an interview. Stockbrokers eat, drink, and snort money, and the mere mention of the word has been known to bring them to the point of orgasm.

Within three minutes, I was ushered into the office of Fred Friedman, a tall, lanky, athletic-looking fellow with thinning blond hair and a king-sized smile stretched from ear to ear across his well-shaved face. The smile began to fade noticeably when I explained that I was not actually there to open a "very large account" with my own money, but instead hoped to open many such accounts later on with money from all the clients I anticipated bringing into the firm during the coming year.

"You … you mean, you're here to apply for a job?"

"As a stockbroker, yes. I've got a lot of contacts in the city, restaurateurs, small-business owners, doctors, lawyers, and I think I could be a great asset to Merrill Lynch."

This type of lunacy went on for fifteen minutes or so when, to my utter astonishment, Fred rose from his desk, stuck out his hand, and asked me if I could start the following Monday. We discussed salary and benefits—yes, he would actually pay me while I was studying to get registered—and I had to restrain myself from running around his desk and embracing this man who had just saved me from bankruptcy and possibly saved my marriage as well. When I asked him one day if he had any leads so that I could build a client base, he tossed the Manhattan telephone directory on my desk and told me to start dialing. "Smile and dial," he said humorlessly. "That's how everybody does it."

I decided there had to be an easier way. That's when I started to write personal finance books hoping that people would take notice and ask me to manage their money for them.

Dave helped me find that easier way to attract a book of clients, with Sandy's backing, after he hired me away from Merrill Lynch. "Sandy wants to mail out fliers about your books to high-level investors and invite them to an investment seminar," he said. "We'll hang posters of your book covers on the wall. You can sign autographs and give a little talk about the stock market."

"Sounds good to me," I said, appreciating this novel marketing approach. "Do you think the legal department will go along with it?"

"Fuck legal! Sandy will take care of legal."

Sandy's marketing program paid off nicely, generating some decent book sales and garnering me a substantial investment clientele within a few months. Shortly afterward, Dave got me promoted to vice president, a move that gave me the privilege of sitting close to one of Sandy's uptown offices, gasping for oxygen in the midst of a toxic cloud of tobacco smoke—not as aromatic as I would have preferred. About six months after I joined Shearson, I noticed that Sandy had begun to put on some weight around the middle.

"Is it me," I asked Dave, "or did Sandy gain about twenty pounds in the last month?"

"He's probably planning to do another deal," Dave said.

"What do you mean?"

"You can always tell when Sandy's going to do a deal. All those lunches every day put the pounds on him. It's a sure sign."

Dave was right. Sandy soon embarked on a buying spree that would have put King Midas to shame. The name of the firm I worked for had changed with dizzying regularity during a few short years. Sandy incorporated other financial institutions under the Shearson umbrella until it reached a point where the brokers had to reprint their business cards every few months or so. How could anyone manage to keep up with the transitions from Shearson to Shearson Hammill to Shearson Hayden Stone to Shearson Loeb Rhoades (which it was when I joined ship in 1979) to Shearson Lehman Brothers to Shearson Smith Barney to Shearson/American Express? Still, no one was complaining. Everyone was making money. I kept writing my financial books and came out with one called *The Money Tree*. On my way into work one day, I turned on the radio and heard a Shearson commercial with the tagline, "The Money Tree: Invest with Shearson."

"Sandy's using my title for his commercial," I said to Dave when I walked in.

"Hey, one hand washes the other. Look at the bright side," Dave said. "Think of how many copies of your book that commercial will sell."

*   *   *

Wall Street has always been a free-wheeling casino with a Wild West culture, but in the 1970s and 1980s the stakes were much smaller than they were thirty years later. When the largest firms got in trouble, like E.F. Hutton, Merrill Lynch, and a host of others did during the silver collapse in 1981, all it took was a mere billion dollars or so to bail them out. Auto giant Chrysler under Lee Iacocca was saved with a billion-dollar loan from the government. Even allowing for inflation, those are pretty paltry sums compared with the trillion-dollar-plus packages required to shore up the financial system after the 2008 meltdown.

But a casino it has always been. Not only Sandy Weill, but virtually the entire financial services industry could flout their legal departments with impunity back then. It was an era when stockbrokers (or whatever euphemism they employed) were rewarded with week-long, all-expenses-paid vacations in Hawaii for churning their clients' accounts and encouraging them to day trade for quick profits when the market was soaring. Back-and-fill, they called it. "Go back to your clients, create a need for new investments, and then fill them." When the market got a bit sluggish, you could always find a floating crap game in many branch offices if you knew where to look for them.

Those were also the days when being a stockbroker was an all-male preserve. With almost one hundred male brokers ensconced at One Penn Plaza, plus countless others spread out among Shearson's innumerable branch offices throughout the country, the federal government finally put pressure on the financial industry to start training a few women to flesh out its ranks. Shearson hired a young divorcee named Debbie, who learned the business at a desk in the middle of a huge bullpen area surrounded by a legion of raucous men pitching their clients over the telephone.

Unfortunately, Debbie got off to an ignominious start when she violated the first rule of investing: don't put all your eggs in one basket. Debbie invested her first client's entire life savings in Municipal Assistance Corporation bonds, which had been floated by New York State in 1975 to rescue New York City from bankruptcy. Most of his nest egg went down the tubes when the state's MAC bonds plunged in value from day to day, as investors grew concerned about New York State's ability to make the astronomical 11% interest rate payments on the debt. At the time, high-level municipal bonds yielded only 6.9%, so the MAC obligations were regarded as junk. Mr. Sorenson came roaring into the office screaming, his mouth foaming over.

"Where is she?" he howled. He spotted her looking back at him, hollow-eyed at her desk in the middle of the bullpen, and dashed over to her. "You! How could you do this to me? A quarter of a million dollars! Everything I had! And now, poof, it's gone! Just like that! Up in smoke!"

And then the poor man collapsed into a chair beside her desk, put his hands up to his face, and started to cry. The entire bullpen was silent. The other brokers stopped their conversations in mid-sentence, phones on their ears, and stared horrified at the drama unfolding before their eyes. It could have been any one of them, they knew. "Thank God it wasn't me," they all thought. Debbie sat stone still observing her defeated client, too terrified to open her mouth. No excuse was good enough for what had happened to him. Finally, she blurted out,

"Oh, don't be such a baby!"

Mr. Sorenson raised his head, looked at her incredulously, and then stood up. With his shoulders slumped forward and his face an ashen mask, he simply turned around and walked out of the office.

It took me a microsecond to rush over to Debbie's desk. Everyone in the office was stunned, just staring. "Debbie, how could you say a thing like that to him?" I asked her.

She looked up, tears streaming down her own cheeks now. "I couldn't think of anything else to say," she said. Then she got up and left for the day. A moment later, all the other brokers returned to their pitches, promoting the latest hot stock they had to offer. After a while, Debbie got through her rookie initiation period without further complications and went on to become one of the more successful brokers at Shearson.

The saddest case of all was a cabdriver who visited the office one afternoon and insisted on investing everything he had saved, $35,000, in one stock—a company named Resorts International, which at the time was essentially two wise guys with a post office address in the Bahamas. To call Resorts a speculative investment is to refer to Jack the Ripper as something of a misogynist. The entire gambling industry was soaring, led by Resorts, which doubled and then doubled again in price every few days or so. There was nothing behind many of the companies, no earnings, no revenues, no cash flow, to drive them skyward, other than the prospect of riches down the road as legalized gambling turned into a national passion. The price of Resorts stock kept climbing, $4, $8, $16, $28, over just a few weeks. The reporter who wrote the "Heard on the Street" column for the *Wall Street Journal* tried to dampen the frenzy, with frequent warnings about Resorts and other gambling stocks having nothing of substance to back them up. But no one wanted to listen; all anyone cared about was the idea of raking in profits from stocks that defied the laws of gravity and sanity. The cabdriver insisted on following suit even though the investment was totally inappropriate for him. So after much deliberation, and the signing of documents relieving Shearson of responsibility for his action, Dave reluctantly allowed the trade to go through.

And the cabbie got rich—at least on paper, at first. He rode Resorts all the way up to $200 and then $300 a share and bought more of it on margin. The $35,000 he started with rocketed to $850,000 on the strength of this one bogus stock alone. Dave begged him to sell at least half of his position, lock in a $400,000 profit and let the rest ride if he wanted to, but the cabbie refused.

"I've always wanted to be a millionaire," he said. "When my account hits a million dollars I'll sell. But not before."

That was about two days before the gambling market tanked. The balloon burst, letting all the air out with one enormous, instantaneous hiss. It was the last fool theory at work; people woke

15

up one morning and said, "This is crazy. These stocks aren't worth that much. Get me the hell out now before the market craters." Resorts and the other gambling stocks plunged to earth at breakneck speed, destroying net asset values all the way down. The cabbie's account shriveled to $35,000, the amount he started with, before he sold out. At least he salvaged his original investment. He walked out a chastened but wiser man, never to be heard from again.

The energy stocks were next to skyrocket along with interest rates and super-inflation in the final years of the Carter administration. Traders would walk in off the street, buy 1,000 shares of Mesa Petroleum at ten in the morning and sell them by noon with a $4,000 profit. Mesa was just one of many oil stocks you could not lose money on. Apache, Hess, Marathon—they were all racing to the moon. You could throw darts at a list of them and end the day with a smile on your face. And then that craze also ended as abruptly as it started. Paul Volcker started to raise interest rates to tame the inflationary spiral, and the oil and gas stocks turned to sacks of molten lead. Shearson's office at One Penn Plaza turned into a graveyard as stock prices continued to plunge. One broker stood up in the middle of the bullpen and tore up a stack of order sheets.

"The party's over!" he yelled at the assemblage of investors who came in every day to watch the tickertape rattling on the wall overhead. "The party's over! It's time to go home!"

His performance sent Dave charging out of his office as though his pants had caught fire. "Shelley!" Dave called as he raced into the bullpen. "A little decorum, Shelley! What the hell's wrong with you?"

*　　*　　*

16

Well, the party was over temporarily, but not for Sandy Weill. Falling stock prices translated into meager pickings for brokers and most of the industry, but Shearson had done well under Sandy's stewardship, generating record profits even when the market doldrums descended with full force. He had already gobbled up most of the financial institutions that appealed to him—a case of a minnow swallowing sharks in the earlier stages—and he was not yet done. He started to put on weight again, a sign that something was in the offing with those daily lunches he ate at the Four Seasons and other expensive restaurants. Mortgage rates hit the mid-teens, the prime rate soared to more than 21 percent, inflation began to resemble the pace experienced in the Weimar Republic after World War I, and the Dow Jones Industrial Average dipped below 800. But the party was not over for Sandy.

In 1981, he called a meeting in headquarters downtown to announce that he had just done another deal, but this one was a shocker. After absorbing other institutions into his growing empire for two decades, Sandy said that he was *selling* his company to financial titan American Express. We sat around the aircraft carrier-sized conference table too dumbfounded to speak. *Selling!* Did Sandy actually say that he was selling the conglomerate he had put together since he started out in the business in 1960? Not even Dave, who had grown up with Sandy in Brooklyn and had been with him every step along the way, had an inkling that this shocking turnabout was in the cards. We took it all in silently and then left in shock, wondering what this could possibly mean for our futures in the industry. Acquisitions always involved cost-cutting, which translated into a loss of "redundant" jobs.

Early the following year, Sandy summoned us to another one of his frequent, anytime-of-the-day meetings that he liked to call on the spur of the moment. This time, with the sale to American Express now a done deal, Sandy wanted everyone to meet his new executive assistant, a good-looking young man in his mid-twenties whom he introduced as a Harvard Business School graduate named Jamie Dimon. We were familiar with the last name, since Jamie's father Ted had been a Shearson stockbroker for as long as anyone could remember—in fact, he was Sandy's personal stockbroker. The Dimons and Weills socialized with one another in Greenwich, Connecticut, where both families had weekend retreats, and Jamie and his siblings got to know Sandy's offspring well as kids. We welcomed Jamie on board the Shearson/American Express bandwagon and wished him well.

The easy interpretation at the time was that he was a privileged rich kid, who had landed his envious position just out of business school because of family connections. None of us gave him much thought beyond that in the beginning. Little did we know that Jamie Dimon would go on to surpass his new boss, in many ways, as a major power in the financial services industry.

Chapter Two

On the surface at least, Sanford I. Weill and Jamie Dimon appeared to be a study in opposites. Sandy, who was gruff by nature and rough around the edges, liked to talk about his working-class roots growing up in Brooklyn, New York, and how he propelled himself up the corporate ladder until he occupied the top rung through his own cunning and daring. It was true—to a point. But in reality, he was not quite the self-made man from a poverty-stricken family that he liked to portray himself as. He was born in 1933, the year the Glass-Steagall Act became law, delineating the line separating investment banks and commercial banks. Essentially, investment banks were restricted to underwriting and trading securities, and commercial banks were limited to accepting deposits and making loans. The law remained in effect for sixty-five years, until Sandy—with Jamie by his side—got it overturned in 1998 to accommodate their own ambitions.

Sandy's parents, Mac and Etta Weill, were Polish Jews who gave their first-born son the middle initial "I" in the hopes that he would flesh it out with a name of his own choosing when he turned twenty-one. "My mother wanted to name me after somebody whose name started with an 'I,' but she couldn't think of a name she liked," Sandy explained. He never did get around to finding one that *he* liked either. In the beginning they were poor, living in a large, but cramped, house with their extended family during the early years of the Great Depression. Sharing the two-family structure on Bay 26th Street with Sandy and his parents were Etta's mother, father, sister, and brother.

Mac was eager to start his own business, and in 1936 he launched a dress-making factory in the heart of Manhattan's Garment District with his father-in-law Louis Kalika. Their timing couldn't have been worse. Within their first week of operation, the garment workers went on strike, nearly plunging Kalika and Weill Dress Manufacturers into bankruptcy. Sandy tried to help out paying the bills by delivering newspapers and taking on various odd jobs where he could find them. During the war, the dress-making business began to boom and the Weill family coffer grew fatter. But when Sandy was eleven years old, his father was driven out of the business for good when he pled guilty to violating wartime wage-and-price controls for underpaying workers and overcharging for his merchandise. He was hammered with a $10,000 fine—which he somehow managed to pay off in three installments by depleting his wartime profits—and a suspended three-year prison sentence. In 1945, Mac moved his family to Miami Beach, Florida, to make his fortune in the steel business. The Florida sojourn ended in another disaster.

"I hated it there and did lousy in school," Sandy said.

So back to Brooklyn they went, this time to a house on 12th Avenue, skirting the boundary separating Flatbush and Borough Park. With the war now over and the economy back on an even keel, the Weill family fortunes took a turn for the better again. Mac and Etta were in a comfortable enough position to send fourteen-year-old Sandy up the river—up the Hudson, that is—to the Peekskill Military Academy, a few miles south of West Point. There was enough money flowing in to the family treasury to pay the tuition, but there was another reason why his parents wanted Sandy out of the house.

"Sandy's parents had a marriage that wasn't going too well," said Stuart Fendler, one of Sandy's roommates. "We went there because every kid was a problem." The Weills' marriage did end in divorce a few years later, when Sandy was in college. Marc left Etta for a younger woman before moving on to wife number three.

Sandy found his niche in sports, however, surprising even himself with his prowess on the tennis court. Sports at the military academy meant either swimming or tennis. Despite growing up near the ocean in Brooklyn and spending two years in Florida, Sandy had never learned to keep his head above the water, let alone propel himself at speed down the length of an Olympic-sized pool. So he picked up a tennis racket for the first time in his life and discovered that he liked thwacking balls at an opponent on the other side of the net.

"We just hit ball after ball," Fendler said. "We'd just keep playing. I could never beat Sandy in tennis."

Sandy became the star of the team and was good enough to be invited to try out for the Eastern U.S. Junior Davis Cup team. His Big Man on Campus status earned Sandy his father's respect. Mac had been an aloof father until now, totally absorbed in his own rising and falling fortunes throughout Sandy's life, and he had never paid much attention to his son, who was more like him than he cared to admit. Mac suddenly found the time to drive up to Peekskill most Sundays to watch his first-born child kick butt on the tennis court.

"He'd walk up the hill, this big guy smoking cigars," Fendler recalled. "He seemed a hard, serious guy."

In 1951, at age eighteen, Sandy graduated third in his class from the academy and began to scout around for a college that would prepare him for a lucrative career. He had a natural gift for numbers, and he believed that space travel was the wave of the future. America needed engineers, and a so-called "engineering gap" was widening between the U.S. and the Russians, who had soared ahead in what promised to be a booming industry with serious military consequences. His grades were high enough to gain him admittance to any number of universities, including Harvard and Cornell.

He chose Cornell. "It had an engineering school and Harvard didn't," he said simply.

Cornell was also more welcoming to minorities, including Jews, African-Americans, and women, while Harvard and the other Ivy League enclaves were largely WASP-dominated institutions for the scions of Old Money families at the time. Sandy felt more comfortable in the liberal Cornell environment, but he soon discovered that adding up numbers and spitting out the answers was not a sufficient requirement for mastering Cornell's rigorous engineering program. On the verge of flunking out, he abruptly switched his focus to government and political science, which he labeled "a good bullshit major." He underestimated the influence of politics as a young man, since he later learned that government just looked like bullshit from a distance, but it paid off mightily when you had friends in positions of great power.

Just as Sandy's parents' marriage was unraveling beyond repair, Sandy met the woman with whom he would share the rest of his life. She was a slim, attractive education major with auburn hair named Joan Mosher. The two got together on a blind date set up by friends and clicked immediately. They were both bright and ambitious, interested in the same things, and the chemistry between them blended smoothly. Their courtship was brief, culminating in a Conservative Jewish wedding in June 1955. Ironically enough, Sandy's father Mac married his second wife the following day and failed to make his son's wedding or reception at the Essex House on Central Park South in Manhattan.

*   *   *

Now Sandy had to establish a career, and his Bachelor's degree in government didn't really prepare him for anything enticing. His big interest was numbers, particularly numbers that added up to lots and lots of dollars. He knew he wanted to make money more than anything else. Money was the name of the game; without it you were just an ordinary piker.

"Sandy was driven by money," his public relations director at Citigroup commented years later. "How he made it wasn't important. If there was a fortune to be made selling shoelaces, he would have done it."

He stumbled across the world of stock-trading serendipitously. Stocks were all about money. The higher they went in price, the more money you made. Wandering around Manhattan one day, without giving much thought to where his feet were carrying him, he spotted a branch office of Bache & Company on Forty-first Street and Seventh Avenue, just a few blocks north of his father's and grandfather's old dress business in the Garment District. Why he had headed in this direction, he couldn't say. He stepped inside and was instantly mesmerized by the spectacle of numbers clicking by on the overhead tickertape, and a bullpen full of brokers pitching their clients frantically over the phone on one stock after another. It was like a casino. It was exciting. It made his heart pump faster. Damn it! This business was made for him.

In those days, Wall Street was segregated into two major factions. The dominant one by far was the Old Money WASP machine, whose powerhouse companies were J.P. Morgan, E.F. Hutton, and others of that ilk that wouldn't hire Jews. The second contingent, created in self-defense as it were, was the Old Crowd German-Jewish establishment, including such stellar firms as Goldman Sachs, Lehman Brothers, Salomon Brothers, and others like Bache & Company, which didn't hire WASPs or Eastern

European Jews. Sandy got his first lesson in intra-ethnic bigotry when Bache refused to hire him for its stockbroker training program.

"Nobody said it was because I was not the right kind of Jew, but the message came through loud and clear."

Sandy was not the type of person who was going to let an impediment like that stand in his way. By his own admission he didn't know much about the financial world. "Hell, I didn't know that savings banks didn't allow you to write checks," he said. "That's how much I knew." But what he did know was that he was going to get his foot inside the door of one of these private clubs one way or another. He was not of the Old World or of the Old Crowd. But there had to be an opening out there for someone from the New Crowd, and he was determined to find it if he had to carve it out for himself.

He kept pushing, paying his and Joan's living expenses by selling some of their wedding presents, until he found the crack in the façade he had been searching for. He started off on the lowest rung of the ladder, as a "runner" for Bear Stearns, carrying buy and sell order slips from the brokers to the traders on the floor of the New York Stock Exchange. His salary was $150 a month, a puny sum even back then. But the slips he carried from the brokers were worth their weight in gold to him. They conveyed the best education he could hope for. He quickly learned which stocks were hot and which were not. His dream was to put together a stake of his own.

"I remember thinking that if I had $10,000, I could buy all the stocks that I'd ever want to buy," he said.

*   *   *

Jamie Dimon had it easier from the start. Born in 1956, he was young enough to be Sandy's son. Jamie's grandfather, Panos Papademetriou, was an ethnic Greek who emigrated to the New World from Smyrna in 1919 with barely a penny in his pocket. His first stop was Canada, but he knew from the start that his ultimate destination would be New York City, the citadel of American finance and capitalism. He had been a banker in his homeland before Greece's war with Turkey, but breaking into that profession in the U.S. was more difficult than he had hoped. First of all, his last name was virtually impossible for most Americans to pronounce. And, second, he lacked the proper educational credentials and family background. He swallowed his pride and applied for a job as a dishwasher, after changing his last name to Dimon, which he thought sounded vaguely French. He was fluent in French and Greek, and quickly picked up enough English to qualify for a low-paying job.

With his intelligence and drive, however, it was just a question of time before he worked his way into his industry of choice. The National Bank of Greece opened a subsidiary in New York under the name of the Bank of Athens. Panos landed a job as a clerk, married a woman of Greek descent, and quickly discovered that the most lucrative area of any commercial bank is the loan department—particularly residential mortgages. Within twenty years, he had risen to the exalted level of vice president in charge of the bank's lending operations. Along the way, he and his wife fathered a son, Theodore, and in 1949 Panos exited the banking business to take a job as a stockbroker at Shearson Hammill.

Theodore, or Ted as he preferred to be called, followed his father into the brokerage arena four years later, following his marriage to Themis Kalos, also the child of Greek immigrants. Panos had a thriving book of clients by then, and he greased the way for Ted to prosper as well, introducing him to the world of Greek restaurateurs and entrepreneurs who had grown wealthy in the fertile American economic soil. Ted and Themis produced three sons: the oldest was born in 1954 and was named Peter, and he was followed by fraternal twins born on March 13, 1956. They were christened Ted, Jr., and James, who would go on to achieve a level of fame and infamy as Jamie Dimon. Over dinner one evening when Jamie was nine, his father asked his sons what they wanted to be when they grew up.

"A physician," Peter replied without hesitation.

"I don't know," young Ted responded.

"I want to be rich," said Jamie.

It was apparent even then, Jamie's father later said, that Jamie "wanted to run something and have power."

Jamie was the apple who fell closest to the tree planted by his grandfather and nurtured by his father. All three placed the pursuit of money—and in Jamie's case, money combined with power—foremost on their list of worthwhile human endeavors.

* * *

The Dimon family lived in a small town in East Williston, a few miles east of the Queens border in Long Island's Nassau County. But as the family's wealth grew over the years, the Dimons set their sights on pricier real estate, first in Jackson Heights, Queens, then in tonier Larchmont in Westchester County, north of the city. From there, Ted commuted by car to his office at Shearson Hammill on Fifth Avenue and 44th Street, and his sons attended the Murray Avenue School, a public elementary school, while they lived there. Jamie's reading tastes told the story of his real interests in life, ranging from math and other quantitative subjects to J. Paul Getty's *How to be Rich*. His favorite pastime, aside from sports, was memorizing long lists of figures, including a virtual encyclopedia of telephone numbers. Family conversations also fostered his passion for the subject.

"I learned a great deal about the brokerage business across the kitchen table," he later said.

Ted, Sr., got tired of commuting after a year in Larchmont and decided that he could afford the really good life closer to his job—a lot closer. Never a man who believed in borrowing money, he paid cash for a four-bedroom co-op apartment at 1050 Park Avenue, between 86th and 87th Streets, a brisk walk to his brokerage office when the weather was good. Otherwise, he drove the forty blocks rather than take the subway. He could also afford to finance an upscale education for his boys, so he sent them to a small private prep school located in a converted town house at 52 East 62nd Street. The Browning School was founded in 1888 by John A. Browning and boasts among its alumni Howard Dean, who went on to become Governor of Vermont and a candidate for president, and Christian Herter, who served as Governor of Massachusetts in the 1950s. Jamie completed high school at Browning, earning high grades in history and math, and playing varsity basketball, baseball, and soccer.

From Browning, where he graduated fourth in his class, it was on to college for Jamie, which turned out to be Tufts in Massachusetts when Brown in neighboring Rhode Island turned him down. Along the way Jamie had developed a near-fluency in French at a language immersion school in France, and he had developed physically during hiking and climbing vacations out west, particularly in the mountains of Colorado. Jamie didn't care that much for Tufts at first—although he changed his mind about the institution before he graduated—and he took on the look of a Marlon Brando-style rebel, distinctive in his tousled long, dark hair and leather motorcycle jacket. He applied himself enough to his classwork to earn top grades; one of his classmates described him as one of those annoying people who do well without trying too hard, but his major interests quickly evolved toward extracurricular analytical subjects. He was brazen enough to send a long critique to Nobel Prize-winning economist Milton Friedman, challenging some points the Chicago School economist made in his book *Capitalism and Freedom*. Jamie was stunned when Friedman responded with an eight-page rebuttal, taking on Jamie's thoughts point-by-point.

"I was blown away by it," Jamie said. "Partly as a result of that, I always try to reply when someone sends something to me."

Another one of Jamie's papers earned him a face-to-face interview and a summer job with the man who was to become his future mentor. Jamie's father was Sandy's broker, and Jamie took it upon himself to write a detailed analysis of the merger between Hayden Stone and Shearson Hammill, where Ted worked. Jamie crunched the numbers and concluded that much in the way of cost savings could be achieved when a strong company like Hayden Stone took over a floundering, inefficient one like Shearson Hammill and eliminated the fat while retaining the viable assets. Ted got Sandy to review Jamie's paper.

"I have never seen the merger from this point of view," Sandy admitted. "Can I show it to people here?"

Jamie not only agreed, but talked Sandy into hiring him during his sophomore year summer break at Tufts in 1976, working on budgets for the retail brokerage operations. When Sandy bragged to Jamie that all his branch offices were profitable, Jamie corrected him by showing him the data and replying, "No they're not. Four of them are losing money."

Some, including Sandy in the beginning, saw Jamie as arrogant even at this young stage of development, but others

28

defended him as a brilliant, impatient young man on the move. "Brashness is a characteristic that is hung on a young person who is succeeding quickly," said Frank Zarb. Zarb had streamlined Sandy's all-important order fulfillment operations and went on to become the so-called "Energy Czar" with the Ford administration, before being appointed chairman of the Nasdaq Stock Exchange.

Jamie's summer job with Shearson turned out to be the start of a long, close business and personal relationship that would endure for more than two decades, as the U.S. financial system soared to the pinnacle of success and the envy of the world, and then imploded with the biggest bang heard around the globe since the days of the Great Depression.

Chapter Three

The Dimons and Weills had developed a tight social bond that went well beyond Sandy's penchant for wining and dining his closest allies among the growing army of people who entered his orbit. The families sometimes spent summer weekends together in the Hamptons on the South Fork of Long Island, and the Weills hosted the Dimons at their luxurious retreat in Connecticut. In 1977, Sandy bought a huge Tudor home situated on eight rolling acres in the posh "Back Country" of Greenwich. Jamie and his brothers spent a good part of their college years hanging out there, where they developed close friendships with Sandy's and Joan's son Marc and their daughter Jessica. The Dimons liked visiting Greenwich well enough that they bought a second home of their own there not far from the Weill family compound.

Jamie had a big decision to make when he graduated summa cum laude from Tufts in 1978: what should he do with the rest of his life? Should he plunge ahead and complete his education, or should he test the waters first with a job to see what sort of industry suited him best. He needed time to think it over, and get paid while he did it, so he took a job with a small data-crunching outfit in Cambridge, Massachusetts, called Management Analysis Center. The next two years convinced him that he was heading more or less in the right direction, doing profit analysis and budget projections for the firm's clients. Harvard Business School seemed like the next logical step for him, and in 1980 he entered the prestigious institution with the goal of getting an MBA, the requisite degree for a serious career in finance. Steve Burke, the future president of Comcast and JPMorgan Chase board member, remembered that Jamie was still sporting his Marlon Brando look when he arrived on campus. Standard-issue dress called for preppy button-down shirts, blazers, and a briefcase.

31

Then there was this one guy wearing blue jeans, a T-shirt, and a leather jacket, carrying his books in a gym bag.

"He didn't look like anyone else, and when he opened his mouth he had total confidence," Burke said.

His classmates included men who would constitute a veritable Who's Who of American business leaders. Besides Burke, attending HBS alongside Jamie were future GE CEO Jeffrey Immelt; future hedge-fund manager Stephen Mandel; future billionaire private investor Seth Klarman; and future chairman and chief investment officer of T. Rowe Price Brian Rogers. Throughout their lives, their paths would keep crossing and crisscrossing. Notably, Jamie as chairman and CEO of JPMorgan Chase helped Immelt downsize an unwieldy GE in 2015, earning Jamie's bloated bank a hefty profit in the process.

Jamie not only looked different than everyone else, he actually did things that set him apart from his fellow MBA candidates. One of his professors wrote a list of numbers on the blackboard one day that didn't quite add up in Jamie's mind. Instead of swallowing his doubts like any understandably terrified and insecure business neophyte would do, Jamie shot up his hand and blurted out, "I think you've made a mistake."

The silence was deafening. Ninety sets of eyes wheeled around in Jamie's direction, and the esteemed professor glared at this impetuous student who had dared to call him out so cockily. His own response was to hold up a piece of chalk and step to the side, silently inviting Jamie to come up to the blackboard and risk humiliating himself in front of the class. Jamie accepted the challenge. He took the chalk and filled the blackboard with his own numbers for more than five minutes, without uttering a word. The professor followed the sequence of digits that Jamie laid out with interest and realized that, while he didn't necessarily agree with everything the young man was doing, Jamie had a unique way of tackling a classic issue of the pros and cons of zero-coupon bonds—bonds that pay no interest but sell at a discount with an implied yield to maturity. Buying those bonds at the right price involves computing their return in terms of capital appreciation versus the total return an investor would receive with a combination of interest payments and a gain or loss of principle.

"You could see he earned the professor's respect," said Burke. "There was this glass wall of sorts between the teacher and the students, and Jamie was bold enough to run right through it. He relieved a lot of tension in the air by doing that."

Jamie also managed to impress his professor when he arranged for family friend, Wall Street wheeler-dealer Sandy Weill, to address the class during one of his visits to the area. Sandy had never been a gifted speaker, and he tended to freeze when he was at a podium staring out at a sea of anonymous faces. But his name carried cache among the business students, and his mere presence at the institution was a coup for the young student who succeeded in getting him there. Despite his insecurity about addressing a group of strangers, Sandy always managed to warm up to his theme when he got rolling on the ins and outs of real-life stock trading. Students and professors tend to live in a theoretical world, and Sandy's stories about life in the financial trenches were akin to reports from the actual battlefield compared with dry lectures about combat theory.

*   *   *

Harvard was not all business all the time for Jamie. Social animal that he was, with an eye for attractive women, he set aside enough time for fun and games as well. He organized a drinking club that normally met on Thursday nights at The Kong on Harvard

Square, where the members consumed rum-laced fruit punches out of oversized scorpion bowls. During his second year at HBS, Jamie's eye wandered over toward a group of women at a nearby table. His gaze settled on one of them, Judy Kent, a slim, beautiful brunette with a broad smile and a glow of intelligence blazing from her steady dark eyes. Jamie's friends noticed her as well, but Jamie was the one who caught her attention.

"In the middle of this group was this one guy wearing all black and sunglasses," she said. "I was just so drawn to him." And he was to her as well, although he tended to observe, listen, and evaluate before letting anyone penetrate his facade.

Jamie ran into her a few days later at a snack bar on campus, and they struck up a conversation. They were both athletic, avid hikers and skiers, who also enjoyed the competitive challenge of the tennis court. It took Jamie a short moment to set up a tennis date with her the next day. Jeffrey Immelt was one of the first of Jamie's friends to realize that any interest he might have had in Judy had been batted over the net before he had a chance to swing his own racquet.

"Judy was by far the best-looking, sexiest, and smartest girl in the class," he said. "Jamie got to her first. That's about it."

Judy hailed from Bethesda, Maryland, attended Tulane, and took a job in the nation's capital with the Beltway management consulting giant, Booz Allen Hamilton, while she worked on a graduate degree at Catholic University. From there it was on to HBS, where she also worked part-time crunching numbers on a project for Sandy's firm Shearson. She and Jamie had more in common than swatting tennis balls; her passion for working with raw data and analyzing the results matched his.

"In many ways, as smart as Jamie is, I think Judy was at least his intellectual equal," said Hardwick "Wick" Simmons, former president of Prudential Capital and CEO of the Nasdaq Stock Exchange.

The couple became inseparable after their first time out together, and by the end of their second year at HBS, they knew they wanted to spend their lives together. Jamie proposed to Judy during a long weekend at his parents' house in Greenwich, and she accepted without hesitation. There was no question of where they would live after they were married. Wall Street was where the money was, the heartbeat of New York City, the engine that powered the machine that drove the global economy. Jamie knew from the start that he wanted to make pots of money and run something important, and Judy was in total sync with his ambitions. They both needed to be at the center of things, the focal point of the empire, rather than off in the provinces somewhere. As a Baker Scholar who had graduated in the top five percent of his class from HBS, Jamie had his pick of Wall Street jobs. The most prestigious firms beckoned for his talents. He could have named his ticket and started his career with an income that would have been the envy of ninety-nine percent of his fellow citizens. But instead, he listened to a sales pitch from Sandy Weill.

*   *   *

"What's more important to you?" Sandy asked Jamie. "Making a lot of money or getting on a faster learning curve? Sure, you could take a job at Goldman or Morgan Stanley or Lehman, and they would pay you a lot more money than I can pay you. But if you come here and be my assistant, I can teach you a lot and we could learn more together about how the system works. You'd have a chance to actually *build* something instead of taking just another high-pressure job."

Jamie was actually on the brink of accepting one of the offers that had fallen into his lap, but he was intrigued by the logic in Sandy's pitch. Yes, Sandy was a salesman, a seasoned stockbroker in his soul more than anything else, but he was also a deal-maker nonpareil, who had started with next to nothing and created a growing empire of his own. He was a *builder* who had made a lot of money along the way, goals that Jamie had set for himself when he was still a kid learning the trade from his father and grandfather. He had learned a lot from both of them, and he knew he could learn even more from Sandy, for whom his father had the highest regard. The quick buck from Goldman or one of the other financial Goliaths was appealing, but Jamie was a brain-picker who sat back and listened until he had absorbed everything someone had to teach him.

He discussed the situation with Judy, his soon-to-be wife and partner, and he found her supportive about any decision he made. Judy respected Sandy as well and thought a short-term sacrifice of income could be worth it in the end. Sandy had a track record that was worth taking seriously by a young man about to launch his own career in the industry. From his first job as a runner with Bear Stearns, Sandy had hooked up with three other ambitious New Yorkers—Arthur Carter, Roger Berlind, and Peter Potoma, the oldest of the group at thirty-two. They formed Carter, Berlind, Potoma & Weill in 1960, after drawing straws to determine the order of the names in the fledgling company. Potoma was more seasoned than the others, and he instructed them all how to dress, with dark three-piece suits, dark hats, and umbrellas.

"Dress British, but think Yiddish," he advised them.

They had to start small out of necessity. While the big boys on the Street focused on institutional clients who were always hammering them to cut commissions, thereby battering their profit margins, Sandy and his cohorts decided that lots of small retail clients—individual investors and mom-and-pop businesses—were the path to their future success. They marketed heavily among their neighbors on Long Island and in the Boroughs around Manhattan, pitching their firm as the one that looked after the "Little Guy," the salaried workers who trudged off to work on the subway every day, and the owners of struggling businesses with less than fifty employees. In the beginning, they measured the firm's revenues in the tens of thousands, and the partners took home less than $20,000 a year each for themselves. The bull market helped them build a book of nickel-and-dime clients, most of whom didn't know what stocks they were buying or the difference between a debenture and a convertible preferred stock.

"What's the name of the stock I bought yesterday?" was a typical question from their neophyte investors.

"Pop Shoppes."

"Pop...Pip...Pip Pop? What does the company do?"

"What's the difference? The stock's up six percent overnight. Just sit back and enjoy the ride."

They sailed along smoothly until their senior partner, their sartorial adviser if you will, ran into a wall called the Securities Exchange Commission, the SEC, the government watchdog agency responsible for keeping things relatively clean on Wall Street. In 1962, Potoma was forced to "retire" early when the SEC charged him with free-riding—that is, using his clients' money to fund his own stock purchases and pocketing most of the profits in his own account. So now the dynamic foursome was down to a terrific threesome, not enough for a round of golf. In 1963, they fleshed out the hole in the partnership by luring Arthur Levitt, Jr., onto the roster. Levitt's father was New York State Comptroller, so the addition of his name to the fledgling brokerage firm was a bonanza in more ways than one. Not only did the son of a major New York politician add some heft to the company, but the young Levitt was the antithesis of Potoma in many ways. He was a straight arrow who would eventually become the longest-serving chairman of the SEC, and one of its most effective. A few years later, the partners shortened the official name of the company to CBWL, the partners' initials, which their haughty competitors lengthened again to Corned Beef With Lettuce. In a way, the derision was a sign of success of sorts; it meant that CBWL had crossed the radar screens of the large, established Wall Street institutions.

*   *   *

Conditions changed rapidly in the financial world throughout the 1960s. Mergers and acquisitions took off as leveraged buyouts— takeovers of other companies financed by debt—expanded at a breathtaking pace. Sandy and his partners knew that if they wanted to grow their company beyond the provincial realm of small, individual stock brokerage, they needed to get in on some of the action. In 1968 they pulled off their first real deal, positioning CBWL as an investment banker in Saul Steinberg's takeover of Reliance, a floundering insurance company, and earning a $750,000 fee for the effort. While not quite the big time yet, the experience whetted Sandy's appetite for expansion into other areas of the business.

"The next day Saul Steinberg had a business," Sandy said, "and we had to start all over again." He knew he had to broaden out and try to build the company by making his own acquisitions "rather than just working on deals for other clients."

After that Sandy went on a tear, largely made possible by the stock market meltdown of the late 1960s. The bull market turned into a "salami" market, as investors lost another "slice" off their net worth in every day of trading. Then the market skidded further in mid-1968, with investors heading for the exits as the war in Vietnam escalated, and assassins' bullets claimed the lives of Martin Luther King and Bobby Kennedy. The major Wall Street firms, which still cleared their stock trades manually, could not keep up with the volume as investors stampeded to get out of their stock positions and into the safe haven of Treasuries and short-term fixed income.

"It doesn't make any sense," Sandy said. "You're supposed to buy low and sell high, not the other way around. You've got investors who couldn't buy enough of a stock at fifty who won't go near it at fifteen. But you know what? This is either the end of the world or a buying opportunity. I'll take the chance that the world's not coming to an end."

While other Wall Street firms gagged on the volume, finding themselves unable to clear their stock trades fast enough, Sandy and his cohorts hired Frank Zarb, another savvy working-class guy from Brooklyn, to set up an electronic clearing operation. Zarb got it up and running at breakneck speed with Sandy peering over his shoulder from day to day, and within months CBWL's state-of-the-art clearing operation was the envy of Wall Street.

"In those days, most people thought the back office was for people with green eyeshades," said Roger Berlind. "But Sandy was fearful of anything going wrong down there. He became familiar with it."

"The idea was simple," said Zarb. "We had to conquer the back end of the business as well as the front end. If we didn't, we really couldn't be a leader."

Most of Wall Street hemorrhaged money, but CBWL prospered as other firms turned to it to clear their own trades. With stock prices plummeting, and the book value of established financial institutions sinking with the rest of the market, Sandy decided it was time to buy cheaply and expand his company's horizons. In 1969, he seized upon the Beverly Hills brokerage office of McDonnell & Co. Though barely remembered today, McDonnell & Company was a top-drawer brokerage firm back then, with $33 million in revenues and twenty-six brokerage offices sprinkled throughout the U.S. and France. Its CEO, Thomas McKay, regarded the firm's clearing operation with the same disdain most people have for their perpetually damp basements.

"Like many Wall Street executives of this era," remembered one of his colleagues, "[McKay] regarded the back office as a rather dirty, smelly warren, a realm in which a man of his abilities and attainments should not involve himself unduly."

That shortsightedness and outright snobbery cost McKay dearly. CBWL, with Sandy driving the deal, picked up McKay's Beverly Hills office at a bargain-basement price, thereby positioning CBWL as a growing bicoastal threat to the rest of the industry. A couple of years later, the entire edifice of McDonnell & Company tottered over the abyss and shattered on the rocks of bankruptcy court. To Sandy & Company, the notion of a bunch of guys who had grown up near Coney Island establishing a beachhead in glamorous Beverly Hills was one to be savored.

Chapter Four

The stock market tumult continued into the next decade. Vietnam. The unraveling of the Nixon administration. The combination of mounting inflation and a stagnating economy, labeled by the media as stagflation. Antiwar demonstrations rocking the very heart of the nation's crumbling political center. All of it came together to punish the stock market like a new black plague that had poisoned the soul of the American dream. Stock prices swooned, creating a classic buying opportunity for those who did not believe that the world as we knew it was ending, and did not subscribe to the view that a new counterculture revolution would succeed in killing off the American political and economic Goliath. Sandy was perhaps foremost among the optimists who gambled that the country would steer its way through the noise and mess and emerge upright and unbroken on stable ground down the road. So he looked around for something of value to buy on the cheap.

He found what he was looking for in the once-sterling brokerage house Hayden Stone. The company had counted itself among the Wall Street elite, but in 1970 it was heading pell-mell toward bankruptcy. In a prelude to the carnage that pummeled the global financial system in 2008, Hayden Stone's precarious position occurred against the background of more than one hundred Wall Street institutions being liquidated, hundreds of others being forced to merge with marginally healthier firms, hundreds of millions of dollars rushing from the market in a flight to safety, and seventeen thousand financial jobs blowing up in the midst of the chaos. Felix Rohatyn, known in the industry as "Felix the Fixer," entered the breach in an effort to find a buyer for Hayden Stone, believing that the venerable firm's demise would be too much for the system to handle. In other words, the company was "too big to fail" at the time—an eerie forecast of things to come in an industry that appears destined to rerun the most sordid aspects of its own history every seven or eight years. Rohatyn would later earn a dubious distinction when he created the Municipal Assistance Corporation to bail out New York City, an effort that failed miserably in the end. Rohatyn practically begged Sandy and his partners to buy Hayden Stone, a seventy-eight-year-old company where Joseph Kennedy had started in business.

"The lack of credibility had the potential to engulf the whole industry," said George Murray, Hayden Stone's president in 1970. "It was a very, very precarious time. Frankly, we had run out of gas."

Yes, and when Wall Street runs out of gas and sputters to a halt, the rest of the world crashes into a wall.

On the surface, the deal seemed laughable. CBWL, a tiny operation with two branch offices and five thousand clients, was being asked to bail out a foundering powerhouse with eighty branches and numerous foreign operations, manned by several hundred stockbrokers. But the key difference was that Hayden Stone could no longer clear its own trades, while miniscule CBWL had constructed an electronic clearing house that could handle trades effectively not only for itself, but for most of its competitors as well. Sandy smelled blood in the water and talked his partners into chomping at the opportunity to propel their company into a major Wall Street player with a stroke of the pen. Sandy played his hand like a true poker player, holding out for terms that allowed CBWL to acquire Hayden Stone's more viable branches without assuming any of the larger company's debt. As icing on the cake, CBWL received a $6 million cash infusion and paid for the takeover by issuing new CBWL-Hayden Stone shares to Hayden Stone's investors. Overnight as it were, CBWL's two-branch base expanded to thirty branch offices, and its five thousand clients rose ten times to fifty thousand commission-paying investors.

"It was an instant blend of what really were opposites," said George Murray. "Hayden Stone was the grand old lady on hard times. Some would refer to it as very WASPy. Whereas, CBWL was viewed as a super-aggressive, small, opportunistic boutique."

Sandy lost little time in urging his partners to take their new company public. On October 4, 1971, they floated more than ten million shares at $12.50 a share. With each of the former partners owning 284,000 shares, twelve percent of the total, Sandy and the others became multimillionaires the day after the offering. A year later, the corporation dropped the CBWL from its name and adopted the Hayden Stone moniker. The grand old lady was back in business, but this time with a new set of footwear to replace her tattered old tennis shoes.

*   *   *

Surviving the 1970s was a struggle, as investors shunned stocks as though they were toxic bacteria that threatened to pollute their entire wellbeing. In many ways they were. The economy was in ruins, and corporate earnings—the ultimate driver of stock prices—were on life support. Buying stocks today inevitably meant losing money tomorrow. And with inflation on a tear, interest rates rose to the level where it made far more sense to park cash in safe securities like CDs and short-term bonds and capture their returns without losing any sleep over them. Barnard Baruch once said that the easiest way to make a small fortune is to start with a large one, and most of the 1970s gave testimony to his sound advice. Hayden Stone, now under the guidance of Sandy and his colleagues, struggled to find new business along with the rest of Wall Street. But at least the company was able to weather the financial storm by trimming expenses (read, eliminating jobs) and building a solid financial base to see it through the prolonged rainy day that drenched the industry.

Hayden Stone was also in a position to pick up other failing institutions in the midst of the crisis, gambling that buying once-solid firms cheaply now would benefit the company's bottom line when the market eventually turned around. Hayden Stone rescued the 117-year-old Hentz &Company from oblivion in 1973, adding $11 million to Hayden Stone's assets while shunning Hentz's debt obligations.

"It was the turning point of my career," Sandy said. "I was forty years old and it was time for me to see if I could do it." He meant, it was time to see if he could continue to strike lucrative deals in the midst of the turmoil. "I didn't know if I had the guts."

He had more than guts; he was a street fighter with cunning and foresight. He pounced again in 1974, buying Shearson Hammill, the brokerage firm where Jamie's father Ted plied his trade. The move propelled Hayden Stone onto the top rungs of the financial ladder, number ten in size beneath such venerable institutions as Merrill Lynch and E.F. Hutton. The new company adopted the name Shearson Hayden Stone and boasted a network of one hundred and fourteen domestic branch offices and fifteen hundred stockbrokers. Sandy immediately went to work cutting jobs, mostly on the Shearson Hammill side of the business, eliminating almost all of its ponderous and antiquated back office clearing operation and replacing it with the one created by Zarb. The salesforce was largely left intact as long as the brokers were producing—that is, generating commissions for the company by "backing and filling" their clients alleged needs. The word *churning* had more relevance in the financial world than it did in the kitchen.

"Obviously, there are a lot of areas of duplication," Sandy said. "You don't need as many people as you start with." In addition, mergers inevitably involve culture clashes between newly

44

conjoined companies, and Sandy's culture was the one destined to dominate as the acquisition moved ahead toward completion. Sandy's style "bruised some people," said George Murray. They wanted to wait a bit longer to see how things worked out, but Sandy "moved so much faster than most people. Usually Sandy was right. Not always, but very often"

The main occasion on which Sandy was terribly wrong was during his 1977 attempt to take over an insurance company, Orion Capital, putting him in direct conflict with the long-standing Glass-Steagall Act, which created a sharp divide among various financial operations. Basically, it prohibited commercial and investment banks from crossing over into each other's bailiwicks, and subjected brokerage houses and insurance companies to separate regulatory jurisdictions. But Sandy became enamored of the concept of cross-selling, allowing stockbrokers to peddle insurance and insurance agents to market investment vehicles.

The problem with the idea, aside from Glass-Steagall, was that the salesmen hated doing it to the core of their being. Stockbrokers are essentially stock jockeys who love swinging their clients' cash in and out of the market like a yo-yo on the end of a string. And insurance agents are slow-motion death dealers who take their time bleeding their customers of hard-earned savings by luring them into an array of unfathomable products they don't need and never knew they wanted. The notion could not work under any circumstances, but Sandy became convinced that Glass-Steagall was restricting him from doing the kinds of deals that would help him expand his empire. He gritted his teeth and vowed that one day, when he had *his* kind of people in power, he would work to abolish what he viewed as a confining piece of legislation.

*   *   *

Sandy, however, had little choice but to seek out ripe pickings on his own side of the business. The ripest plum that entered his sights was Loeb Rhoades, founded in 1931 by John Loeb. In 1978, Loeb Rhoades looked like a punch-drunk fighter staggering on the ropes after suffering a series of blows inflicted by the market and its own cumbersome back office. Loeb Rhoades was gasping for air at the same time that Shearson's profits were tripling, thanks to Sandy's cost-cutting, streamlined clearing operations, and a pickup in business. Acquiring Loeb Rhoades was a deal that *had* to be done, and Sandy had the motivation and the ability to make it happen. The negotiations took place at Sandy's estate in Greenwich, Connecticut, over the Mothers' Day weekend in 1979.

"Was it a tough negotiation?" John Loeb's nephew Thomas Kempner asked rhetorically. "All successful people are tough, or they aren't successful. He made the best deal he could for Shearson, and I made the best deal I could for Loeb. And I think it worked out pretty well."

The acquisition turned out to be the largest merger in Wall Street history up to that point. After combining their assets, the new Shearson doubled in size again, harboring thirty-five hundred stockbrokers under a single umbrella, fleshing out two hundred and eighty domestic and twenty-five foreign branch offices, with a total capital base of $250 million. Sandy cut out twenty percent of the work force to streamline his new prize possession, eliminating "redundant" personnel and nonproductive stockbrokers. When Sandy's old sidekick from Brooklyn, Dave Dworsky, lured me over to Shearson from Merrill Lynch in 1979, the sign hanging over the door read Shearson Loeb Rhoades.

Shearson prospered as never before when the gambling stocks took off that year, followed by the oil stock craze a year or two later. The company's own stock price almost quadrupled in price, from $10 to $37 a share, during the same period, making Sandy and others holding a sizable slug of Shearson equity even richer than they had become over the years. Still festering in the recesses of Sandy' mind, however, was the notion of cross-selling. He just couldn't let go of the idea that his company's future growth depended on the ability of his brokers to peddle insurance and other products, and for the salesmen at those other institutions to sell stocks and bonds to their own clients. So when James Robinson, the CEO of American Express, came calling in 1981 with the intention of buying Shearson, Sandy shocked the financial world by admitting he was interested in a merger. On the surface, the two men were as different as day and night.

"You're combining Jewish guilt with Southern aristocracy," said George Sheinberg, former CFO of Shearson. James Robinson III was a smooth, debonair, old-school executive with blue blood flowing through his veins. Sandy, as president of the combined company, was a rough-and-tumble working-class stock-slinger, whose style would rub Robinson the wrong way every time they chaired a meeting together.

Souring the deal a bit for Sandy was Robinson's condescending manner. In no uncertain terms, he informed Sandy that he, Robinson, would run the show once the merger was complete. "And what would be my role? Who would report to me?" Sandy asked.

"You'll have to prove yourself," said Robinson, as though Sandy were just some ragamuffin who had wandered in from the beach at Coney Island. Uncharacteristically, Sandy swallowed the insult, so blinded was he by the lust of expanding his empire via the magic of cross-selling. American Express's customer base of thousands of credit card holders appeared to him like a vision in the desert, befalling Saul on his way to Damascus. Once he turned their names over to his stockbrokers, there would be no limits on the amount of product his best producers could unload on them. But it was little more than a pipedream from the beginning. Robinson had no intention of allowing that to happen. What interested him most about Shearson was its capital base and topnotch retail brokerage operation, which he could use to *his* advantage.

"At the end of the day, the credit card people were not going to open their business to thousands of salespeople," said Howard Clark, an American Express executive at the time. "They just weren't about to do it. The credit card list was called 'the crown jewel of American Express,' and the thought of having a couple of thousand salespeople calling credit card holders to try and sell them common stocks, unit trusts, annuities, and partnership interests just never worked."

"Sandy and Robinson don't seem to get along very well," I said to Dave one day.

"Don't underestimate Sandy," Dave said. "I've known him all my life. You'll lose your shirt if you bet against him. He'll eat Robinson's lunch before you know it."

Well, Sandy would *eventually* eat Robinson's lunch. But not just then. It would take him a few years to get back at Robinson. As the Sicilians say, "revenge is a dish best served cold," meaning don't retaliate immediately, but pounce out of the shadows with your stiletto drawn when your adversary thinks his victory is assured. Though Sandy got richer yet as a result of Shearson's sale to American Express, he was unhappy from the start. Accustomed to doing things his own way for the past two decades, he now found himself in the role of president of a subsidiary, reporting to a man who barely had the time of day for him. He was Pontius Pilate relegated to a minor fiefdom at the edge of the empire, ignored by the emperor in Rome as long as he didn't create any disturbances.

*   *   *

So there was Jamie, hitching his wagon to a star that was losing luster in the firmament, joining Sandy's team at a time when Sandy had little if anything of substance to do. Sandy was nothing if not a persuasive salesman. Jamie, with the pick of the plushiest Wall Street jobs, listened to Sandy's pitch, took stock, analyzed his options carefully, studied Sandy's track record as a man who had started with next to nothing and created a burgeoning financial colossus, and decided to sign on as Sandy's assistant. The bottom line for Jamie was that he could advance his career further over the long run by apprenticing himself to a master and building something of his own than he could as part of an overpaid army of smart, ambitious HBS graduates climbing all over one another on a scramble to the top. As Jamie figured it, he was giving up some easy money in return for a spot on the inside track.

"My goal in life was not to be an investment banker," Jamie said. He was not interested in shuffling other people's money around and grabbing a piece of the action. "I loved the concept of helping build a company. Something that was yours over a long period of time that you could be really proud of. And Sandy had done it before with Shearson." Jamie knew he was taking on considerable risk since Sandy was not top dog at American Express, but he thought it was worth the gamble. And he appreciated Sandy's forthrightness in leveling with him.

"I'm not sure it's going to work out here," Sandy said. "But I think you're a smart kid and we'll see how it develops."

Jamie was not exactly giving up a fat payday in exchange for a life of poverty. Before the ink was dry on his contract with American Express, he and Judy went apartment-hunting in Manhattan. For most couples that's an ordeal, thumbing through the

49

vacancies in neighborhoods they could afford. But Jamie and Judy had the wherewithal to select their own pricey digs, and they settled for a comfortable spread in the Bristol, a thirty-three story high-rise at 300 East 56th Street near tony Sutton Place.

That same year, I decided to give up the commute and move my own base of operations closer to home in the Greenwich, Connecticut, office. I wasn't there long before the branch manager introduced us to a new employee who had just joined the firm. She was young, attractive, and smart, a recent graduate of Cornell. Word got around in a flash that Jessica Bibliowicz was not just any new hire. Her maiden name was Weill and she was Sandy's daughter, just starting out in the business. She was a few years younger than Jamie, and she and her brother Marc had socialized with Jamie and his brothers during their weekend jaunts to Greenwich. Jamie's path would cross hers many times during the coming years, but no one would have guessed at the time that they were on a collision course that would end in a head-on crash a decade and a half later. The ensuing detonation would resonate throughout the financial world, littering the maimed and battered along the side of the road.

"Have you met Jessica yet?" Dave asked me over the phone one day.

"Yes. She seems very bright."

"She looks like her mother but thinks like her father," Dave said.

"She's got the best of both sets of genes then."

"Sandy would appreciate it if you showed her the ropes a bit. He wants her to learn the business, and she can learn a lot from a seasoned vet like you."

It was hard to picture myself as a "seasoned vet" at that stage of my life, more than thirty years ago, but you either learn the tricks of the trade early in this business or get crushed under the Wall Street juggernaut.

Chapter Five

It was inevitable that a few wags in the business would start referring to Sandy and Jamie as Batman and Robin. It was a natural tag bestowed upon the older superhero and his loyal apostle, but Jamie gave no indication that he was troubled by the imagery. He was as tough as he was smart. He knew he had a lot to learn about the business despite his education around the dinner table at home when he was a kid, and Sandy was the right man to mentor him, a father figure in his own right. Jamie settled in, rolled up his sleeves, and aligned his fate with Sandy's on a journey into the unknown future.

Jamie could not have started out in the financial industry at a better time. The era of stagflation was drawing to an end, with inflation reined in by Paul Volcker's sky-high interest rate policy, and the economy's precarious slide down the side of a cliff was finally arrested. With Ronald Reagan now occupying the White House, the president primed the pump with a huge tax cut coupled with a military spending program that would have put Genghis Khan to shame. Economist Arthur Laffer and Congressman Jack Kemp, the latter of whom wrote an introduction to my own book on the first Reagan tax law, convinced Reagan that lower taxes would lead to higher government revenues and eventually to a balanced budget. Well, the federal budget deficit never did tighten on Reagan's watch, but the stock market reacted to the Republicans' stimulus program by awakening from its slumber like Lazarus from the crypt.

The party started in earnest in August 1982. The Dow Jones Industrial Average scraped bottom at 777. With the prime rate peaking at 21.5 percent and precious metals prices plummeting, signaling that the worst of times were over, stocks took off like rockets from their launching pads. Shares of Merrill Lynch were selling for six dollars each, and anyone with the guts and foresight to pick up a thousand shares at that price would have made enough money to retire on less than fifteen years later.

"Sandy says it's a classic buying opportunity," Dave said to me over the phone one day.

"Either that or it's the end of the world," I said.

"Don't bet against Sandy. He's always right, at least most of the time."

The difference between Sandy and the rest of the world is that he wasn't afraid to follow his own advice, which is one reason why he is superrich and almost everyone else is not. Aside from soaring stock prices, however, all was not fun and games for Sandy and Jamie during the next couple of years. The cultural and personality differences between Sandy and Robinson intensified, with a dark cloud of tension descending from on high every time the two principals occupied the same conference room together. Robinson resolved the issue by dispatching Sandy as far away as possible within the lower forty-eight states, out to San Francisco with the onerous responsibility of rescuing American Express's subsidiary Fireman's Fund from extinction. There was only one word to adequately describe the assignment: *exile*. Sandy made no effort to hide his humiliation.

"Your mind is made up, then?" he asked Robinson rhetorically.

"It's the best solution."

"What about Shearson?"

"Shearson can report to me. Don't worry about that, Sandy."

Sandy had no choice but to accept the assignment from his boss—the very word made his skin crawl—and prepare to depart on his mission to the frontier. His assistant Jamie would accompany him on a journey that was not on his radar screen when he signed on with Shearson American Express, but not before he took care of some personal business at home. He and Judy had settled on a wedding date a year after his proposal. To accommodate Judy's religious background, Jamie agreed to be married by her family rabbi, although he drew the line at actual conversion to her faith.

"You don't need to actually convert to become a Jew," the rabbi told him. "The religion passes down to your kids from the mother's side."

"I am what I am," said Jamie, expressing his distaste for any organized religion at all.

The couple was married in Bethesda, Maryland, on May 21, 1983, and Jamie packed his own bags for his move to the west coast. Judy had taken a job at Shearson working for the larger-than-life director of sales and marketing, Joe Plumeri, which would keep her anchored in New York while Jamie relocated to San Francisco with Sandy. The sudden downturn in fortune and the separation it dictated forced Judy to reconsider her husband's decision to cast his lot with Sandy, the former master of his own fate.

"I wasn't even speaking to him at that point, I was so mad," said Judy. "Things were getting pretty tense."

*   *   *

Jamie's assignment as Sandy's sidekick out west pushed both men into commuter marriages, with them putting in twelve- and fourteen-hour days and flying home on the redeye on Friday nights.

Saving Fireman's Fund from bankruptcy required skills that Sandy had honed well over the years, and also came natural to Jamie who didn't let emotions get in the way of the raw, cold data. Fireman's costs had spiraled out of control, and to make the company's condition even more appalling, its accountants had tried to conceal losses caused by an unexpected spurt in insurance claims. Jamie pored through the numbers, went over them with Sandy, and they both agreed that the once-great company was rotting away at its core. Their solution was to fire about fifteen percent of the workforce and hike premiums, which stanched the bloodletting early in 1984. Still, their tough medicine was not enough. Later the same year, Fireman's Fund required another cash infusion to keep it up and running, and Robinson decided to unload the moribund outfit that weighed on his balance sheet like a malignant tumor. He scoured the waterfront for a willing buyer.

Sandy saw an opportunity to get out from under Robinson's boot and be his own man again, and Jamie was more than eager to do the kind of deals he envisioned when he signed on with Sandy two years earlier. They enlisted the support of Warren Buffett, who was always on the prowl for insurance assets in particular that he could buy for pennies on the dollar, and they also secured the financial backing of Morgan Stanley. Sandy put together terms that he thought all parties could live with, but in the end the deal never got off the ground. No one was more disappointed than Jamie, who was just as eager as his mentor to break free of Robinson's stranglehold—although Jamie held no personal animosity toward Robinson.

"Someone said at the time that American Express couldn't do a deal if Sandy, Morgan Stanley, and Warren Buffett were on the other side," Jamie lamented. "That's part of the reason Sandy had offered to let them keep forty percent, so if they thought it was a little cheap, they'd make it back on the back end. But I really hope that wasn't the reason they didn't do it, because that would have been pretty stupid."

His failure to lock up the sale was a deal-breaker for Sandy in more ways than one, and ultimately for Jamie as well. While Jamie had managed to develop a reasonably cordial relationship with Robinson, Sandy couldn't abide the sight of him. Beginning in August 1984, Sandy began to dump his American Express shares by the cartload. A firm believer that an entrepreneur should invest heavily in the company he worked for, Sandy was signaling to the world that he was no longer interested in being an insider at any enterprise run by Robinson. Sandy owned more than 600,000 shares, and he timed his sales carefully, letting most of his position run out in 10,000 share blocks so as not to spook the market with his selling program. Still, there was no way to completely hide his activity, since insiders are required by law to report their trades regularly. His major fear was driving the share price down as various institutions followed suit and sold their own stocks. By March 1985, Sandy had relieved himself of about three-quarters of his total American Express holdings for more than $6 million.

"Mr. Weill sold his American Express stock as a result of personal financial planning that includes diversification of his portfolio," a company spokesman dutifully told the media, a standard cover-up that, while not totally truthful, nevertheless remains within the bounds of strict legality. Yes, Sandy's sales involved personal financial planning—and career planning as well, since he had been planning to extricate himself from Robinson's orbit after the Fireman Fund's deal fell through. Sandy achieved escape velocity on Monday, June 25, 1985, when he turned in his resignation to Robinson. No one around him was surprised by the move.

"Sandy never fit in there," said Alison McElvery, Sandy's secretary at the time. "On the one hand, you had all these upstanding, pressed, and beautiful people like Jim Robinson who just reeked of money. And then you had Sandy who would yell down the hallway to ask someone how their weekend had been."

Sandy's decision placed Jamie in something of a bind. He had joined forces with the older man a few years earlier to grease his own glide path to entrepreneurial glory, but now at age twenty-nine, a time when he could have been raking in big bucks at a top Wall Street job, he was contemplating the prospect of unemployment if he failed to change the course of his own life. His wife had just given birth to their first child—the first of three beautiful girls, Julia, Laura, and Kara—and Judy had long ago had second thoughts about Jamie's loyalty to Sandy, which so far hadn't panned out the way either of them anticipated. Robinson, with Sandy's blessing, presented Jamie with an escape route of his own if he chose to take it, offering him a vice presidency at American Express with real responsibilities. Sandy urged Jamie to take advantage of Robinson's offer.

"You get along pretty well with the guy," Sandy said, "so why not grab it or take another good offer on the Street?"

Sandy was not normally an introspective man, but he did experience a tinge of guilt about luring Jamie off the straight and narrow path to guaranteed success and onto the garden path of rosy promises that failed to come to fruition. "I was in a different stage of my life than he was," Sandy said. "If I ever did anything again, it would be possibly okay. I didn't have that pressure that I had to go back to work. Jamie was just starting his career. If he decided to leave with me, he would basically be hanging his hat with an unemployed person."

Jamie wavered. He had a complex decision to make, which was not made easier by the doubts expressed by Judy and some of

58

his closest friends. During a weekend getaway with their families at Bethany Beach on Delaware's eastern shore, HBS buddy Peter Maglathlin asked Jamie point-blank, "Is this guy washed up? Does he even have another act?"

Jamie thought the questions over long and hard in the silence that followed. They were questions he had asked himself many times during the past few years. Finally, he made up his mind on the spot. "I have faith in Sandy," he said. "Something's going to happen."

Peter might as well asked himself if *he* had another act. Their roles were reversed years later when Jamie's firm at the time, JPMorgan Chase, purchased the assets of Highbridge Capital Management, the hedge fund where Peter had labored for a while, following the 2008 crash. The lifelines the kingpins of Wall Street extended to one another in times of financial distress underlined their incestuous relationship.

In the end, Jamie decided that he was no more suited to taking orders from a boss than Sandy was. Learning the trade at the foot of a mentor, and vacuuming his brain of all he had to offer, was one thing. But allowing his life to be proscribed by someone else's dictates and operating at his forbearance held no appeal for Jamie. He was determined to be a builder and to get very rich while he was at it, and who better to do that with than a man who had already proved his mettle on the deal-making path? Perhaps Sandy was a bit past his prime. Perhaps he didn't have another act left in him. But Jamie was willing to gamble that he did and that he would be better served in the long run by hopping aboard for the ride. He chose to align his fate with Sandy's.

*   *   *

Sandy's departure from American Express into the unknown void left the rest of us in something of a quandary as well. The culture at American Express under Robinson's rule was markedly different from the free-wheeling casino atmosphere that characterized Shearson when Sandy was in charge.

"What are you going to do?" I asked Dave.

"I've gone along with Sandy since we were kids together," he said. "But I've got to cut bait now. I still have teenagers to get through college. I can't take the risk yet. I need the steady income, so I'll hang on here at American Express. And you?"

"I've got an offer to take my business over to Gruntal and work out of their Scarsdale office."

"You've got a job here as long as I'm around," said Dave.

"I appreciate that. If Gruntal doesn't work out I'll give you a call. We'll stay connected in any event."

So Dave remained at Shearson American Express and I moved on to Gruntal, a smaller regional firm with headquarters down on Wall Street. And Sandy and Jamie joined the ranks of the unemployed—although the meaning of the word *unemployed* had a different connotation for them than it did for their fellow Americans.

It was at Gruntal that I met the diamond trader from Antwerp, Sigmund Larsen. He showed up at my office one day with a perplexed look creasing his brow. "What's your problem I asked him?"

"Interest rates are coming down. A few years ago I could get twelve, fourteen perzent dividends on my stocks and bonds. Now it's shit. Everything is coming down."

"So that's a good thing," I said. "It means inflation is under control. Rates don't have to be so high anymore to contain it."

"But I want more income."

"I can get you eight percent with some safe utility stocks."

"Eight perzent is shit. Can't you do any better?"

"Well, South African gold stocks are paying fourteen percent."

"Fourteen perzent! Now you're making me hot."

"But the country's on the verge of a revolution," I warned him. "If they shut the mines down, you'll wind up with nothing."

"I'll make a call and get back to you," he said.

Three days later he called me back. "I spoke to a friend of mine, a diamond trader in Johannesburg," he said. "He told me the government can hold out for another three years before the shit hits the fan. So I tell you what I want to do. Buy me a basket of South African gold stocks paying fourteen perzent, and I'll sell them in two-and-a-half years before the revolution starts. What do you think?"

I thought he was nuts, playing with fire like that. But what did I know? I was just a seasoned pro who thought he had learned a few things about Wall Street. And he was a bona fide risk-taker, a diamond trader, who made his living traveling all over the world with a suitcase filled with diamonds for sale. He did what he said he would do. He collected his dividends for two-and-a-half years or so, then sold his entire portfolio months before the noxious apartheid South African government went to hell in a handbasket.

Chapter Six

The question for Jamie and Sandy was where to hang their hats next. They wanted to remain in New York City, the apex of the financial world, the capital of the empire. In July 1985, Sandy rented space from American Express in the Seagram Building at 375 Park Avenue between 52nd and 53rd Streets, just a short walk to his favorite restaurant, the Four Seasons, where he was a regular customer. The Four Seasons was the mandatory midtown hangout for serious deal-makers, and those who wanted to be perceived as such. The game for those who were either past their prime or still on the outside looking in was to be spotted there by reporters sniffing around for a scoop on who was breaking bread with whom, while those who were actually in the midst of serious negotiations hid from the spotlight in one of the remote corners of the restaurant.

Sandy and Jamie, and a few others who tagged along for the ride, put in twelve and fourteen hours a day on their non-job, poring over annual reports and other financial documents, searching for signs of distress within major institutions. They met with Ivan Boesky, the legendary arbitrageur and takeover king, to see if they could get a handle on the kinds of situations that caught his eye. While Boesky was obviously successful at the way he operated, his eccentricity is what struck Jamie the most about the man.

"He seemed totally paranoid," Jamie said. "He listened in on all his employees' conversations, and he had cameras all over the place so he could keep an eye on them from his office that looked like a cockpit. It was totally bizarre."

Finally, in the fall of 1985, Jamie and Sandy spotted what they were looking for, a major financial institution that was struggling to stay alive. Ironically enough, the outfit in distress was another San Francisco company, this one the second-largest bank in the country after Citibank, BankAmerica. Amadeo Pietro Giannini founded BankAmerica's predecessor in 1904 before merging it into the Bank of America. He was the son of Italian immigrants who migrated to the New World to seek their fortune in the California gold rush. The bank prospered for decades after his death, but in 1985 it was gagging on a series of bad loans it had made to Latin America and various Third World countries. BankAmerica's losses in fiscal 1985 amounted to $337 million, and the company eliminated its dividend for the first time since the Great Depression.

It was time to pounce, like a fox on his prey. "BankAmerica appeared to be the biggest troubled financial thing around," Sandy said. "It was a shame what was happening to a great old institution." Sandy and Jamie couldn't do the deal on their own, so they swallowed their pride and approached Jim Robinson about his interest in injecting a $1 billion capital infusion into the San Francisco bank. For his part, Sandy would put in $10 million of his own money if the BankAmerica board installed him as CEO. Robinson was so anxious to beef up his west coast exposure that he went along with the proposal—or so it seemed on the surface.

But Robinson knew that it was up to Sandy and Jamie to cement the deal with the San Francisco Sanhedrin, who considered the two New Yorkers rabble-rousers intent on turning over the money-changing tables in their temple. Robert McNamara, a board member and the former defense secretary, advised Sandy to put his intentions in a letter to Sam Armacost, BankAmerica's CEO. McNamara knew that Armacost would view being displaced by Sandy like Job welcomed a vindictive God inflicting another blow on his rapidly crumbling world. On January 31, 1986, Armacost stared at the envelope containing Sandy's letter for an interminable moment, sensing by osmosis as it were what lay inside it. Armacost panicked. He seemed to feel that the longer he refrained from opening the envelope, the longer he could claim that he never received it. He needed advice. He called a meeting with Sandy, Jamie, and some top investment advisors who gathered in New York at—where else?—the Four Seasons. To everyone's astonishment, the twenty-nine-year-old Jamie dominated the meeting, peppering the assemblage with a battery of questions. Sandy sat back and let his protégé have the floor.

"Who's this young pup?" investment adviser Mike Holland asked afterward.

In the end, the consensus was that Sandy and Jamie were trying to buy themselves jobs. The investment team, which included Joseph Perella of Wasserstein Perella, recommended that the board turn down the offer. On March 3, 1986, the board did exactly that. Seventeen of the twenty-one directors voted against the proposal. San Francisco investment banker Warren Hellman described the mood at BankAmerica, characterizing the board's mindset as, "Nobody is going to tell us who the CEO of this bank is going to be. How dare this guy come to San Francisco and offer himself up to be the CEO of our most important institution?"

A telling side-story to Sandy's bid for BankAmerica starred his wife Joan, who couldn't resist inserting herself into her husband's business dealings with close associates. For seven years Joan had been seeing a Manhattan psychiatrist named Robert Willis. Part of her apparent therapy involved passing along insider tips to the shrink, who promptly traded on the information via his stockbroker Martin Sloate, president of a small brokerage firm. In January 1986, Sandy alerted his wife that he was making a bid for BankAmerica—information not yet made public that reached Willis's ears. Willis and the broker got caught in the act, and they were fined heavily for making illegal profits on the BankAmerica trades, plus earlier transgressions. It seemed that Joan had been tipping Willis off about Sandy's deal-making activities for some time now.

According to court documents, "Mrs. Weill, as a patient, regularly confided to Dr. Willis the progress of Weill's plans concerning BankAmerica. What is relevant is that Dr. Willis knew that he was receiving the information in confidence, that it was valuable non-public information, and that by disclosing and using the information for his personal benefit, he was breaching the duty of trust and confidence that he owed to his patient," Judge Miriam Cedarbaum wrote in her ruling. "It is difficult to imagine a relationship that requires a higher degree of trust and confidence than the traditional relationship of physician and patient." One can only wonder if Willis charged Joan his regular fifty-minute hour fee for his services, or agreed to accept payment in trade alone.

Sandy and Jamie took the blow from the BankAmerica disappointment like two street fighters who had been knocked off their feet, but were not yet out for the count. For Jamie's part, he did wonder if he had made the right decision by following Sandy to the edge of a cliff. "I was looking into the abyss a little bit," he admitted. "I was pretty much a kid who was not getting experience nor making money in the meantime. Of course I thought I might have made a mistake."

*   *   *

If someone had told Jamie when he was in Harvard Business School that his path with Sandy would lead him south to a working-class Mid-Atlantic town, trying to resurrect a low-end loan company catering to people who shopped at Walmart, he would have glared at him as though he had taken leave of his senses. The town was called Baltimore, and there were just two places to work in the financial services industry if you really had to be there: T. Rowe Price and Legg Mason. The rest of Baltimore's economy, such as it was, depended on blue-collar jobs on what was then a smelly harbor with spice manufacturer McCormick & Company, Domino Sugar, and a few other enterprises. Most of Baltimore's workforce was unemployed, and the welfare rolls were bursting at the seams. Jamie did not go to Baltimore to work for Legg Mason or T. Rowe Price. Jamie, in effect, journeyed to Baltimore to resuscitate a moribund lending company from the throes of death.

The opportunity, if you could call it that, came in the form of a phone call that Sandy had been hoping to get when he joined the ranks of the unemployed. Bob Volland, the treasurer of Commercial Credit, went over his bosses' heads and telephoned Sandy from his Baltimore office late in the summer of 1986. Volland told Sandy, in effect, that his company was gagging on bad loans to unqualified buyers. Yes, as proof that there is nothing new under the sun, Commercial Credit specialized in subprime loans more than two decades before those words became a catchphrase following the global financial meltdown of 2008. One of the company's programs initiated car loans for ex-convicts—"Cars for Convicts," as they were somewhat unfairly labeled. Sandy invited Volland to come to New York to discuss the situation, and Volland met with him and Jamie in their office in the Seagram Building. Sandy immediately rocked Volland back on his heels when he told him his company was "a piece of crap."

What Volland didn't know at the time was that Sandy and Jamie had already discussed a possible deal with Bob Price, the CEO of Commercial Credit's parent company, Control Data, and had made plans to fly to Minneapolis, the company's headquarters, to meet with Price and his staff. Control Data had acquired Commercial Credit in 1968 to finance its own computer sales, but the plan never worked the way it was conceived. Both parent and subsidiary were on their knees in 1986, and their lines of credit had dried up.

"We were down to where we had nothing left to sell and we would have run out of money and closed up shop by the end of 1986," said Charles "Chuck" Prince, Commercial Credit's chief counsel then and future CEO of Citigroup. "It felt like Dunkirk." Famously enough, Prince later admitted that he never saw the 2008 crisis coming and was happy enough to go along for the ride. "As long as the music is playing, you've got to get up and dance," he said. For his remarkable lack of foresight, both while he was helping to run the ship into the ground at Commercial Credit and later at Citigroup, Prince was rewarded with an exit package worth $12.5 million. On Wall Street, the road to great wealth is often paved with a series of missteps.

Jamie knew that Commercial Credit, if run properly, was not a piece of crap; that was just Sandy's way of negotiating for the best terms he could wangle. Bob Lipp, Commercial Credit's head of consumer finance and former president of Chemical Bank, was particularly impressed by Jamie's acumen at the time. "He's as smart as can be," he said. "He's a quick learner. He did a great amount of study and analysis on his own. If we were signing a lease, Jamie would end up reading the lease himself that night."

Control Data had no viable option but to unload the Baltimore subsidiary and receive a quick cash infusion if it were to rise from the grave it had dug itself into. Sandy and Jamie clearly occupied the catbird seat in this negotiation. On September 12, they announced a deal allowing Control Data to retain 20 percent of Commercial Credit and Sandy and his cohorts to assume ownership of the other 80 percent, which they would spin off in an initial public offering a month later. Sandy would be installed as CEO of Commercial Credit with a base salary of $500,000 a year, and Jamie and the rest of Sandy's team would occupy key management roles and receive stock options and other benefits. Jamie's official titles were senior vice president and chief financial officer.

Jamie was not altogether happy with the job Sandy bestowed on him. He assumed, as Sandy's assistant for the past few years, that he would occupy the second rung down the corporate ladder below Sandy. Instead, he discovered that he would be reporting to former Merrill Lynch chief financial officer F. Gregory Fitz-Gerald, who joined the company as executive vice president. Many of the older executives whom Sandy lured on board still regarded Jamie as "the kid," a youngster with a big mouth and strong opinions who had yet to earn his stripes on the financial battlefield. Their attitude, and his perception that Sandy had betrayed him, planted the seeds of the rivalry that would end Jamie and Sandy's relationship thirteen years later. Jamie had no choice but to buckle under and accept his role. But Sandy would find Jamie breathing down his neck from that moment forward.

"Jamie was in a hurry to run right through Greg," Sandy said, "but he ended up having to be a little patient."

In any event, the announcement did wonders for Control Data's stock, driving it from $1.75 to $27 in a few weeks. Sandy, Jamie, Fitz-Gerald, and the rest of the team embarked on a dog-and-pony show, pitching their company to institutional investors in eighteen cities across the country. Sandy believed in investing heavily in any company he controlled, and Jamie borrowed money from his parents to acquire a stake of his own. The insiders got shares at a discount to the public offering price, which hit the market at $20.50 a share on October 29. When the dust settled in the days and weeks after the IPO, Commercial Credit—the down-at-the-heels outfit that specialized in risky loans to its busted-out-slippers clientele—suddenly had a market capitalization of close to $1 billion. It was nothing less than financial alchemy at work. It was a lesson in how you turn nothing into something with a lot of hype and salesmanship in an industry filled with smoke and mirrors. Sandy was back in business again, and Jamie's gamble on Sandy had finally begun to pay off, obliterating his doubts in the blink of an eye. The IPO enhanced Sandy's net worth and turned Jamie into a rich man—at least on paper for the time being.

*   *   *

Now it was time for Jamie to roll up his sleeves and really go to work again. The first order of business was for Jamie and Sandy to descend on Baltimore and shore up the bottom line. They stayed at the Harbor Court Hotel, with Sandy taking up residence in a one-bedroom suite and Jamie occupying another across the hall. Sandy started the day with his trademark cigar, a newspaper, and a cup of coffee, while Jamie smoked cigarettes in his own digs, chafing at the smell of Sandy's cigar smoke, which always found a way to swirl into his room from under the door. The others on the team stayed in a nearby hotel.

"We all left Jamie to deal with Sandy's cigar smoke," said Bob Lipp, laughing. "It was his way of getting Jamie's attention first thing in the morning." And Sandy knew exactly what he was doing. "Here's how I'd wake him up," he said. "The first thing in the morning I'd have a cup of coffee, read the paper, and then light up a cigar, and that awful cigar smoke would go right under his bedroom door." The kid, it seemed, still had a lot to learn about the way his mentor operated.

Putting Commercial Credit in order meant winnowing the wheat from the chaff—which meant firing about one-third of the staff, trimming the payroll from about six thousand to close to four thousand employees. One of the first people to be tossed out was Bob Volland, whom Sandy regarded as disloyal for doing an end run around his bosses. Sandy regarded loyalty as a primary virtue and believed he couldn't trust anyone who violated his cardinal rule.

Once again, the dynamic duo were involved in commuter marriages, although the commute to Baltimore was not quite as onerous as flying back and forth from New York to San Francisco every week. They hopped aboard a Piedmont Airlines flight out of LaGuardia on Monday morning, put in long grueling days in their Baltimore offices, jetted back to New York on Thursday evening, and showed up bright-eyed and bushy-tailed for marathon meetings at the Seagram Building on Friday. Sandy often extended the workweek at his estate in Greenwich over part of the weekend.

Jamie, who was a bit more of a family man than Sandy and some of the other team members, decided to move his family to Baltimore for what promised to be an unpredictable stay after Judy became pregnant with their second daughter. They moved into a ground-floor apartment in Cross Keys, a veritable small village in itself complete with upscale shops, restaurants, tennis courts, and other amenities somewhat isolated from the grimy underside of downtown Baltimore. Jamie quickly developed a reputation for his aggressiveness and assertiveness. He was still pouting over his secondary role under Fitz-Gerald and often interrupted others, including Sandy, when they tried to make a point.

"I know, I know, I know," he would respond dismissively. Sandy usually sat back silently, watching the interplay between Jamie and the older executives, admiring his protégé's intelligence and skills, but understanding at the same time that he was an impatient Young Turk who needed to be carefully watched and restrained. Jamie's only saving social grace, if you could call it that, was that he treated everyone with the same disdain. When he tried to lecture Sandy the same way he hectored the others, Sandy drew the line and said, "OK, I get it," and walked away, which sometimes drove Jamie into a screaming fit. Jamie also resented the more-or-less mandatory dinners with Sandy after they had finished for the day. Sandy treated them like a command performance of sorts; if you were in town that day, you were expected to have dinner with Sandy in a private room at Marconi's at 106 West Saratoga Street, not far from the office at 300 Saint Paul Place, a few blocks north of the harbor. Marconi's, now closed, was an old Baltimore watering hole where literary icon H.L. Mencken wined and dined regularly in the early years of the twentieth century.

"There was no social life," said Robert Willumstad, a member of Sandy's team. "Everybody would come in at seven-thirty or eight and just work all day. Then, if you didn't have a good excuse, you'd have to have dinner with Sandy."

"You had to be careful," said James Calvano, another member of Sandy's team, "because if you didn't get there in time, Sandy would order your meal for you. He had these set ideas about what people should like." Sandy also drove the rest of them nuts, since he believed the "No Smoking" signs were a mere suggestion that didn't apply to him. He lit up a cigar after dinner, and the owners said nothing because—well, because he spent a lot of money there every night, picking up the tab for six or eight hungry and thirsty patrons. Jamie usually countered with a cigarette of his own, inhaling deeply as he glared at the others, but it failed to fully compete with Sandy's less-than-aromatic effluvia. Jamie clearly did not find it amusing to have his balls broken by Sandy or anyone else.

Chapter Seven

The next eighteen months were a blur of activity as Batman and Robin and the rest of the crew worked overtime to put Commercial Credit's finances in order. In addition to trimming the bloated payroll and cutting expenses overall, their essential job amounted to eliminating non-profitable areas within the company and shoring up the balance sheet to create a healthier financial profile. Presenting a "fortress" balance sheet to the world was a policy Jamie often discussed with Brian Rogers, who later put the concept to better use at T. Rowe Price—a company that normally harbored a large cash reserve and rarely kept any debt at all on its own books. Yes, net profits are important, but an impregnable balance sheet showing assets well in excess of liabilities was a better reflection of a company's true health.

"If there are any insurmountable problems, we haven't found them yet," Sandy said at the time. Their major goal was to get Commercial Credit in a position where it was able to acquire other assets when the opportunity arose. As usual, Sandy was waiting for a substantial stock market correction to mark down share prices to a level where he could load up on them cheaply—a lesson Jamie had learned well at this stage of the game.

Jamie had his own agenda as well, which he quickly put into operation. The first order of business for him was to get rid of Fitz-Gerald by staging what amounted to a palace coup of sorts. He simply rewrote the org chart on the blackboard one morning, erasing all of Fitz-Gerald's personal reports and putting them under his own name. When Sandy failed to overturn Jamie's act of defiance, Fitz-Gerald decided he didn't need to put up with the grief. He already had plenty of money, and he had little trouble finding a lucrative spot as director of Dain Rauscher, a brokerage firm catering to high-net-worth investors. Royal Bank of Canada acquired Dain Rauscher in 2001 and integrated it with its U.S. brokerage house Tucker Anthony Sutro, where I worked as a supervisory analyst until 1994.

The stock market refused to cooperate with Sandy and Jamie's grand design during the early months after their acquisition of Commercial Credit. Stocks entered blast-off trajectory at the beginning of 1987 and kept on soaring to giddy heights into the summer, when they finally began to lose momentum. The Dow Jones Industrial Average peaked at 2722, 44 percent higher than it had been a year earlier. The widely followed average then proceed to sink back into the atmosphere, falling 500 points by October. This rather gradual slide was only the precursor to the infamous Black Monday crash on October 19, when U.S. stocks plummeted 508 points, or 22.6 percent, in a single day, triggering massive selloffs across the globe. It was another end-of-the-world situation, except that Sandy didn't believe in end-of-the-world scenarios—and Jamie had learned not to believe in them either. To them it was a proverbial buying opportunity. Think about it: if it really is the end of the world, then what the hell does anything matter anyway?

The crash took no prisoners, decimating the stocks of sound and weak companies alike. Commercial Credit's share price lost half its value, which temporarily rattled the crew in Baltimore, but Sandy quickly recovered and encouraged the troops to buy more stock on the dip. "Buy more! Buy more!" was his familiar mantra. "We'll bounce back from here." Sandy purchased a bushel of Commercial Credit shares at the lower prices, and Jamie borrowed more money to do the same. "In for a nickel, in for a dime," was how he viewed the situation. Share prices of other companies were falling all around them, putting many prestigious financial firms in dire straits, but Commercial Credit was better positioned to survive the carnage thanks to its cash reserves and solid balance sheet.

"This is the time to find out what else we can buy on the cheap," Sandy said.

Jamie pored through the numbers to look for firms that were struggling to survive the devastation, and he found literally hundreds of them gasping for air in the toxic environment. "What are you finding?" Sandy asked Jamie impatiently.

"Lots. Look at this one. Look at that one."

The one Jamie liked best was the once venerable brokerage firm E.F. Hutton. Hutton had started out as an honorable institution in 1904, but in 1980 key executives were indicted for check "kiting"—writing checks for larger amounts than they had on hand, then covering them later, in effect giving the firm an interest-free loan. The real black mark on the company was its involvement with the Patriarca crime family based in Providence, Rhode Island, the overlord of the Boston mob. Early in 1987, prior to the crash, the firm's Providence branch was found to be laundering money for the crime bosses, an act for which the entire firm was facing imminent indictment. In addition, Hutton was technically in violation of the Glass-Steagall Act, since it had crossed the line separating various financial functions, operating simultaneously as a brokerage firm, an investment bank, and a lending institution.

When Sandy examined Jamie's numbers, a bell went off in his head. Sandy had never been in favor of Glass-Steagall in the first place. He regarded the law's restrictions as a set of handcuffs that kept him from doing the kinds of deals he really wanted to make. The law boxed him in. He was still enamored of the concept of cross-selling—a one-size-fits-all financial firm that sells stocks and bonds, peddles insurance, makes loans, puts together IPOs for fledgling companies, and in effect acts as a one-stop financial powerhouse that takes care of all the financial needs—real or created—of a wide variety of customers. E.F. Hutton, once shed of all its troublesome baggage, fit that profile handsomely.

"Let's see if we can do a deal," Sandy said. "I see a chance for a return to the securities business."

With Jamie at his side, Sandy approached Hutton's board of directors, who were anxious to unload the tainted institution and bolster their own equity position in the firm, whose common stock was losing altitude every day. But Sandy and Jamie were a day late and a dollar short, as it were. They were not the only ones who recognized blood on the water when they smelled it. Peter Cohen at Sandy's old company Shearson American Express topped their offer with a bid of $29 a share to their $21 proposal, and Cohen carried the day with little further discussion. The deal was announced on December 3, and Hutton was merged into the larger and sounder institution a few months later.

Down but not yet out, Sandy and Jamie went hunting again. Sandy was the leader of the expedition, and Jamie was his sharpshooter. "Jamie, where do we put the decimal point here?" Sandy often asked Jamie, whom he depended on more and more to target in on the bull's eye. Their hunt took them farther afield into the insurance industry, where they spotted a sagging behemoth staggering on the ropes.

*　　*　　*

When Shanghai-born Gerry Tsai was flying high on Wall Street, he lived like a monarch in a sprawling palace situated on a spit of land jutting into Greenwich Harbor, with a commanding view of Long Island Sound. Not far from him, in another posh estate overlooking the water, reigned the Queen of Motown, Diana Ross, the lead singer of the Supremes. Across a narrow inlet at the eastern edge of another peninsula sat a huge retreat owned by Donald

Trump and his first wife Ivana. Donald Trump was in a snit because Gerry Tsai had a helipad on his own property, from which his personal helicopter pilot ferried him over New York's snarled traffic to his Wall Street office every day.

"Donald is driving me crazy," A former first selectman of Greenwich (the equivalent of mayor, who shall remain nameless) said over lunch one day in 1987. "He's livid that Gerry Tsai has a helipad on his property and the town won't give Donald a permit to build one for himself."

"What's the big deal?" I asked.

"I told him we couldn't have helicopters taking off from Greenwich every morning so all the fat cats could fly over other commuters on their way to work. Helicopters are noisy. They disturb the peace. The town would be up in arms over it. They don't like Trump very much anyway."

"What about Tsai?"

"He got grandfathered in when he bought the place. But I told Trump that was it. No more permits for helipads."

"So what's Trump going to do about it?"

"He said he's going to sue the town and me personally. Should I be worried?"

"I'd transfer all my assets into my wife's name if I were you. Assuming you trust your wife, that is."

The unfortunate first selectman had a penchant for dressing up as a policeman in his time off and speeding through the streets in a patrol car with the lights flashing. When he pulled over a motorist for a traffic violation shortly after our lunch, and the motorist discovered who he actually was, he called the real cops who arrested the politician on the spot for impersonating one of their own. The incident put a dent in the good man's political career, but not Donald Trump's business career or Gerry Tsai's high-flying career as one of Wall Street's savviest and richest investors—at least not quite yet.

Gerry Tsai detested Glass-Steagall with the same passion that Sandy, and now Jamie, did. He felt that the restrictive law was just restraining him from doing business his own way. So he pretty much proceeded to ignore it. He started small, but with big dreams. He was an aggressive growth investor, one of the first momentum traders, who specialized in jumping on a handful of stocks that were already moving up, without concerning himself too much about such fundamental niceties as corporate earnings or share price valuations. And the strategy worked wonders for him over the course of several decades. He applied his momentum style diligently to the Fidelity Capital Fund in the late 1950s, attracting a large following of investors, then founded the Manhattan Fund in 1965 with even more impressive results.

But he wasn't content to rest on his laurels there. Insurance struck him as an impressive bailiwick to expand his burgeoning empire, so he sold the Manhattan Fund for a huge profit and bought a small insurance firm, Associated Madison, for $2.2 million in 1978. Four years later, he sold Associated Madison to American Can Company for $162 million, another whopping profit. He remained with American Can as vice chairman. American Can was essentially a container and food packaging outfit, as its name implies, but it also crossed the line into insurance with its acquisition of Associated Madison. Gerry waited until what he believed was the right moment to take full control of American Can and transmogrify it into a full-fledged brokerage-insurance-financial services supermarket, a model that had become increasingly prominent in his mind over the years. In that regard, he was something of a soul brother to Sandy and Jamie.

But his timing turned out to be lousy. He loaded up on debt and bought Smith Barney at pretty near the top of the market in May 1987, just a few months before stocks leveled off and began their descent that August. Smith Barney was just the kind of conglomerate that Gerry—and Sandy and Jamie—had been lusting after. It was an amalgam of brokerage operations, insurance services, mutual funds, and quasi-banking lending functions. As such, it tottered on the peak of the financial Intercontinental Divide separating the types of businesses that financial firms were allegedly proscribed from engaging in. American Can was hardly an apt name for such an institution, so Gerry changed it to Primerica after shedding the company's manufacturing business. With the market in tatters, Sandy and Jamie approached Gerry about making an offer for his company.

Gerry expressed interest—in fact, he was also negotiating with other potential buyers including Merrill Lynch, which Sandy found out about shortly afterward. Gerry and Sandy respected each other but harbored no warm feelings in their relationship; perhaps they were too much alike in the way they did business. But Gerry's timing had been off, and Sandy's had been impeccable, putting him in the driver's seat. The talks went on for several months in 1988, with each side enlisting major support, Gerry from Felix "the Fixer" Rohatyn at Lazard Freres, and Sandy and Jamie calling on Bob Greenhill at Morgan Stanley and legal firm Skadden Arps. Gerry got to know Jamie well during the negotiations and was struck by the young man's tenacity with numbers. Both sides agreed that the deal had to go through if Primerica was to be saved; Smith Barney alone had suffered losses amounting to hundreds of millions of dollars in the past two years with a staggering pile of debt on its books.

On August 24, 1988, they came to terms. Sandy and Jamie would acquire all of Primerica with a combination stock-cash transaction totaling $1.7 billion. "This is an old-fashioned merger done by old-fashioned people," Rohatyn announced to the media. But it was hardly a merger in the strictest sense of the word. Tiny

Commercial Credit was *subsuming* the much larger institution in a proverbial case of the minnow swallowing the whale. The agreement allowed Gerry to remain as a director of the new company and head of the operating committee with a tranche of stock in the firm, but his titles were mere honorifics with no responsibilities.

"It was mostly Jamie who structured the deal," said Gerry. "He crossed most of the T's and dotted most of the I's. You could see Sandy had come to rely on him more and more during the few years they had worked together." Sandy, Gerry thought, "seemed a bit distant and removed."

While Gerry recognized Jamie's contribution to the merger, Jamie had yet to earn his stripes with the media. When reporter Robert Coles of the *New York Times* asked for a meeting with Gerry and Sandy to discuss the deal, Sandy brought along his brash sidekick to listen in. Except that Jamie was not very good at listening. Coles looked askance at him when he stepped into the room, and when Jamie interjected with a detailed analysis of how it all went down, Coles snapped at him immediately. "I'm sure you're smart," he said to Jamie. "But I already have two geniuses here to answer my questions. I don't need to hear from the junior genius as well."

The big question was how Sandy was going to take a motley collection of disparate businesses, many of which were losing money, and turn them into a whole that was greater than the sum of its parts. That was Sandy's job, with Jamie's help. Their first step was to drop the less-than-desirable Commercial Credit handle and change the name of the new conglomerate to Primerica, which had more panache notwithstanding its recent stumbles in the marketplace. Sandy's second concern was what to do with Gerry Tsai. He already had one upstart to worry about, Jamie, his erstwhile protégé, who had launched one palace coup—with Sandy's blessing—to get rid of a superior who stood in his way. Sandy recognized that, as much as he admired Jamie and relied on him, he, Sandy, was the next one up on the food chain. Was it just a question of time before…well, anyone could fill in the blanks.

Gerry represented a different kind of problem. He was a predator like Sandy, a shark circling in the water waiting for the best opportunity to close in for the kill. It wouldn't be long before he attempted to regroup after his poor timing and displace Sandy as the hungriest fish in the financial waters. Sandy was not about to let Gerry have that chance. So he simply kissed him goodbye with a $40 million exit bonus. With a solid gold parachute like that to soften the landing, you don't need to apply for unemployment insurance to pay the bills.

For Jamie and Sandy both, the acquisition meant they could pack their bags and head north up the pike to New York City, for good this time. Judy had delivered her and Jamie's second daughter, Laura, on June 16, 1987, and it was time to move their growing family back home. And Sandy and Jamie had a new beast in chains, a beast called Primerica that had to be tamed. Tamed, and trimmed, and transformed into a lean, mean insatiable eating machine that could gobble up and digest anything that crossed its path.

PART TWO

THE BEAST AWAKENS

Chapter Eight

Gerry was not the only one who thought the Primerica deal was mostly Jamie's doing; Jamie thought so too. He was determined from that moment onward not to play second fiddle to anyone. Sandy still regarded him as his "assistant," his gifted intern in training, but in Jamie's mind his success at the negotiating table elevated him to the rank of equal partner with his former mentor. When Sandy told Jamie that they needed to cut costs, Jamie responded with a precise figure. "We need to slice out $50 million," he said. "And that's just for starters. The final amount should go much higher. And we should start cutting at the top."

Sandy had no problem with that, nor did most of the senior level people he brought on board. Most troubled firms are top-heavy with redundant executives who enrich themselves with lucrative perks while they mismanage the entire operation. Sandy knew that better than anyone else, although there was an ulterior methodology at work in Jamie's calculations. He didn't want any unnecessary competition around to deter him in his rise to the top. His likely competition, however, came from those whom Sandy recruited into the new Primerica with him, not from those who were already ensconced there before the ink was dry on the final deal. Bob Lipp was one of those who followed Sandy and Jamie to New York.

"Our heroes have been those who cut costs, who increase margins, and who run a tight ship," he said. "For the most part, our most talented people are not marketing people, not new product people, but operations people." His statement was unambiguous. He was announcing to anyone keeping score exactly whose heads were going to roll.

Frank Zarb concurred. He epitomized operations to the core of his soul, having established a state-of-the-art back-room operations system for Sandy that became the envy of the industry years earlier. He put on his green eyeshades and zeroed in on Smith Barney, a dinosaur that provided its parent company with 27 percent of its revenues but only 11 percent of its net income, largely because of back-office inefficiencies. Operations were clearly inadequate there, and the new team hoisted its collective scalpel and got ready to slice off the dead wood and replace it with green shoots. Sandy was shrewd enough to know that he had to reward Jamie as well for his contributions. He named him Primerica's chief financial officer and the senior executive vice president in charge of Smith Barney, reporting directly to Sandy. There would be no intermediaries standing between Jamie and Sandy this time around. One palace coup was quite enough to suit Sandy's tastes.

Their next move was to relocate Primerica's headquarters from Greenwich, where Gerry had planted it after he changed the company's name from American Can, to midtown Manhattan near Pennsylvania Station, ten blocks south of Times Square. Sandy felt at home there, close to the Garment District where his father and grandfather had set up shop during the Great Depression. The offices of the top executives were packed tightly together, cheek by jowl not far from Sandy's, which made it easier for him to get everyone's attention with a loud yell down the hallway. Jamie would have preferred more elegant digs, with a bit more breathing room so he could pore through his data in peace and quiet, but that was not Sandy's style.

"He expected everyone to listen to his rants when things were not going well," Jamie said, "so we had no choice except to wait ten or fifteen minutes until the storm passed over."

Primerica North was Sandy's house in Greenwich, where he often called impromptu meetings during the weekend, whenever the mood suited him. It was an all-hands-on-deck performance. Very little short of death excused one's absence. His team was expected to drop everything else that might be going on in their lives and head north to suburbia. Not that Sandy was without his charming side. He could laugh and joke along with the best of them. But to him his closest associates were family, and families had to put up with the good and bad, the pats on the back along with the criticisms. That's what loyalty was all about, and to Sandy loyalty ranked up there at the top of the highest virtues known to man.

"Sandy didn't get ulcers, he gave them," said Jamie, who had gotten to know Sandy as well as anyone did but was beginning to resent being yanked around like a pet poodle on the end of a leash. Sandy's number-one poodle was not a title he aspired to.

"Sandy has no filter. If it's on his mind it's on his tongue," said Jeff Lane, who had followed Sandy to Primerica from American Express.

*   *   *

American Express, and Jim Robinson, were never far from Sandy and Jamie's thoughts as they worked to shore up Primerica and put it on more solid ground. If the Sicilians believed that revenge is a dish best served cold, Sandy and Jamie did them one better with the notion that it is not enough to merely get even; the real goal is to pull even and then get ahead. They saw an opportunity to put that plan in motion shortly after they took over Primerica. Drexel Burnham Lambert, a once-stalwart fixture on Wall Street, found itself gasping for oxygen (money is oxygen in the financial services industry) following a string of misadventures by junk bond king Michael Milken. Milken had perfected the black art of taking over other firms with astronomical loads of debt, and along the way his insider trading activities led to an indictment on racketeering charges. It was a mind-numbing reversal for a company that had been the most profitable investment bank on Wall Street as recently as 1986. Drexel's losses in 1989 amounted to $60 million, plunging it to the point of ruin.

Under Milken's guidance, Drexel had become a primary player in the takeover battles that swept corporate America during the previous decade. With Drexel's bonds, smaller companies that could never have obtained financing were able to make bids for some of America's largest corporations. But things started to come unglued for Drexel in 1986, when the firm was caught up in the scandals that swept Wall Street after the fall of Ivan F. Boesky, whom Jamie had described as weird after their first meeting. Boesky paid $100 million to settle insider trading charges and agreed to testify against Drexel and Milken. As a result, Drexel pleaded guilty to six felony counts, agreeing to pay $650 million in fines. Milken was indicted on ninety-eight counts of racketeering, securities fraud, and other charges.

"It was another golden opportunity for Sandy, and for Jamie as well since he put together the deal," said Joseph Califano, a former top adviser to President Lyndon Johnson, who sat on Primerica's board of directors.

The terms of the deal were almost laughable. A firm that could have fetched eight figures in a normal transaction two years earlier was now on the auction block. Sandy and Jamie approached Fred Joseph, Drexel's stunned CEO who had been battered into semi-consciousness by Milken's flamboyant excesses, and who had been rendered almost speechless by the experience. "I had no choice," he said. "It was either sell or watch my company go down the tubes." What he sold was sixteen of Drexel's healthiest branch offices, along with five hundred of his most productive stockbrokers and their books of clients, for $3.5 million. Jamie presented Joseph with the take-it-or-leave-it offer, which Joseph accepted with little fanfare on April 8, 1989. The deal hardly elevated Primerica to the level of American Express, which enjoyed $19 billion in revenues, more than four times those of Primerica, and assets totaling $117 billion, compared with $17 billion for Primerica. But there was little doubt that Sandy and Jamie were gunning for bragging rights as top dog on the street.

"There was no question in my mind that Sandy and Jamie were looking at the American Express model and turning their company into a mini version of the company," said Fred Joseph.

They had a way to go to catch up with American Express's size and financial clout, but there was no mistaking the target they were shooting at. What remained of Drexel, aside from the cream that Jamie and Sandy had skimmed off the top, crashed onto the shoals of bankruptcy a year later. The once-proud firm that had given free rein to Milken and his excesses filed for protection under Chapter 11 of the federal bankruptcy laws on February 13, 1990, after it failed to secure an emergency loan from the New York Federal Reserve to pay off $100 million in debt.

"After it's all over, Drexel will be left with no cash and a lot of laid-off employees," said one soon-to-be-unemployed Drexel executive. Other sharks in the industry began to circle in, examining the remains of the bodies floating in the sea to find out if there was anything left worth picking over. Not much, they quickly discovered; Sandy and Jamie had already walked away with most of the meat a year earlier. The final collapse of Drexel triggered concerns about the bankruptcy's potential effect on the financial markets and the economy in general.

"This is a sad day for New Yorkers and a sad day for the American financial system," said then Representative Charles E. Schumer, before he was elected to the Senate. "It represents a significant blow to New York City's economy and marks the end of an era in American finance. Drexel could end up taking some other companies with it." He might have added that it was a potential blow to his campaign coffers as well, since he got most of his election money from the barons of Wall Street.

Jeff Lane, however, took the news in stride. "This is the nature of the financial services business," he said. "'You go into a steady decline, and then you fall off a cliff." Well, he, Sandy, or Jamie were not about to fall off a cliff. And neither was the rest of the Street. The market absorbed the news in stride, with the DJIA actually *rising* five points to close at 2,624.

*   *   *

Jamie's star was also rising with the market. Judy had given birth to their third daughter Kara on June 20, 1989, completing their family's contribution to society, and his income was ascending as well to more than $600,000 a year in base salary plus bonuses and stock perks that far exceeded salary, as it does for most chief executives. Sandy, as top dog, earned more than twice as much in total compensation. Primerica's stock also defied the laws of gravity. As the overall economy began to lose momentum during the early years of the George H.W. Bush administration, Primerica's stock price continued to go up, propelled by profits from their assorted business units. Commercial credit was now on sound footing following a major financial overhaul; the brokerage and investment banking side of the business at Smith Barney and Drexel was sailing smoothly, largely through the efforts of Jamie, who was "among the top three people who were the most instrumental" in turning them into profitable enterprises, according to Frank Zarb; and the insurance hub at Primerica, along with its assorted financial services, had been streamlined into fighting trim as it functioned as the brain center of the entire conglomerate. Sandy, Jamie, and the rest of the team now presided over a burgeoning financial conglomerate that they worked hard to transform into a cohesive entity.

Whether it was all legal or not was a different question entirely. They had worked so hard to patch the beast together during the past couple of years that Jamie, at least, lost sight of the idea that they might technically be in violation of Glass-Steagall. "The administration had so many other things to worry about that they weren't overly concerned about what was happening on Wall Street," said F. Clifton White, a political consultant to the first President Bush. "George had always been focused on foreign policy, like Nixon was, and he figured the economy could look out for itself."

Glass-Steagall, however, was never far from Sandy's mind even if Jamie turned a blind eye to the law's restrictions. So Sandy grew more than a bit nervous when his chief lieutenant started loading up on Citicorp stock. While Primerica's share price kept rising, problems at Citicorp sent its common stock into a nosedive. Jamie couldn't resist what looked like easy pickings when Citi fell to $8.50 a share, and he bought $50 million worth of the stock for Primerica's portfolio.

"What are you doing, Jamie?" Sandy asked his underling when he found out about the purchases.

"Can you imagine taking over Citi?" Jamie enthused. "Wouldn't that be the mother of all deals? It's time to buy it."

"Sell the position. We can't go there." Sandy, the old stockbroker, had a lot more experience in this area than Jamie did. He was concerned about Glass-Steagall, yes, but he also knew that stock prices didn't levitate forever; sooner or later the flagging economy and stock market tailspin would catch up with Primerica's stock too. And he wanted to be in a solid cash position when that scenario unfolded. Reluctantly, Jamie pulled the plug on the Citi position, reaping Primerica a $30 million profit. Sandy's timing was spot on. Months later, the recession took hold, dimming Bush's prospects for reelection and slicing the value of Primerica's stock from a high of $37 a share in 1990 to just under $17 later the same year. The profit from the Citi trade helped cushion the downfall, beefing up Primerica's cash reserves while the economy sagged further.

Jamie learned from the experience, but he was hardly humbled. Humility was simply not his style. He was quickly gaining a reputation as Sandy's pit bull on the end of a leash, nipping at his master's heels, a brash and increasingly arrogant pretender to Sandy's throne who preferred to talk when he should have been listening. When Sandy appointed Jamie president of Primerica, some board members complained that Sandy was advancing him too quickly. "He could do five sets of computations in his head," one said. "But given his mandate from the get-go, he had few interpersonal skills. He never had to learn them. Most of us have to go through the ranks and learn some humility. But he never had to. He was dictating to everybody from day one."

But there was a method to Sandy's apparent madness. He knew he had to reward Jamie if he wanted to keep him from jumping ship and setting up shop as master of his own fate. While everyone else speculated that Sandy was creating a succession plan with Jamie set to replace him when the time was right, retirement was the furthest thing from Sandy's mind. "I don't feel very old," he laughed. Simultaneously, he lifted Jamie up and raised his hopes with one hand but put obstacles in his path with the other.

"Sandy will never let go until they carry him out feet first," said my old boss Dave.

"Guys like Sandy don't roll over and play dead when they're still in their fifties," said Joe Plumeri. "Jamie may have been a bit naïve if he thought Sandy was going to step aside anytime soon."

Instead, while Jamie saw himself positioned on the inside track, ready to accelerate ahead of the pack as soon as Sandy flashed the green light, Sandy constantly brought other executives into Primerica from outside the firm with responsibilities that overlapped Jamie's. One new hire was Bob Druskin, the chief financial officer at Shearson, an accomplished executive in his own right who was a decade older than Jamie. Bob was not one to step easily into the younger man's shadow and help ease his way to the top of the Primerica ladder. He and Jamie locked horns almost instantly. Jamie fumed visibly over what he regarded as Sandy's duplicity, but his mentor's carrot-and-stick approach to management served his purposes well. Jamie had little choice but to fight for supremacy on the corporate battlefield along with the rest of the hungry wolf pack.

For the moment at least, Sandy was pleased with how much progress he had made since his less-than-pleasant sojourn at American Express. With a new decade dawning, he and his entire team sat back and analyzed the playing field while they planned for the immediate future. The past few years had been a breathtaking whirlwind of fevered activity. As Sandy and Jamie took stock of what they had accomplished during their eight years together, one deal stood out as the lever that made everything else work together.

"I'm happy with all our businesses," Sandy said. "But the one that really shot the lights out was Smith Barney."

Chapter Nine

It took a hurricane to get the next big deal done. A hurricane named Andrew, plus a slew of bad real estate deals by Travelers Insurance Company just as the housing market got caught up in an avalanche that did not subside until 1996. Travelers was founded in 1864 in Hartford, Connecticut, to provide travel insurance to railroad passengers at a time when that form of transportation carried a high level of risk. Over the years the company expanded its mission, underwriting automobile policies, airline insurance, and the first coverage for space travel. So far so good. Travelers was unique in its industry and enjoyed hefty profits from its innovative franchise,

Then, in a classic case of a company venturing beyond its familiar boundaries into uncharted territory, Travelers invested much of its income from relatively safe investments known as guaranteed investment contracts into mortgages that paid higher yields, which the company then repackaged as securities for investors looking for better rates of return. If this sounds like a prequel to the carnage that jolted the markets in 2008, you'd be right in assuming that things don't change all that much on Wall Street—except for the severity of the impact.

The problem for Travelers, then the eighth-largest insurance company in the U.S., was that it made most of its real estate investments in the early- and mid-1980s, close to the peak of the market. When housing prices nosedived in 1986, Travelers was stuck with a slew of defaults on its mortgage securities, a problem compounded by its obligation to make ongoing payments to its investors. The final straw that broke the camel's back was Andrew, a brute of a hurricane that roared ashore along the west coast of Florida on August 24, 1992.

By the time Andrew had completed its job of ravaging much of Florida and the Gulf Coast of Louisiana, Travelers was facing more than $400 million in claims, on top of the few hundred million it owed investors on its bum mortgage loans. The load was too much for Travelers to bear. The company was on its knees, staring into the cold, dark eyes of bankruptcy proceedings, and Sandy talked to Jamie about the idea of moving in to rescue it from insolvency. Jamie ran the numbers and didn't like what he saw.

"It doesn't add up," he said. "We'd be taking on too much risk."

But Sandy would not be deterred. To Jamie's dismay, Sandy brought in Bob Greenhill, the merger specialist at Morgan Stanley whom they had worked with on the Primerica deal, to approach Travelers CEO Ed Budd about making an offer for the troubled insurance firm. Jamie fumed openly. He didn't like Greenhill all that much to begin with. They had managed to rub each other the wrong way during the earlier negotiation. And Jamie viewed Sandy's inclusion of Greenhill in this later instance as just one more example of his mentor's penchant for erecting roadblocks in his path. Sandy's pattern of rewarding him with one hand while undermining him with the other was emerging as a major irritant between them. It was an issue that would only worsen over the years until it finally exploded into open combat.

Budd was more than receptive to the idea of a bailout; he had little choice considering the circumstances. But he didn't want to let go entirely, feeling that he still had a role to play in Travelers' future. "I don't think that because things won't always be what they were tells the whole story," he said rather vaguely. Jamie had little choice himself but to hop aboard the bandwagon, once he understood that Sandy was determined to move forward with it despite his own objections. But this time it was Greenhill who drove the deal, which came down to Primerica paying $723 million for a 27 percent stake in Travelers. Sandy assuaged Jamie's bruised ego to some extent by naming him a director of Travelers, but Bob Lipp was the executive whom Sandy tapped to oversee operations at the beleaguered insurer.

As for Ed Budd, he didn't last too long after the merger was announced on September 20, 1992. So much for the role he thought he might be playing. Sandy ushered him out the door a year later, as he had done with Gerry Tsai after the Primerica takeover, cushioning his exit with a handsome bonus package. "We have made excellent progress since the merger of the Travelers and Primerica," Budd said anticlimactically as the exit door swung behind him. The rest of the Travelers staff did not fare quite as well. Jamie and Sandy went to work cutting thirty-five hundred jobs from the payroll, and they forced those facing early "retirement" to pay for their own health care benefits—or do without them. Sandy's compensation package alone exceeded the savings on health care costs by more than 33 percent. Pure math is without emotion, but it tells the story better than anything else on how to turn a company around.

*   *   *

Sandy and Jamie didn't have to wait long for their dream deal to present itself. Jim Robinson and American Express had never faded from their cross-hairs, and Sandy and Jamie had been waiting for a clear shot at their ultimate target since their inglorious departure from Robinson's empire almost a decade earlier. Now that empire was under siege, much like Rome's was around 400 A.D., when the barbarians stormed out of the forests and charged southward toward the citadel of the civilized world. In Robinson's case, as in Ancient Rome's also weakened by bankruptcy, American Express's plight was one of his own making. He proved that he knew how to run a credit card company, but what he didn't know much about was how to navigate the rough seas of the brokerage industry. Shearson Lehman Brothers had devolved into a mess under Robinson's tenure. Shearson lost $116 million in 1992 alone, mainly because of bad deals cobbled together in the form of tax-sheltered investments, including oil-and-gas, equipment leasing, and real estate limited partnerships. The problem was that Reagan's second tax law, enacted in 1986, tossed most of those write-offs out the window in exchange for lower overall tax rates.

Reagan's attempt to simplify the tax code wreaked havoc on the tax shelter industry, in which Shearson was a major player. Most of those tax-sheltered investments went belly-up, inflicting heavy damage on Shearson's bottom line—as well as on their clients' net worth. Robinson as chief executive should have been able to anticipate the changing tax environment; rumors about the government putting an end to "abusive" tax shelters had been circulating well in advance of 1986. Indeed, the government had even set a target date of July 1, 1986, for brokerage firms and other financial institutions to put limits on cash transactions and to flush bearer bonds—those not registered in investors' names, making it easy for them to collect interest without paying taxes on it—out of the market. One of my favorite memories of the time was of a bar owner, whose account I managed, coming into my office before the July deadline with a paper back stuffed with cash that reeked of stale beer and whisky.

"Tommy," I said, "my office smells like two o'clock in the morning in Shanahan's Bar and Grill."

"Where the fuck do you think it came from?" he said.

Another client came by to cash in a few hundred thousand dollars' worth of bearer bonds before the deadline. "What are you going to do with the money?" I asked.

"I'm buying a house in the Hamptons," he answered. "Three-fifty cash. But the deal will go down as two-fifty and I'll slip him a hundred grand under the table to help him with the capital gains tax."

"Shit, Roger! I don't need to know all that."

Then there was the mob guy who operated out of JFK Airport, who came in once a week to deposit $9,999 in cash—just under the legal reporting limit—in his account. When the government changed the rules to no more than once a year, then later to any cash transactions on a regular basis, that game ended as well. Many clients took their business elsewhere, never to be heard from again.

The point is that Robinson should have known what was going on, since every brokerage office in the country had been experiencing similar scenarios long before Shearson Lehman Brothers' tax-tainted investments crashed into the rocks. All he had to do was walk into any branch, smell the air, and listen to some of the conversations taking place. But he remained oblivious to it all until it was far too late, like an absentee landlord presiding over his plantation house while his sharecroppers tear his rental properties apart.

Most major corporations function on crony capitalism. The CEO and other top executives stuff their boards of directors with old-school buddies, who rubberstamp their compensation packages and enrich themselves in the process. But Robinson's mismanagement was too much for any board to put up with; the declining stock price was hurting all of them. So, on September 20, 1992, crony capitalism took a holiday. The board met at the St.

Regis Hotel in Manhattan and decided that it was time for Robinson to hit the road.

That's when Sandy and Jamie came calling. For Sandy, revisiting Shearson was like a family reunion. His father Mac worked as a clerk in the Miami office, and his daughter Jessica and son Marc were still employed by the firm. The board of directors replaced Robinson with Sandy's old friend Harvey Golub, another graduate of Cornell. Golub opened the entrance door with a smile on his face when Sandy said he was interested in doing a deal, and Jamie was right beside Sandy this time around. He was not about to let Greenhill get in line ahead of him as he had on the Travelers negotiations, and Jamie was just as anxious as Sandy was to gobble up their old firm and expand the horizons of their growing empire.

But as eager as Golub was to rid American Express of the Shearson Lehman albatross that weighed like an anchor around his neck, he and his team proved to be savvy negotiators in what turned out to be a fairly complicated merger. The talks went on through the night, from the time the markets closed for business until six o'clock in the morning. They centered on American Express divesting itself of the Shearson side of the operation, the brokerage side, while maintaining Lehman Brothers' investment banking division, which had no appeal in its current condition for either Sandy or Jamie. It was tantamount to splitting conjoined twins apart at the hip without killing both patients.

"This was Jamie's shining hour," said Frank Zarb, who ran Smith Barney for Sandy. "It was by far the most meaningful contribution he made while I was there."

Sandy's and Jamie's goal was to integrate Shearson and Smith Barney into a single brokerage operation, which would propel it alongside Merrill Lynch as the two dominant players in the industry, with about twelve thousand stockbrokers each. The deal would also beef up Primerica's mutual fund assets under management to more than $100 billion, putting it fourth in the U.S. in that category. When the deal was announced in March 1993 after a long stretch of all-nighters, the numbers fell into place with both teams saying they were satisfied with the terms. Sandy and Jamie got precisely what they wanted, plus Shearson's building at 388 Greenwich Street just south of 14th Street in Greenwich Village, for $1.5 billion.

Primerica's stock jumped on the news, as the investment community welcomed the return of the ultimate stockbroker to his old company. And the brokers welcomed Sandy's return as well. When he entered their midst after the deal was final, many stood on their desks and cheered him with a standing ovation. A few shouted, "We keep leaving and you keep buying us back! We surrender! This time we'll stay!" Sandy grinned widely, with Jamie at his side, relishing the role of the conquering general accepting his tribute as he slowly approached Rome along the Appian Way. The victory was made even sweeter, since Robinson had already left involuntarily with his tail between his legs. The *Economist* noted in its March 1993 issue that Sandy had "proven himself mightier and richer than Mr. Robinson. It would be naïve to think the point was lost on either of them."

*   *   *

The aftermath of the deal, however, left a sour taste in Jamie's mouth in more ways than one. First, the media failed to acknowledge the full extent of his contribution to the highly successful negotiation. Rather, they focused by and large on Sandy and Zarb smiling at the cameras and clasping hands in celebration of the coup. Jamie resented being relegated to the background; no matter how much he accomplished as Sandy's sidekick, he had yet to earn the respect he felt that he deserved from the architects of public opinion. He was now thirty-seven years old, no longer just the kid at Sandy's side, with flecks of gray beginning to weave a pattern through his thick, wavy hair. Understandably, he was growing increasingly anxious to step closer to the limelight and be recognized as a major player in his own right.

Jamie's second point of contention was the now-overcrowded field of top executives, all of them jockeying for Sandy's attention, as a result of so many mergers. The problem was exacerbated further a few months later when Sandy, basking in the glory of his most recent acquisitions, decided to buy the rest of Travelers—the 73 percent he had previously left behind—for $4 billion. He also changed the name of the parent organization to Travelers, which he thought carried more panache.

So now the financial conglomerate, the beast in the making, was not only top-heavy with redundant executives, all of them trying to avoid being labeled as disposable leeches with no viable reason for continuing to bleed the payrolls dry, but it also harbored an army of rank-and-file employees who failed to generate revenues to assuage the financial Frankenstein's insatiable appetite. Many of them would have to be let go and find new employment. The brokers were a different story; they remained the lifeblood of every brokerage operation as long as they generated a minimum of a quarter-million dollars—preferably double that—in gross commissions for their firm, 40 percent to 50 percent of which went into their own pockets.

The new Travelers operated in every conceivable arena of the financial services sector. It sold stocks and bonds; it peddled insurance; it ran mutual funds; it packaged annuities and foisted them on unsophisticated investors, usually with an 8 percent sales charge tacked on upfront; and it skirted the outer edges of investment banking, mainly because the company's principals were leery of violating the strictest restrictions of Glass-Steagall. That law remained a sticking point for Sandy and Jamie, one they hoped to rub away as soon as they had the opportunity to do so. The biggest problem for Jamie was that the beast had grown to a size that it was now hydra-headed. It was no longer just a Sandy-and-Jamie creation. Sandy had just turned sixty, but there were no signs that he was ready to name a successor. And doubts emerged in Jamie's mind that he really did have the inside track to succeed Sandy with so many other prominent contenders for the throne positioning themselves for dominance.

Sandy hardly clarified the murky waters swirling around him when he replied to a question about who might succeed him, "We don't have that sort of stuff" around here.

Making matters worse for Jamie was that, in addition to the people whom he had worked with and gotten to know over the years, new ones came on board that he had to contend with. The old faces included Zarb, whose original job of running Smith Barney was now broadened to heading up the life insurance and money management services under the Primerica bailiwick; Lipp, who also moved over to Primerica to manage consumer finance operations; and Plumeri, now president of the as-yet-to-be-integrated Smith Barney Shearson brokerage businesses, who never ceased to wonder at the lack of structure at the top of the conglomerate. Sandy gave Jamie the titles CEO and president of Primerica, with the main task of expanding the company's trading facilities into 390 Greenwich Street, the building next door to the one they acquired from Shearson.

It was the newest face in the lineup, however, that concerned Jamie the most. The face belonged to Bob Greenhill, who Jamie tolerated as much as he would a thorn stuck in his side. Sandy and Greenhill had a long history together, and Sandy lured the merger specialist away from Morgan Stanley in June 1993 with the titles of chairman and CEO of Smith Barney Shearson. His perks included a $20 million annual salary, plus a percentage of the company's profits. Reporters at the time commented that Sandy "displayed Mr. Greenhill like a trophy" at a press conference announcing his hiring. Greenhill's major task was to beef up Smith Barney Shearson's investment banking operations. Sandy apparently decided that Glass-Steagall be damned; he was going to expand into that profitable corner of the financial universe one way or another.

As for Jamie, "I was not that interested in investment banking," he said. It was a business fraught with risk, and high expenses into the bargain. Jamie was more concerned about the bottom line, while Greenhill carried with him a reputation as a free-spending, dice-rolling, nonpareil leveraged buyout specialist. And he now hovered like the new glamor boy standing tall at Sandy's side. Greenhill did not arrive alone, since he insisted on bringing with him thirty-two investment bankers from Morgan Stanley, insisting that they were more accomplished than anyone Smith Barney Shearson had in place. Suddenly, there was a legion of Greenhill bankers moving in with high compensation packages, amounting to more than an additional $50 million a year in salaries and benefits, threatening the profit margins of the unwieldy financial colossus, all of it with Sandy's blessing.

Jamie took it all in with increasing alarm. Greenhill was more than a potential threat to Jamie's medium-term career goals. He loomed over the horizon like a hostile invader, in Jamie's mind, one that had to be vanquished before he and his hordes trampled across the financial landscape that he and Sandy had worked so hard to cultivate.

Chapter Ten

Bob Greenhill was a Wall Street creation right down to his well-manicured cuticles. Like Jamie, he was a Baker Scholar, a graduate of Yale in 1958 before he made the requisite move to HBS, from which he graduated with his MBA four years later. He wasted no time putting in an apprenticeship at the feet of an older mentor, but rather accepted a job offer immediately from Morgan Stanley, rising through the ranks quickly as a leveraged buyout specialist and becoming a partner in the firm in 1970. He was just a few years younger than Sandy, an energetic Master of the Universe on the move who was not accustomed to being reined in by a younger colleague who had not yet, in Greenhill's mind, stepped outside of Sandy's shadow. He enjoyed Sandy's full support, which added even more ballast to the role he was hired to play at Smith Barney Shearson.

From the start, however, the roles that Jamie and Greenhill took on were not only contradictory, they were mutually antagonistic. Jamie's goal was to cut costs and turn the beast into a lean, mean, fighting machine, while Greenhill was used to spending however much money it took to expand his own theater of operations. His investment bankers had no restraints on their own spending; indeed, they believed that worrying about such trivialities as unfettered spending was beneath their purview while they shouldered the Smith Barney people aside as though they were mere underlings who were better suited for pushing mail carts down the hallways.

Jamie wanted to trim the payrolls and consolidate space, but Greenhill believed the firm needed international exposure, with new branch offices in Hong Kong and Beijing. Smith Barney bankers took taxis to the train station at night, while Greenhill's minions hired a fleet of town cars to take them to their favorite hotspots before squiring them home. Smith Barney's people flew coach overseas, while Greenhill's lieutenants flew first class—on the same flight. Greenhill held Monday morning briefing sessions for his troops to keep them abreast of what was going on, to which Smith Barney's bankers were not invited. Jamie was a bottom-line guy, looking to beef up net earnings; Greenhill was more focused on the top line, hoping to attract gross revenues no matter how much money he had to spend to do it. They were two bulls in a china shop, butting heads and locking horns with neither willing to give an inch. Theirs was a corporate marriage forged in hell, destined to fail from the start, and Sandy observed the proceedings with amusement, like a referee watching to see which combatant would land the more serious blows.

It didn't help Jamie's standing with Sandy that he had taken to teasing him openly in front of the other top executives during Sandy's monthly meetings at his estate in Greenwich. Sandy sat back with a forced smile on his face, pretending to accept Jamie's barbs with good humor, while the rest of the team chuckled nervously. The tension between them was growing thicker by the day, a dark cloud with a palpable presence of its own. At the end of the year, Sandy held an annual meeting at a retreat on Saranac Lake in upstate New York. After a few rounds of drinks, Jamie picked up an empty box and hurled it into the roaring fireplace, where a rush of air sucked it up the chimney. The box clogged the passageway, sending a storm of black soot down into the room, forcing them all to clear out while the hired help cleaned up the mess.

"That was a stupid stunt," Lipp said to Jamie after he pulled him aside from the other execs.

Jamie just smiled and shrugged. The expression on his face indicated that he really didn't give a damn. He was determined to bring the Greenhill issue to a boil, and if he needed to shower the assemblage with a dark cloud of soot to do it, so be it. It was just another ingredient added to the ominous cloud of tension that had descended on all of them.

The major problem with the entire operation, aside from Jamie and Greenhill pulling each other in opposite directions and Sandy's attempts to put a happy face on all of it, was that the integration of Smith Barney and Shearson was not going well. The cultural clashes were just too jarring. The Smith Barney brokers disdained their counterparts at Shearson as though they were so many shoeshine boys who should be polishing their masters' shoes while they checked out stock quotes in the *Wall Street Journal* or the *Financial Times*. Add to that another layer of hostility, imposed by Greenhill and his bankers, who looked down on everyone else as though they were unfit to breathe the same air that the big boys did. So, while investors rewarded Travelers by buying its stock and jacking up the share price, behind the scenes none of it was working like a well-oiled machine. The gears were stuck, and Plumeri had more than he could handle trying to impose a note of harmony over the clashing cultures.

*   *   *

In 1993, I was working in Boston, wearing two hats for Tucker Anthony, a regional brokerage and investment banking firm. I had given up my brokerage business and switched over to the research side of the industry, where I headed up the communications department and also functioned as a supervisory analyst. The second job had more downside associated with it than its name implied. Not only was I charged with rewriting and editing stock reports generated by the company's analysts, but I was also responsible for signing off on their financial projections along with the legal department.

Most of the analysts played by the book and followed the rules; if, for example, Tucker Anthony was bringing a new company to the market, which it did with great regularity, the analysts made reasonable forecasts on where the stock price was likely to be a few years down the road. None of these companies had yet to earn a dime, and the analysts peppered their reports with warnings that the stock carried a high degree of risk and could be worthless if the fledgling company failed to meet its financial goals. Signing off on those reports was the easy part of the job.

But one analyst, whom we'll call Rob appropriately enough, was one of those rogues who keep supervisory analysts and legal departments awake at night. His typical report carried a projection about how this untested new company, whose stock was being brought public at $5 a share, would soar to $50 within the next three to five years. Buried in the footnotes, in type so small you could hardly read it, was a standard caveat that Rob owned fifty thousand shares of the company's stock in his own account. I always gagged when I got one of Rob's reports. If I put my signature on it, indicating that his financial forecast was reasonable, and the company went belly-up a year or so later, I would be exposing myself not only to a hefty fine, but possible jail time as well.

"I can't sign this," I told Rob one day, explaining my objections.

"You *putz!*" he screamed at me over the phone. "Who the fuck do you think you are anyway? How much money do you make? I make ten times more than you do."

"Good. You can pay my fine and bail me out when I go to jail."

108

"I'm not wasting any more time on you. Put Hal on the phone."

Hal was my boss, and he invariably backed the analysts. "Sign the report!" he ordered. "How do you know Rob is wrong?"

"I don't *know* he's wrong. I just think his numbers are off the wall. He's also got a conflict of interest owning such a big slug of stock himself."

"This is a risky business," Hal said. "Investment banking and corporate finance are the lifeblood of this firm. We all take our chances."

"Well, I'm drawing the line with this prick," I said. "I'm not sticking my neck out for him."

Needless to say, my days at Tucker Anthony were numbered after that. It was just a question of time before Hal decided to drop the hammer on me. Fortunately, I was saved by the bell, as it were. My phone rang one day and my old Shearson boss Dave Dworsky was on the other end of the line, calling from New York. He had remained with Shearson from the time Jamie and Sandy departed seven years earlier. After we caught up a bit, he got to the point.

"Are you happy up there?" he asked.

"Um, no, Dave," I answered, explaining what was going on.

"Well, a spot has opened up down here. We need a supervisory analyst who's also a good writer and editor. You won't have any problems like that here. The legal department is too tough. Are you interested?"

"I'm already on my way," I said.

I flew to New York a few days later and met Dave in his office on Greenwich Street. He looked much the same, except that he had packed on another thirty pounds or so, giving him the appearance of Sandy just as he was priming himself for another big deal. Dave introduced me around to the Shearson people, many of whom I already knew. The interview process went smoothly; Dave's word was good enough for them. If he wanted me back there, they all seemed ready to make me an offer. The first sense I got that there might be a fly in the ointment occurred at the end of the day, after I had already met with four or five of the Shearson lineup.

"It looks good," Dave said, shaking my hand. "Just as a courtesy, I'll set up some interviews for you next week with a few of the Smith Barney crowd. They have to give the thumbs up too, but it's just a formality."

A week passed, and then another, and finally I got a call from Dave who had arranged an appointment with his Smith Barney counterpart. Again, I flew down to meet with her, and I felt as though I had walked into a meat locker. The reception I received was frigid and barely cordial. It was apparent from the get-go that she would not give the green light to anyone recommended by Shearson, even if I was able to walk on water down the Hudson River to meet with her. No, she would be hiring one of her own, someone whose name had been put forward by one of her Smith Barney minions. I left New York with the distinct feeling that I had traveled into a parallel universe, one that *looked* a lot like the Shearson world, but was as different in tone and texture as matter is from antimatter. These were two different firms, with two distinct cultures, integrated under the same banner in name only. There was no telling how long it was going to take for Smith Barney and Shearson—not to mention the real Masters of the Universe serving under Lord Greenhill—to get their collective act together.

The beast was not only hydra-headed, it was schizophrenic as well.

A resolution to my dilemma came in the form of another phone call, this one from a headhunter trying to find out if I was open to a slot in Charlotte, North Carolina, with a financial services powerhouse we'll call Bull, Banks, Forbes & Trotsky here—BBF&T for short. I needed little encouragement, particularly since my relationships with Rob and Hal at Tucker Anthony had deteriorated from merely stormy to tornadic. Having headed north from New York to Boston, I now made a U-turn south to the heartbeat of the Mid-Atlantic region. At BBF&T there were no culture clashes to be concerned about. There was only one culture, the BBF&T culture, at a firm I thought I could fit into. I took that as a good sign.

The headhunter had set up interviews with five or six key people at the company for what turned out to be a whirlwind day of nonstop meetings, punctuated only by lunch. The last interview was with the most important person at the company, aside from its then chairman and CEO Jeffrey Peters. His name was Bob Dorian, who managed one of BBF&T's bellwether funds and would go on to become the company's chairman.

Just to put some perspective on the state of technology when I started there, e-mail and voice mail did not yet exist at BBF&T, and there was no access to the Internet. Secretaries—later called admins—answered the phones and wrote messages down on little blue memo pads. Most interoffice communication was done by fax machines, on shiny wax-like paper that invariably distorted what came through. A year later the firm announced that it would be experimenting with something called the Worldwide Web, which had everyone snickering in the hallways as though it were just another crazy fad they had to put up with. Edits and rewrites were made on the margins of hard copies of the reports, since there was no way to do them electronically at the time.

Looking back, it's hard to believe that this was the world as people knew it just a bit more than two decades ago. It was closer to the world of the 1950s and 1960s, portrayed in shows like "Mad Men," than it is to modern western society. Cigarette and cigar smoke floated freely down the hallways as employees lit up wherever and whenever they felt like it. Everyone wore a suit and tie or a dress to work, compared with the mind-boggling attire they put on today, which pushes the description of business casual to the outer limits. This would be my home until I retired twenty-two years later.

Chapter Eleven

Jamie did not have to remove Greenhill, the main roadblock on his climb to the pinnacle of the corporate slag heap, on his own. Greenhill took care of that himself. "The bottom line, or maybe I should say top line, was that Greenie failed to deliver," said Plumeri. "Sandy didn't mind loosening the purse strings for him as long as he saw some results. But Greenie didn't deliver the revenues Sandy expected after all the spending. That was it in a nutshell." Greenhill's failure to produce became a public embarrassment when the *Wall Street Journal* ran a front-page story in 1994, trumpeting Smith Barney's inability to sell more than $250 million worth of RJR Nabisco stock to the public out of a total offering of three times that amount.

In Greenhill's defense, RJR Nabisco's CEO James Johnston didn't make Greenhill's job any easier when he testified before Congress on April 14, 1994, that "cigarettes and nicotine clearly do not meet the classic definition of addiction." "I, too, believe that nicotine is not addictive," he reiterated, leaving Representatives Henry Waxman and Ron Wyden glaring at him and other tobacco company bigwigs with their jaws agape.

A serious shortfall in revenues was one thing, but public ridicule was quite another. Sandy began to trim the borders of Greenhill's fiefdom after that, shutting down his Hong Kong and Beijing operations and dividing Greenhill's dual roles at Smith Barney between him and Jamie, appointing Greenhill chairman and Jamie CEO of the firm. The shared job responsibilities were tantamount to pitting two male Bengal tigers against each other in the same cage. It was just a question of time before they ripped each other apart with bared fangs and sharpened claws, until only one of them was left standing. But, while Sandy was effectively demoting Greenhill, he was growing increasingly annoyed with Jamie, who was openly hostile not only toward Greenhill, but toward other top executives whom he viewed as obstacles on the road to achieving his career goals. Jamie complained about *everyone* on the team to Sandy, making his boss's job more difficult than it already was.

"Somehow, it seemed as though Jamie had a serious problem with anyone with whom I shared a close relationship," Sandy wrote, "as though it amounted to a personal threat. I understood the legitimacy of many of Jamie's points, but it bothered me that he couldn't operate more collegially." Jamie's hit list had lengthened to include Zarb, Plumeri, and others who had left safer pastures to take their chances in the combat zone with Sandy.

Greenhill was the first to blink. Sharing a job with Jamie, the pit bull straining to break free on the end of Sandy's chain, was not what he had bargained for. He resigned from Smith Barney on January 10, 1996, pulling most of his investment bankers with him to establish his own company, Greenhill & Company, at 200 Park Avenue. When a Smith Barney banker asked one of Greenhill bankers where he was going, the latter replied, "Over to Greenhill & Company with Greenie."

"Where is it?"

"Just get on the elevator and follow the groove," the Greenhill loyalist said.

*   *   *

114

The tension between Jamie and Sandy had become a toxic cloud that threatened to poison what was left of their unraveling relationship. Jamie managed to fire Sandy's blood to the boiling point when he positioned himself in front of Sandy in a *New York Times* feature story in July 1995, appearing to all the world as though he was the one who was actually running the show at Travelers. Califano threw more fuel on the fire when he told the reporter that Jamie was the one who actually "runs Smith Barney" and was increasingly the central figure at Travelers overall. Sandy exploded, storming into a meeting the day after the story appeared and demanding to know, "Who the fuck told Joe Califano to say that? And who chose that photo?"

Even Sandy's wife Joan, who had always been inordinately involved in her husband's business affairs and was instrumental in refining his public persona, objected to Jamie's perceived usurpation of authority. "It's not good for Jamie to be getting this kind of publicity," she said.

Sandy was not the only one on the Travelers team who resented Jamie's lust for more and more power. Jamie had taken to showing up at the office as early as six o'clock in the morning to see who among his colleagues was already in. Jamie's "bed checks," as the other execs called them, pressured them into getting in earlier themselves to show they were working as hard as he was. Some began to complain to Sandy about Jamie's autocratic behavior, something Sandy was increasingly aware of, but when Jamie began to criticize Sandy at meetings in front of everyone else, Sandy could barely rein in his temper.

"You're making a mistake. You, Sandy," Jamie exclaimed when Sandy expressed interest in buying a division of Aetna in 1995. Sandy glowered at him, feeling that his underling had gone way too far. "We'll discuss it later," he snapped. Sandy moved ahead with the deal despite Jamie's objections, acquiring Aetna's property-casualty operations for $4 billion in May 1996. Later, when the *New York Times* speculated about the "father-son" relationship

115

between the two men, Jamie was the one who bristled. "I've got my own father, thank you," he said, apparently determined to completely sever the cord binding the two men together.

The situation only worsened when the growing animosity between the two of them spilled over to include other members of their families. Joan Weill had already weighed in with her own thoughts on Jamie's ambitions, and Jamie's wife Judy was equally protective of her husband's medium-term prospects at the company. At one point she suggested that he might be better off working for someone else instead of waiting for Sandy to roll over and play dead. In an attempt to reconcile their differences, Sandy invited Jamie and Judy to lunch during a company outing in Puerto Rico early in 1996.

"You need to behave," Sandy told Jamie in front of Judy. "If you do, all of this can be yours one day."

"But, Sandy, you're not giving Jamie enough credit," Judy answered for her husband. "He's been working incredibly hard, and you don't appreciate him."

Sandy wrote later that he was flabbergasted that his junior partner had "come to see himself as my equal." Neither of them was prepared to retreat an inch. So, the impasse remained, with the gulf between them growing wider every day.

It was not their wives, however, who created an insurmountable breach between them that would prove impossible to repair. Sandy had high hopes for his own offspring, particularly his daughter Jessica to whom he felt especially close. His son Marc functioned as Smith Barney's chief investment officer, overseeing a $3 billion portfolio for the firm. Jamie had no problem with him as long as his returns were good. Jamie had even helped Marc navigate his way through the thickets of the firm's competitive, warring cultures. But Jessica was a different story. Stronger-willed than her brother, she had joined Smith Barney in 1994 and reported directly to Jamie as the director of sales and marketing for the company's mutual fund division. They began to clash immediately, primarily over the question of whether or not Smith Barney should introduce a line of no-load mutual funds—those with no commissions or sales charges added—which had become popular with investors in firms like Vanguard and T. Rowe Price.

As it turned out, Jamie was on the right side of this issue, since Smith Barney's lineup of funds with their relatively heavy loads had been losing market share to the no-load companies. But Jessica resisted the idea on the grounds that the loads were a primary source of Smith Barney's profits. "Where are your numbers to back that up?" Jamie challenged her. "We're *losing* market share, not gaining it."

"The brokers like selling our funds because they put more money in their pockets," she answered defensively.

"*Their* pockets, not the firm's. Again, where are your numbers?"

Numbers were not Jessica's forte, marketing was. Jamie won that argument, and in July 1996, Smith Barney became the first major brokerage house to introduce its own lineup of no-load mutual funds. But he had alienated the boss's daughter in doing so. When Jessica asked to be promoted shortly afterward, Jamie turned her down against the advice of some of his chief allies at the company who didn't think it was a good move for him to make politically.

"She's not ready," Jamie replied. In discussing the question with Sandy, Jamie explained that his daughter had the "soft skills" like marketing, but "she doesn't understand the numbers of the business." Sandy was stunned and infuriated over Jamie's intransigence.

The final straw was a decision Jamie made in February 1997 to exclude Jessica from a three-person advisory board he established to plan for future strategic moves at Smith Barney. Jessica complained vociferously to Jamie, but instead of giving in, he offered her a slot overseeing retail operations at a network of branch offices in California. In effect, he was talking about exiling her to the outposts of the empire—comparable to Pontius Pilate the prefect of Judea trying to keep the peace in the desert. Sandy blew his stack when he learned about it.

"You insulted her!" he screamed at Jamie.

That was it for Jessica. She had clearly reached a dead-end at her father's company. Sandy expected Jamie to patch things up, which he failed to do, and Sandy refused to intercede directly to avoid the appearance of nepotism. Jessica jumped ship in June 1997 and accepted an offer from a small money management firm named John A. Levin & Company. The company had only one-tenth of Smith Barney's assets under management, but it provided an escape route for Jessica. She accepted the offer to come aboard as president and chief operating officer. The news made the headlines of the financial pages throughout the country.

"Jamie, did you miss the class at Harvard when they said you never fire the boss's daughter?" asked Stephen Burke, a long-time friend, after he read the story in the *Wall Street Journal*.

"I had to tell her she wasn't going to get a job she wanted," Jamie replied deadpan. "She didn't like it and she left the company. I couldn't do something I didn't think was right."

Others felt that Jamie should have found a way to compromise, particularly when the boss's daughter was involved. "It wasn't like she was incompetent," said Robert Willumstad, a colleague of Jamie's since the Commercial Credit sojourn in Baltimore.

"As businessmen, we all have to live with this stuff occasionally," said Arthur Zankel, a close friend of Sandy.

But Jamie viewed the situation differently. He was tired of living in Sandy's shadow at this stage of his life. He felt a need to move on and run his own show, his own way. He was determined to force an ultimate confrontation one way or another, even if he had to "fire" the boss's daughter to do it.

* * *

All the while, the booming stock market had been good to Travelers, generating handsome profits and boosting the stock price, and it put Sandy and Jamie in a mood to feed the beast by buying more assets. Indeed, the beast was growing fatter and more aggressive, and it was time to pounce again. In July 1997, Travelers bought BankAmerica's consumer finance division for $1.6 billion as a warm-up exercise for one of the best opportunities of the decade, which arose a few months later. Sandy and Jamie agreed that they needed to establish a strong international presence to put together deals that they were incapable of doing otherwise. Greenhill had been right in setting up beachheads in Asia, although his efforts had fallen short of Sandy's expectations. What Travelers really needed to do, Jamie and Sandy reasoned, was to acquire a powerhouse institution that was *already* successful in foreign markets—particularly if they could get it for an attractive price.

Salomon Brothers had precisely the right pedigree. For better or worse, it had a reputation for being the most aggressive institution on Wall Street, a place where the investment bankers called themselves "big swinging dicks" and threw telephones at rookies who screwed up. In that regard, Salomon was more honest than other firms, which camouflaged their ravenous cultures with a phony veneer of gentility. Salomon had prospered over the decades by becoming the biggest and best-fed shark in the financial seas, but in 1991 the company bit off more than it could chew—almost literally. The government charged the firm with buying more bonds than it was legally entitled to, and then altering its books to hide the transgression. As a result, the firm was slapped with a $290 million fine, and the biggest swinging dick there, its chairman John Gutfreund, was forced to resign.

Enter Warren Buffet. The Oracle of Omaha's Berkshire Hathaway had owned 20 percent of Salomon since the crash of 1987, more than enough to give him significant clout. He had been a straight shooter all his life with no tolerance for dishonesty. He liked playing poker, but Liar's Poker—a game Gutfreund liked to gamble on to the tune of $1 million a hand—was not Warren's style. The 1991 debacle forced his next move, and he stepped in as temporary chairman to protect his company's investment and restore confidence in Salomon. He worked overtime to clean up the mess, and then tapped a straight-arrow, old-school executive named Deryck Maughan to step in as chairman and CEO in May 1992. Maughan was an Englishman who had served as an advisor to the British treasury from 1969 to 1979, before joining Salomon to run its Tokyo office.

Maughan had moved to New York, where he worked diligently to complete the job Warren had started. He made good progress, but by 1997 he realized that Salomon as presently structured could not make it all the way back on its own. "The economics of investment banking are that if you are not in the first tier of three or four firms, it's problematic to generate a satisfactory return on capital, and we were stuck just below that tier," he explained. "And given that we were a somewhat smaller firm, with a somewhat smaller footprint, I didn't know what the chances were of us penetrating that first tier, occupied by Goldman, Morgan Stanley, and Merrill Lynch. They were larger, they were generating more profits. I thought it was a race I might not win."

The man was honest enough to state his problem clearly and succinctly. Clearly enough, Salomon Brothers needed more size to achieve its goals. The old cowboy, bond-trader culture, compounded with skullduggery, had nearly wrecked the firm six years earlier. And now, for Salomon to reinvent itself and play credibly in the international investment banking arena, it needed a partner with deep pockets. Maughan compiled a list of potential suitors and put Sandy's name near the top. Sandy had been shrewd enough to invite Maughan for lunch shortly after he had relocated to New York after being placed on the top rung of Salomon five years earlier. The two of them hit it off well despite their diverse backgrounds, and talks about merging their companies progressed smoothly over only a few months. On September 24, 1997, with Warren's imprimatur, they announced that Travelers would acquire Salomon for $9 billion.

The deal was mind-boggling to most observers. Hadn't Sandy characterized Salomon and its bond trading atmosphere as "just one big casino" a while earlier? And now he was putting himself in the role of King of the Casino, changing the name of the merged operation to Salomon Smith Barney and folding it into his sprawling array of financial services products that encompassed banking, brokerage, insurance, mutual funds, investment banking—everything, in short, except loan sharking and outright mugging.

His next move is difficult to analyze clearly. Perhaps he regarded Maughan as a less-than-dynamic leader who required an able cohort by his side. Perhaps he still thought that he needed Jamie close by to get the numbers right in the vain hope that Jamie would file off some of his sharp edges and not lacerate Maughan too much. Or, then again, perhaps Sandy was just exercising his own somewhat sadistic sense of humor while he sat back and enjoyed the forthcoming show.

In any event, Sandy appointed Maughan and Jamie as co-CEOs of Salomon Smith Barney. Even the normally staid *Business Week* ran a story entitled "How Long Can These Two Tango?" in its October 1997 issue. The magazine might well have substituted the word *tangle* for *tango*. Maughan tried to put a gentlemanly face on it when he replied that "we want to operate as a team. The idea of partnership is not foreign to us." Jamie was less committal, saying "There's plenty of work for both of us to do around here."

Yes, well time—a very short time at that—would tell a different tale. The mayhem that followed would make the Jamie-Greenhill match look like a preliminary bout for the main event.

Chapter Twelve

Travelers' acquisition of Salomon Brothers turned out to be an undercard exercise for the real deal of the century shortly afterward, the biggest Wall Street merger ever announced to date and by far the grandest—if not the most grotesque—episode in Sandy and Jamie's long careers on the Street. Travelers and Salomon Brothers together were huge enough, especially when enfolded into all the other ingredients in Sandy and Jamie's metastasizing financial stew. But, when political gadfly Ralph Nader heard that Travelers was interested in swallowing the largest leviathan of all, Citicorp, into its insatiable maw, he warned the Administration and the Congress against even thinking about approving the gluttonous meal.

Allowing such a merger to go through, Nader said, would be to grant those Wall Street firms a vast concentration of power, enabling them to insulate themselves from the risks of the financial markets. It would be "an example of state capitalism or corporate socialism" run amuck, he testified at a Congressional hearing on financial reform. "What we are seeing here is not only explicit, ongoing, often subtle subsidization of the banking industry by government federal agencies, but we are seeing the 'too big to fail' approach…"

In using that description eleven years before the Great Recession of 2008, Nader was repeating a term popularized by Congressman Stewart McKinney in 1984, when he warned of the potentially dire consequences of the government's $4.5 billion bailout of Continental Illinois. And now, a new proposed merger was up for consideration, a $70 billion acquisition that would concentrate a stunning array of assets under a single umbrella, which staggered the imagination just to contemplate it.

Ironically enough, Citicorp was the financially healthier institution in the months before the discussions commenced. The

Jamie-Maughan partnership had failed to gel from the start, as most wags had predicted, and Salomon's trading losses overseas burgeoned as the arbitrage department got sandbagged on the wrong side of the bet during one crisis after another. Sandy promptly shut down Salomon's New York risk arbitrage department and was on the verge of pulling the plug on the London operation. Jamie blamed the losses squarely on Maughan, making their relationship even more inflammatory before it had barely begun. But the rest of the company was prospering, boosting the share price, and putting Sandy and Jamie in a position to pull off another acquisition, "the mother of all deals," Jamie boasted. Sandy, however, was not about to let Jamie get credit for it.

"I'm Batman, he's Robin," he said, having decided that he liked the imagery after picking it up from the rumor mill.

The big question was: would such a merger even be legal with Glass-Steagall still the law of the land? Financial analyst John Keefe brought that issue to the fore when he clearly stated that, "Under the current thinking, the ideal combination would be a commercial bank with investment banking capability with some kind of retail arm to complete the circle to distribute the products and reach into the consumer market."

That sort of combination was precisely what Glass-Steagall prohibited, and every key Wall Street player was aware of it. So, no, there was no way for the deal to go through unless someone got assurance beforehand that the law would be demolished.

*   *   *

If Jamie and Maughan looked like the Odd Couple to the financial world, Sandy and Citi chairman and CEO John Shepard Reed stretched that characterization even further. Sandy was as different from Reed as Sandy had been from, well, from American Express head Jim Robinson. Reed was a patrician, pin-striped banker, born in Chicago and raised in South America. He was also a

124

great visionary, the originator of the concept of ATMs so customers could access their accounts electronically, and he had been an astute manager who successfully navigated Citi through the ubiquitous financial storms that erupted throughout the 1990s. Unlike Sandy, Reed was an introvert by nature who found unnecessary contact with other people painful.

"Reed did not like people," said one of his colleagues at the time. He preferred "an office where he didn't have to associate with humans. Mind you, if he did run into you, he'd try to prove to you every day that he was smarter than you were."

Reed sat atop a colossus that generated just under $22 billion in revenue and $3.6 billion in net earnings in 1997. He was pushing sixty years of age and was as rich as Croesus, and unlike Sandy who was six years older, Reed was already thinking about a succession plan at Citi. Sandy smelled the opportunity of a lifetime floating on the surface of the ocean. At the end of the year, he invited Reed to meet with him at a mutually convenient time, and the two got together on February 28, 1998, at a conference of prominent CEOs in Washington, D.C. When Sandy proposed merging the two companies, he was astonished to find Reed receptive to the idea.

They met again for a second round of talks at Sandy's apartment in New York City on March 5, this time with Jamie and others at Sandy's side and their counterparts at Citi sitting in with Reed. They cemented the deal at their next meeting, this one in Armonk, New York, during two days of hard negotiations on March 20 and 21. Reed had taken a liking to Jamie, whom he apparently regarded as one of the few people on earth who was almost as smart as he was, and Jamie felt similarly about Reed, about whom he said, "He could be a cold-blooded analytic, and so could I."

It suddenly dawned on Sandy that Reed's primary interest in a merger was to put a younger man in place when he decided to step down. Sandy did not fit that description; for one thing he was older than Reed; and second, Sandy saw himself running the entire show before too long. He had no intention of playing second fiddle to anyone before he turned a corner and ran unexpectedly into a wall. Sandy acted quickly, proposing that he and Reed serve as co-CEOs of the combined firm, with a board of directors composed equally of appointees from each company. Jamie beamed, sensing this as his chance to step into Reed's shoes shortly afterward. As co-CEO with Sandy when that happy day arrived, he would finally be on an equal footing with his mentor and would be in a better position to plan his next move.

Reading Jamie's mind as it were, Sandy dropped a bombshell into the negotiations. Pulling Reed off to the side during a private dinner, he told him, "Don't do this deal in order to get Jamie as a successor. You'll have to see for yourself, but there are issues here you aren't aware of."

Reed did not react at first. Then he replied with a comment that threw Sandy off-stride. "I may not want to work as long as you do, and I don't want you to feel forced to retire. That would give me a guilty conscience. As far as I'm concerned, you don't have to leave with me as we initially discussed." Reed appeared to be assuming that he and Sandy would both step down simultaneously during the next few years, once the merged companies were functioning smoothly—a notion that Sandy may have implanted in his head during the negotiations. Now, Reed seemed to be content to let the cards fall where they may after he departed the scene. But Sandy could smell Jamie's ambition roiling like storm clouds on the horizon, and he was taking no chances that Jamie would step in to steal his thunder anytime soon. He launched his next drone strike into Jamie's lap before the deal was officially announced.

"Jamie, you're not going to be on the new board," he told him.

The comment was essentially a declaration of war. In no uncertain terms, Sandy had informed Jamie that he was being cut out of the loop. Jamie was shell-shocked. "It's absurd! I helped build this company, and I deserve to be treated better than the others," he reasoned, but to no avail. The aging king had picked up his sword and announced that he would fight on to the death. It was kill or be killed for Jamie. The terms of the merger were announced on April 6, 1998, the largest merger of "equals" in financial history, with the new entity changing its name to Citigroup.

Sandy and Reed issued a joint statement, saying that "U.S. financial services companies must be able to offer customers the same array of products and services that their international competitors are now free to provide if we are to maintain our nation's leadership position around the world. This is particularly critical given the rapid pace of consolidation by global competitors."

The financial media immediately poked fun at the notion of co-CEOs working harmoniously together; not even the sons of the Roman emperor Constantine had been able to divide their father's estate peacefully after his death, opting instead to fight one another until there was only one of them left standing. "The betting on Wall Street is that the co-CEO arrangement can't last, and that Weill and his close-knit team will eventually run the entire show," reporter Leah Nathans Spiro wrote in her April 20 article in *Business Week*. At this time, Jamie did not feel as though he were part of Sandy's or anyone else's "close-knit" team. Rather, he felt as though he had been abandoned in the wilderness to fend for himself.

The merger of the two giants created the largest financial services firm on earth, with $700 billion in assets and $50 billion in total revenues. It was also illegal. If there had been any doubts in the past about whether the beast that Sandy had knit together with Jamie's help skirted the edges of legality, there were none now. The very size, scope, and structure of Citigroup clearly pushed it over the line. Reed himself said, "the combination is clearly illegal." Not to worry, though. Sandy and Jamie had friends in Washington, friends named Robert Rubin and Alan Greenspan who, with the help of some Republican congressmen and the stroke of the president's pen, could make those annoying concerns go away.

*   *   *

Sandy and Jamie had the kind of administration in Washington that they had long been hoping for. They had both been lifelong supporters of the Democratic Party, and after eight years of President Ronald Reagan and four under President George H.W. Bush, a Democrat ascended to the catbird seat of the American Democratic Republic in 1993. Clinton came out of nowhere. Not even a tape recording of Bill Clinton engaged in verbal foreplay with Gennifer Flowers and making bigoted remarks about Mario Cuomo's Italian-American Mafioso connections could save Bush and Quayle from their well-earned defeat. In addition, he was fat at the time, he played golf, and he cheated on his wife. In other words, he was a quintessential American male of his era. The so-called New Democrat, packaged to perfection with a glittering surface, assumed the role of the most powerful man on earth. He was a "sweet, undisciplined rogue," as Maureen Dowd referred to him in her *New York Times* column.

Clinton was also a masterful politician, as he demonstrated in 1994 when he stole Newt Gingrich's playbook—the so-called "Contract with America"—and veered to the right with his support of free trade, cuts in the welfare rolls, and a balanced budget. He learned to get along well with Republican Federal Reserve Chairman Alan Greenspan, who thought Clinton was the "smartest president" he ever worked with. As I wrote in *Alan Shrugged*, my own book about Alan published in 2002, "While many of his former libertarian colleagues accused him of compromising his beliefs for the sake of political expediency, Alan maintained that his ideas had not changed since the 1950s. When he recommended to a Senate subcommittee that economic regulations should all be 'sunsetted,' that is, given an expiration date, Senator Paul Sarbanes of Maryland accused him of 'playing with fire, or indeed throwing gasoline on the fire.'

"'Do you also favor a sunset provision for the authorization of the Federal Reserve?' Sarbanes asked Alan, the sarcasm unmistakable in his voice.

"'Yes, I do, Senator,' Alan replied calmly.

"'Do you actually mean,' Sarbanes continued in disbelief, 'that the Fed should cease to function unless affirmatively continued?'

"'That is correct, sir,'

"'All right. The Defense Department?'

"'Yes.'"

Taking the man at his own word, Alan believed that the sun should have set decades earlier on Glass-Steagall.

Clinton also appointed as Secretary of Treasury Robert Rubin, who had been a bona fide Wall Street creature with Goldman Sachs' risk arbitrage department since 1966, when he was only twenty-eight years old. Robert is "the greatest Secretary of the Treasury since Alexander Hamilton," Clinton crowed at the time. Well maybe, if your names were Sandy Weill and Jamie Dimon, that is. To others, Rubin's tenure was more a case of the fox being called in to guard the henhouse.

Jamie and Sandy's common, long-standing bete noire, of course, was the set of handcuffs imposed on the way they both wanted to operate since the dark years of the Great Depression. Glass-Steagall had been the law of the land from the time Sandy was born in 1933, some twenty-three years before the day Jamie had first seen the light of day, and the two empire-builders were frothing at the mouth to break free of its tight restrictions. The beast they had created was already in technical violation of the law, but now they had an Administration and a central bank, the Federal Reserve chaired by Greenspan, in place to absolve them of their sins like a priest in the confession box. Clinton, whom some wags referred to as the best "Republican" president since Dwight D. Eisenhower because of his tilt to the right after 1994, was all too happy to let Greenspan and Rubin take the lead on this critical piece of financial legislation.

Rubin was sworn in as Treasury secretary in January 1995, after he had already helped Clinton navigate some rough financial seas as the president's Director of the National Economic Council. He ushered in the North American Free Trade Agreement with the help of a willing Republican congress and Federal Reserve, and over the objections of the unions and other opponents of globalization. As the head of Treasury, he would soon be dealing with a series of international crises, bailing out Mexico with a $20 billion U.S. loan guarantee, then containing other crises in Russia, Asia, and Latin America with the assistance of the International Monetary Fund. In what has to go down as the irony of ironies, Rubin even rescued Greenwich, Connecticut, figuratively at least, when the Connecticut-based hedge fund Long-Term Capital Management threatened to undermine the global financial structure because of its overleveraged position—meaning it had borrowed more than it could pay back,

"All of the world's capital markets began to lock and to distort," said Deryck Maughan, who was already exhibiting signs of brain trauma as Jamie's latest number-one punching bag. "Funding shut down and all sorts of things started to go wrong."

Well, when all sorts of things are starting to come unglued, and your solution is to hammer together a $3.6 billion package to pay the floundering company's debt obligations, why not take crony capitalism a step further by freeing other too-big-to-fail institutions from their straightjacket? It would take another year for Sandy and Jamie to get their ducks lined up and the hated legislation tossed onto the junk pile of Depression-era legislation. But with Greenspan, Rubin, and others including Texas Senator Phil Gramm, chairman of the Senate Banking Committee, on board, the death knell for Glass-Steagall could be heard chiming in the distance.

Sandy was so sure the law would be overturned that he told financial reporter Lou Dobbs on April 8, 1998, "I feel great about the reaction from the Fed. I think we feel good about the initial reaction from Congress, from both sides of the aisle, and we think this is really the way financial services is going."

Roger Levy, a lobbyist for Travelers, underscored Sandy's comments with a statement of his own on the same day. "We have to take advantage of the current agreement, however fragile, among all of the interested parties. All of these planets are in alignment now, in ways they may not be a year from now."

So the deal came to fruition, creating the archetypical model for the rest of Wall Street's sprawling institutions to emulate as the decade roared to a close. It was now a question of growing fatter and more powerful, or dying. No financial firm that expected to play a major role on the global stage could afford to remain small and fragmented. They all had to evolve into a one-stop financial supermarket where investors could satisfy all their financial needs— a kind of Sam's Club or BJ's offering super-sized packages containing a broad array of goods and services.

The deal was in the bag, and a new law was passed, Gramm-Leach-Bliley, which laid Glass-Steagall to rest on October 22, 1999. President Clinton cemented it with a stroke of his pen on November 12.

Three days later, Robert Rubin quit his job at Treasury and went to work for Sandy at Citigroup. Rubin, the former co-chairman of Goldman Sachs, was back in business again. In making the transition from so-called government regulator to Citigroup honcho, he exchanged his $150,000 annual salary for a compensation package worth $45 million.

"The members of the Rubin clique are extraordinary in the incompetence they displayed during their years in public and private service, and in the financial devastation they left in their wake," said James Rickards, a portfolio manager at West Shore Group and an advisor on insider trading to the Department of Defense and the U.S. intelligence agencies. "Rubin and his subordinate and successor, Larry Summers, promoted the two most financially destructive legislative changes in the past century: Glass-Steagall repeal in 1999, which allowed banks to act as hedge funds; and derivatives regulation repeal in 2000, which opened the door to massive hidden leverage by banks."

Chapter Thirteen

Through it all, John Reed remained distant. The kind of human contact, not to mention arm-twisting, required to deregulate the financial services industry simply did not interest him. He preferred to stay above the fray and let lesser mortals do the dirty work. Had he been forced to take a position himself, he would most likely have voted for the status quo, saying at one point that he was skeptical of all this "Wall Street financial engineering" and "committed to consumer banking and sound commercial underwriting." Skeptical and committed perhaps, but not enough to stand in the way of the deregulatory convulsions taking place in his own backyard.

"Sandy cut Reed out from the start," said Jeff Neufeld, chief information officer of the company who worked on the transition team after the deal was completed that October. "We literally did not know how much money was spent on payroll, on bonuses, other items. It was totally disorganized. We really had to focus on tracking all the data."

With the megamerger now a fait accompli, Jamie honed his scalpel to a fine edge with the intention of slicing away the fat at Salomon Smith Barney. He and Maughan were still jointly responsible for the division's performance, which was less than stellar by anyone's measure, and Jamie laid the poor results directly at Maughan's feet. Increasingly, he complained to Sandy about Maughan's incompetence, in his view, criticizing his co-CEO and Sandy himself openly at company meetings. Maughan was capable of defending himself, but he was especially embarrassed by Jamie's mounting hostility toward their boss.

"After I arrived, I felt there were some differences of opinion and tensions between Sandy and Jamie," he said, "and I did my level best to stay out of it, although that was not easy. I was co-head with Jamie and we both reported to Sandy, and I kept getting pulled into these things. It wasn't that comfortable."

When Jamie was not feuding with Sandy in person, he pointedly chose to operate out of his downtown office instead of moving uptown to the Citigroup headquarters at 399 Park Avenue, around the corner from Citicorp Tower, where the other top executives had set up shop. Sandy viewed it as a direct slap at him.

"Jamie spent more and more time downtown and separated himself from me and his colleagues," Sandy noted. "Everyone commented on it."

The situation could not continue much longer. Jamie was spoiling for a fight if he could not get his own way, and he clearly was not going to get it as long as Sandy remained at the helm. Jamie had been locked off the board of Citigroup, and with that curt dismissal from his boss, Jamie's prospects of succeeding Reed as co-CEO of the parent company evaporated into the ether. Maughan stood in his way at Salomon, preventing Jamie from running that bailiwick the way he wanted to as long as Maughan stayed where he was. It was time for a final shoot-out at the financial equivalent of the O.K. Corral—in fact, what happened next seemed all but inevitable considering the explosive atmosphere that emanated from the beast like a malignant vapor.

* * *

Sandy and Reed had scheduled a five-day offsite event at the tony Greenbrier Resort in White Sulphur Springs, West Virginia, in late October for one hundred and fifty of their top executives and their wives. Greenbrier sat atop a network of underground tunnels and bunkers outfitted with the latest computer technology, which had been created as a retreat for the president and key government officials in the event of a nuclear attack on the United States. The sprawling underground city was decommissioned in 1992, when the media released its secret location, but the original structures were intact when the Citigroup crew arrived for the conclave on October 24, 1998. The symbolism of Greenbrier's survival-of-the-most-powerful functionality could not have been more suitable for the events that transpired over the next few days.

The meeting began amicably enough, according to Sandy, then Deryck "gave a well-received speech that focused on our vision and the need to break down factions within the company. Jamie then followed, and my heart sank as he rambled on incoherently. The talk had no bearing on what we had just heard and lacked focus. At one point, he even lapsed into a strange analogy with the Peloponnesian War. His aloof manner and insulting lack of preparation left the crowd bewildered and seemed anything but presidential."

Jamie did not disagree with his boss's characterization of his talk. "Maybe I didn't give a good presentation," he admitted, "but do you think it's acceptable to judge a fifteen-year career on one presentation?"

Jamie and Maughan's contrasting performances set the stage for the main event of the evening. With the business part of the agenda concluded late Saturday afternoon, the execs and their wives changed into formal regalia for a black-tie dinner dance in the ballroom. The champagne, wine, and spirits flowed freely as the night progressed, and the rival factions within Salomon Smith Barney circled each other warily like two motorcycle gangs spoiling for an all-out turf war. Sandy tried to distance himself from the tension in the ballroom, sipping wine and chatting with his loyal entourage at the bar.

Reed, who had no interest in socializing or making small-talk, had departed earlier, following the conclusion of the business discussions. In the ballroom, Maughan sat at a table with his wife, the former Lorraine Hannemann, a Hawaiian who preferred to use her Samoan name Va, and a couple of his own supporters. Across the floor Jamie occupied a table with his chief lieutenant Steve Black and their wives.

Black harbored no more love for Maughan than Jamie did. In fact, he resented Maughan for treating him as just another one of

Jamie's acolytes whose career goals were beneath his consideration. The night wore on, and the spirits kept flowing, further fueling the heated passions that were ready to erupt like a bubbling volcano. Shortly after ten o'clock, Maughan escorted his wife onto the dancefloor. Black seized the opportunity to sidle over to them with Debbie, his wife at the time, and asked Maughan if he could cut in. Maughan stepped aside, but instead of reciprocating by asking Debbie to dance, he returned to his table, leaving Debbie stranded on the dancefloor. Debbie, feeling insulted and humiliated, started to cry. When Black saw what had transpired, he lost his temper and stormed over to Maughan, grabbing his arm.

"You fucking asshole!" he yelled. "You can do whatever you want with me, but if you ever do something like that to my wife again, I will drop you where you stand."

Black was a burly man, pugnacious by nature, and Maughan stood around six foot three. Va was not diminutive either; she was nearly as large as her husband and she had a propensity for violence and meddling in her husband's business affairs, according to a June 12, 1995, profile of them in *New York* magazine. Black was ready to take on the two of them, but Maughan responded by shrugging and walking away from Black, refusing to be baited into an escalation of the conflict. Black stormed back to his own table with his wife in tow and rejoined Jamie and Judy.

"What was that all about?" Jamie asked.

When Black told him what Maughan had done, Jamie decided to get involved himself. He tracked Maughan down in the foyer of the ballroom as his co-CEO prepared to leave. "Explain yourself!" Jamie demanded. "Was it an accident or did you do it on purpose?"

Again, Maughan turned away rather than letting the situation deteriorate into a physical confrontation. At that point, Jamie grabbed Maughan by his lapel, spun him around and ripped a button from his jacket.

"Don't you ever turn your back on me while I'm talking!" Jamie yelled.

Maughan stared at his damaged jacket and said, rather whimsically, "You've popped my button." He then turned his back again and strode away with his wife, infuriating Jamie all the more.

When word of what had just occurred reached Sandy and his drinking companions at the bar, it took him a microsecond to conclude that a major shakeup was in order. The events of the evening gave Sandy the excuse he needed to make the decision he had been putting off for far too long. One of the chief combatants, Jamie and Maughan, had to go—and it wasn't going to be Maughan, at least not yet. Sandy invited the executives who were drinking with him over to his cabin, where they talked about the Jamie-Maughan rivalry and its effect on company morale. Disagreements between powerful businessmen were par for the course, but a street brawl—or a ballroom tangle in this instance—called for decisive action. Bob Lipp, who had worked with Jamie since their days in Baltimore and admired his talents, was the only one who defended him. The others viewed him as uncompromising and unwilling to improve his relationship with Maughan.

"I think it's time for Jamie to go," Sandy told his wife around three in the morning.

He called Reed the following afternoon to fill him in on what had happened after Reed left Greenbrier. Reed, whose original opinion of Jamie was highly favorable, was shocked. The whole notion of a fistfight between high-level executives was almost inconceivable to him.

"Jamie has become an impediment to making the merger work," Sandy reiterated his decision for Reed's benefit.

"You can't live with this," said Reed. "You're right. Jamie has got to go."

*   *   *

When they returned to New York, Jamie proceeded to do his job in his downtown office as though nothing extraordinary had occurred during the previous weekend. He made no effort to apologize to Maughan or attempt to put the incident behind them. He had reached the point where he was arrogant and self-deluded enough to think that when push came to shove—literally, as it turned out—Sandy would choose him over Maughan. Maughan was the problem in his view, not him, and Sandy would back him in the end.

Sandy did, in a fashion, but not in the way Jamie expected. He decided to demote Maughan, whose performance he was less than thrilled with, to a figurehead position and replace Maughan and Jamie with two other executives who could work together, Mike Carpenter and Victor Menezes. Sandy then called for a meeting with Reed and other top Citigroup executives in the company's planning complex in Armonk, thirty miles north of New York City in Westchester County, on Sunday November 1. Jamie had picked that day to host a brunch for about one hundred Salomon Smith Barney brokers at his sprawling Park Avenue apartment. As they sat around munching eggs benedict, smoked salmon and bagels, and drinking coffee, Jamie's phone rang around noon. Sandy was on the line.

"Jamie, I need you to come up to Armonk now for a planning meeting."

"It's inconvenient," said Jamie. "I've got a bunch of brokers here for brunch."

"It's urgent. We're making some changes that affect you and it's going to be big news."

Jamie apologized to his guests and told them he had to leave, something important had come up. He drove north out of the city, still attired in his company sweat suit. As he headed up the Hutchinson River Parkway in Westchester, past White Plains, he fully expected that Sandy and Reed had decided to get rid of Maughan and turn over sole responsibility for Salomon Smith Barney to him. Sandy had finally seen the light and gotten Reed to go along with him. That's the only thing that made any sense. When he arrived early in the afternoon, he was ushered into a conference room for a private meeting with Sandy and Reed. They got quickly to the point.

"John and I have made the following changes," Sandy told him. They had moved Maughan off to a strategy job. So far so good. It was time they shunted Maughan off to the hinterlands, a meaningless position where he could do no further damage. That was the last stop before the exit door. Then Sandy delivered his first drone strike: Carpenter and Menezes were taking over at Salomon Smith Barney. Jamie stiffened. Wasn't that his job? Finally, Sandy lobbed the second drone into Jamie's lap. "And we want you to resign."

Jamie sat there silently for a long moment. He just then absorbed the full impact of Sandy's words, with Reed's obvious approval. "OK," he said.

"Do you want to know why?" Sandy pressed him.

"Nope. I'm sure you've thought it through."

Sandy told him anyway. The merger could not work as currently structured, and he blamed Jamie's attitude for poisoning the atmosphere. "The status quo isn't good for the company, and it's not good for you either." Reed interjected in his unemotional, matter-of-fact manner that he and Sandy were in total agreement on the decision. Jamie took the blow calmly as the realization hit him that he and Sandy were no longer a team, and that he would definitely not be stepping into Reed's shoes after the latter's planned departure once the company came together as a unified whole.

"Sandy didn't have any choice," said Dave Dworsky, ever faithful to the man he had grown up with in Brooklyn. "First there was the Jessica thing, her having to leave the company because of Dimon. Then all the other stuff. Dimon wouldn't give Sandy any rest until he was running everything himself, and Sandy wasn't ready to let go."

*   *   *

There was little left to do now but work on a press release, which Jamie helped them craft during the next two hours before they

139

went public with it that evening. Then Jamie joined the others who had been called to Armonk that fateful Sunday and waited outside throughout the afternoon. He shook hands, told them essentially that it had been a good ride for him but he had been asked to submit his resignation. "Good luck," he told them. "If I can help you in any way, let me know."

He drove south back into the city and returned to his wife and daughters on Park Avenue about five-thirty. "I resigned today," he first told them, before correcting himself. "I was fired," he said sadly. Judy cried, but the girls took it in stride when he told them they didn't have to move and he could still afford to send them to college.

Being forced out of his home and onto the street was hardly a concern for Jamie and his family. According to the terms of his negotiation with Citigroup, Jamie would receive a total compensation package worth $30 million. The other casualty, if you could call him that, resulting from the Armonk meeting was Jamie's buddy Steve Black. His platinum parachute amounted to $20 million. They occupied a rarified world where the superrich get richer yet for being told to hit the road, your services are no longer required around here.

Oddly enough, Maughan hung around a bit longer than one would expect, laboring away at his non-job for another five years before moving on to greener pastures.

Predictably, Reed was next on Sandy's hit list. Reed had served Sandy's purposes well until then, but it was a foregone conclusion that Sandy wanted Reed out of the way as soon as possible so he could run the company alone. "I felt good about our partnership at the end of 1998," Sandy wrote. "Cooperation, however, didn't mean that I blinded myself to John's quirkiness. I recognized his eccentricities even before we entered into the merger." Sandy enumerated a laundry list of Reed's failings as an executive and a human being. He didn't relate well to investors or the financial markets, according to Sandy. He insisted on working in a nondescript office on a low floor in the Citicorp building, instead of occupying an aerie high above the madding crowd where he could look down on the common folks in the grimy streets. And perhaps most damning of all, Reed was just too candid with the politicians in Washington.

"Citigroup's checking business is criminally profitable," Reed said when he testified before Congress just after the merger was announced. He later told reporter Bill Moyers that he regretted his role in dismantling Glass-Steagall. "I'm quite surprised the political establishment would listen to groups that have been so discredited," Reed said. "It wasn't that there was one or two or institutions that, you know, got carried away and did stupid things. It was, we all did."

No, clearly, Sandy had to wrestle Reed's job away from him before he said anything else that was too candid for public consumption. Reed had planned to step down anyway, fully hoping that Sandy would join him on the exit ramp to make room for younger execs who were champing at the bit to speed up their own progress along the road to greater success.

"I think Reed believed he had a handshake agreement with Sandy during their original negotiations that he and Sandy would step down together and make room for Jamie," said Citigroup chief information officer Jeff Neufeld. "It was a shame to see Jamie go the way he did. You had to admire him for what he's accomplished over the years. He was a real builder while Sandy was an accumulator, buying up failing companies and patching them all together."

But Sandy had other ideas about singing his swan song, and before long Reed decided that he had had enough. He didn't need to put up with this kind of internecine warfare any longer. He announced his resignation in a February 28, 2000, press release, leaving Sandy as the sole steward of the beast they had given birth to.

PART THREE

ARMAGGEDON

Chapter Fourteen

It's hard to believe that someone as smart as Jamie didn't recognize the dark clouds mounting overhead as his tenure at Citigroup came to an abrupt end. Yet, his closest friends say he was truly shocked by the outcome of the meeting in Armonk a week after the Greenbrier affair. Introspection and self-awareness are not necessarily traits associated with power, money, and the arrogance that often goes hand-in-hand with them.

"He was devastated and totally blindsided," said Laurie Maglathlin, the wife of his long-time friend Peter Maglathlin. "I really do believe that when he walked into that office, he had no idea he was going to walk out without a job."

"I never saw it coming," Jamie admitted. "I thought one day we'd have a drink and work it out."

"Sandy had been telegraphing Jamie's demise for some time," said Harvey Miller, a bankruptcy lawyer who had been working with Sandy over the years. "It's hard to believe Jamie didn't pick up the signals."

Money is never the issue for the superrich, but the loss of power, reputation, and prestige takes precedence over everything else. He had all the money he'd ever need for ten lifetimes, but his hands were tied to a great extent by a non-compete agreement prohibiting him from recruiting from Citigroup that he signed as part of his severance package. It was not as though he could lure talent away from his former employer and step in as the head of another money-center bank that competed directly with Citi.

At this point in his life, the industry he toiled in was hardly a bastion of free enterprise, nor had it been since the dark days of the Great Depression when the government intervened to insure depositors and prevent a run on the banks. The financial institutions had become protected utilities, as the government effectively told them they had carte blanche to take greater levels of risk, and don't worry if you roll the dice and lose, because we're here to guarantee your losses. There was little doubt that financial services, along with many other sectors including energy, pharmaceuticals, transportation, you name it, were examples of corporate welfare rather than models of entrepreneurial creativity.

So, because of the non-compete, Jamie was forced into an involuntary stretch of enforced "retirement" from the financial industry, a period in which he took up boxing to work off his hostilities, get back in shape, and prepare for the battles ahead. He spent more time reading—expanding his horizons beyond balance sheets, profit-and-loss-statements, and Machiavellian tomes on how to take over the world, to histories and biographies—and assessing where he really wanted to be a couple of years from then. He took trips to Europe with his wife and daughters, and ventured out west to enjoy an outdoor life of camping and hiking, all the while knowing that in due time he would eventually return to the world of the protected casino where he didn't have to concern himself with the nasty consequences of risks that didn't pan out.

This model had its critics on both the left and right sides of the political spectrum, from 2000 presidential contender Ralph Nader on the progressive left to Congressman Ron Paul on the libertarian right—although they tended to offer different remedies to fix what was wrong in the U.S. financial services universe. Paul placed the blame at the feet of the Federal Reserve, whose long-time chairman Alan Greenspan was at least partly instrumental in the destruction of Glass-Steagall, while Nader advocated new restraints on the colossal power that the industry's cronies in Washington had bequeathed to their major campaign contributors.

"The special privileges granted to Fannie and Freddie have distorted the housing market by allowing them to attract capital they could not attract by pure market conditions," warned Congressman Paul five years before the financial Armageddon of 2008. He was referring to the Federal National Mortgage Association, better known as Fannie Mae, and the Federal Home Loan Mortgage Corporation, or Freddie Mac, both of which were government sponsored enterprises whose major function was to buy loans made to homeowners by the banks. "It is not the market that has failed. It is intervention into the market that has failed. The Federal Reserve and its manipulation of money and interest rates have failed. None of this can be blamed on the free market."

Nader saw the situation somewhat differently, calling for more regulations, not less. He wanted Fannie Mae and Freddie Mac to be disbanded and replaced by stiff regulatory controls. "The banks want a weak oversight panel consisting of their toady regulators, who failed repeatedly and miserably in the past decade to stave off the collapse of Wall Street and its economically lethal consequences for workers and consumers...The banks want their buddies in Congress to drop the standard of reasonableness by which the new consumer protection agency can go after wildly gouging fees and deceptive practices, such as the check overdraft racket that rakes in $40 billion for the banks...The American Bankers Association is crowing like a thousand roosters. The five biggest banks...are crowing the loudest."

A casino that needed free market solutions without confining legislation from Washington, or a casino that needed to be monitored more closely? Neither unfettered competition nor restrictive oversight was acceptable to Jamie or his colleagues, who prospered most when the "right kind" of regulators set the rules. They preferred a political atmosphere in which the banks could operate with impunity, with a guarantee that the taxpayers would be paying the tab when their gambles resulted in obscene losses.

*   *   *

No matter which point on the political spectrum you chose as your vantage point, there was little doubt that the government planted the seeds for the looming economic crisis that gathered like storm clouds on the horizon. And the banks were only too happy to cultivate those seeds. Housing was at the center of the storm, the vortex of the tornado, the spot where the banks were able to profit most with no risk to their balance sheets.

"Home ownership was synonymous with the American Dream," said former representative and 1996 Republican vice presidential candidate Jack Kemp. "It was the only area of the investment universe that was subsidized by the federal government with tax write-offs. Both major political parties bought into the notion that everyone had a right to own a home, whether they could afford one or not."

The liftoff in housing prices began in 1998, following a sharp decline through the late 1980s and early 1990s. Go out and make mortgage loans to whomever wants them, the government told the banks, whether or not the buyers had sufficient income to pay the interest on the loans, and Fannie and Freddie would relieve you of all responsibility for them. The banks were only too happy to comply. It was a no-brainer; roll the dice, and if your gamble pays off, you get to keep all the profits. If you lose, the U.S. taxpayer will make you whole.

"Since Alan Greenspan took office," said economist Antony Mueller, "financial markets in the U.S. have operated under a quasi-official charter, which says that the central bank [the Federal Reserve, which Greenspan chaired from 1987 to 2006] will protect its major actors from the risk of bankruptcy. Consequently, the reasoning emerged that when you succeed, you will earn high profits and market share, and if you should fail, the authorities will save you anyway."

This was the world that Jamie returned to following his forced sabbatical from the financial sector. He briefly played with the idea of switching hats as he considered various offers, crunching numbers for an Internet company for example, but he realized that the financial markets were what he knew best. That's where he belonged. As he studied his options, he discovered who his real friends were in the world he left behind. "A lot of his old colleagues were afraid to be seen with him out of fear of antagonizing Sandy," said Bob Gilmartin, who ran public relations at Citigroup. "They didn't cut him off exactly, but they were cautious about staying in touch with him."

Jamie also joined the boards of several companies, within and outside of the financial sector, where he championed the rights of poor, downtrodden executives to squeeze as much compensation as they could from corporate coffers regardless of their performance. He was lured onto the boards of Lions Gate Entertainment; Japan's Shinsei Bank; Yum! Brands, an operator of fast food chains in the U.S. and Asia; and other major firms. Finally, after eighteen months of sitting on the sidelines and warming the bench, Jamie got itchy to don his armor once again and return to the corporate battlefield. The opportunity that intrigued him most did not come from Wall Street, but rather from a failing bank in the heartland of America, Bank One in Chicago.

Despite its august name, Bank One was not first on anyone's list of financial institutions at this stage of its history. It fact, it resembled more than anything else the moribund shell of the once-dynamic Commercial Credit in Baltimore, which Jamie and Sandy had rescued from the brink of bankruptcy fourteen years earlier. This time, Jamie was out to prove that he could make his mark on his own by visiting the graveyard of sick banks that were about to go under and breathe the gift of life into them again. It would be his way of showing Sandy that he could do his former master one better, without depending on a sidekick who was smarter than he was, in Jamie's view, to make sure the numbers worked out in the end.

*   *   *

At the turn of the millennium, Bank One was a stitched-together corpse of once-austere financial powerhouse. It came into existence as City National Bank, a McCoy family-run operation based in Columbus, Ohio, in 1863, the year of the Emancipation Proclamation. President Lincoln ended slavery on January 1 that year, and the financial world was not yet enslaved to the same degree as it is today by the Wall Street Money Masters. Through various acquisitions over the years, the bank expanded, becoming the first institution outside of California to issue credit cards, namely BankAmericard, the forerunner to Visa.

In 1968, the company created First Banc Group as a holding company for City National Bank, and it functioned as an acquisition machine to gobble up other banks. In the aftermath of the Great Depression, First Banc acquired smaller banks outside its home territory, starting with Farmers Saving & Trust Company in Ohio, and allowed the acquired banks to operate under their own names. First Banc provided cash infusions to shore up their balance sheets and pumped new life into moribund markets. Banc one took its odd spelling from a peculiarity in the law, which prohibited holding companies from using the word *bank* in their charters.

First Banc continued to expand throughout the region, buying Security Central National in 1971 and others throughout the Midwest. In October 1979, as laws began to change, First Banc became the Banc One Corporation, but its member banks were allowed to use the more familiar spelling, such as Bank One Columbus, Bank One Portsmouth, and Bank One Mansfield—all of them Ohio-based. Other acquisitions followed, as the parent company grew into a Midwestern behemoth. 1985 was a pivotal year, with federal and state banking laws undergoing major overhauls that permitted banks to buy other institutions outside state borders. First Banc became Banc One and extended its acquisition campaign farther afield, swallowing Purdue National Bank in Lafayette, Indiana, and a mind-numbing array of institutions in Indiana, Kentucky, Wisconsin, Arizona, Texas, and Louisiana. The name changes continued apace, with Citizens Union National Bank & Trust Co. of Lexington, Kentucky, being reincarnated as Bank One Lexington.

So far so good. But soon the engorged beast swallowed more than it could easily digest, as home prices hit a peak and started to tumble downhill in 1988. Banc One had taken over one hundred and thirty banks during the past twenty years, and not all of them were functioning smoothly. John B. McCoy, the last in the McCoy family dynasty in more ways than one, was starting to gag on his bank's ravenous diet. He unwisely devoured the Fletcher Corporation, a multibank holding company in Indiana, in a deal that gave 20 percent of the voting stock in the new company to the former managers of American Fletcher. As a result of the merger, a change in management followed. Frank McKinney, Jr., the head of American Fletcher, replaced John B. McCoy as president of Banc One Corp. and moved McCoy up to chairman of the combined organization with the creation of an unwieldy two tiered management system that oddly enough reduced McCoy's stranglehold on the entire enterprise.

The deal of deals, which turned out to be the coup de grace for McCoy, was the 1998 merger of so-called equals between Banc one and First Chicago NBD of Illinois, based in Chicago. First Chicago was hardly in better financial shape that Banc One was, and Wall Street analysts compared the two institutions to a couple of drunks propping each other up after an all-night bender. On paper, the two staggering Goliaths controlled $260 billion in combined assets, but their profits were in free-fall due to waning mortgage and other consumer lending and flagging credit card operations. The $29 billion deal, a combination of cash and stock swap, rapidly transmogrified into a $20 billion merger with the share prices of both banks plummeting. McCoy's fortunes plummeted with the stock valuations, calling to mind Barnard Baruch's witticism that the easiest way to make a small fortune is to start out with a large one. The combined board of directors was less than thrilled by McCoy's performance, which was underscored by his laughing-stock image in the media, which started to refer to him as "Fly-by McCoy."

The combined bank, which moved its headquarters to Chicago, now operating under the name Bank One, was a single entity in name only. In reality, the cultures were at war from the beginning, with the former Banc One decentralized and prone to take on great risk through acquisitions, and First Chicago a highly centralized and conservative bank that avoided undue risk as though it were a plague from hell. Talk among the employees was that Bank One was addicted to taking on risks before all the numbers were fully crunched, and First Chicago never got anything done because it analyzed every situation to death. But it was clear that heads were going to roll, the first among them John McCoy's.

"If you had to choose who you were going to be working with for an extended period of time, John certainly had an advantage," said Ron Steinhart, a big investor in McCoy's bank before the merger. "He's someone you can identify with. He's not arrogant, not a know-it-all, just a good people person who gives you a lot of leeway. Perhaps that sometimes came home to haunt him."

In December 1999, the board voted to replace McCoy with an interim CEO, Verne Istock from the First Chicago side of the operation. Two other First Chicago people, John Hall and James Crown, took over as interim co-chairmen. McCoy, who had clearly gotten in way over his head during his buying spree, was genuinely crestfallen by the turn of events, which wrested control of the Civil War-era bank away from his family—although he did attribute much of the blame to an executive named Richard Vague, once viewed as a possible successor to McCoy, whom he allowed free rein with minimal supervision.

"He let me down," McCoy said. "I did what I had to do with Dick Vague, and I don't want to talk about it."

McCoy's board had always backed him despite several stumbles in the past, but this time he was not dealing with *his* board. "In all of his years as CEO, he always had a very supportive board

152

and group of executives working for him, so all this controversy and division was a new thing for him," said Hall. McCoy had no option but to walk away quietly, knowing he was in a battle he couldn't win.

"Instead of fighting, I decided it would be better to take the high road," he said. "My conclusion was that we needed to bring in some outside management, and I worked hard to get that done. When the board had difficulty with that, I said, 'I'll go, but they'll agree to do a search.'"

And so the search for a permanent CEO commenced, with Jamie on the short list of contenders for the job.

Chapter Fifteen

Landing the top slot at Bank One was not a slam dunk for Jamie. His reputation—or rather, his *reputations* had preceded him: cost-cutting data-cruncher who knew how to turn a company around; cantankerous, bull-headed head-banger who knocked people dizzy with his pugnacious manner. In addition, Jamie had been high on McCoy's list of candidates, hardly a good reference from a man who was being ushered unceremoniously out the door. In Chicago, he would be entering a conservative banking culture that viewed brash Wall Street pit bulls with considerable alarm. His feuds with Sandy and the reasons for his abrupt departure from Citigroup were widely known throughout the industry. The Greenbrier Incident, culminating in a near fist-fight with a fellow executive, had been embellished to the level of a TV reality show with each retelling. And for some time after the event, that's *all* anyone wanted to talk about outside of business.

Jamie joined the long line of applicants for the top job at a revered but failing bank with some trepidation. He longed to get back in the game, at the very pinnacle where he felt he belonged. But both Hall and Crown, the two men Jamie had to impress the most, had their reservations about him. "There was from the start some concern that a person from New York, with a New York financial community background, would not fit the Chicago culture," said Hall. "And that Jamie would break too much china. We talked to Jamie about it. He said he would work hard to do the right thing. He recognized that maybe some of them were used to a different style. There were a lot of concerns that we had to overcome on that particular issue."

Crown was also hesitant, but he tended to accentuate the positives. "What was interesting and impressive about Jamie then was if you asked him a question, he thought about it for just a little bit and then he gave you a direct and directional answer," he said. "There was no word-mincing and no circumlocution around the question. Jamie was very direct. Jamie came out of this process as just a white-hot, superior level of intelligence, very knowledgeable about financial services, the financial industry, and banking, and as a tireless worker."

Jamie had his own worries about pulling up stakes and moving his family to Chicago, a prospect that Judy was less than thrilled about. "We had three daughters to consider, where they would go to school, how they would fit in, all of that," she said. "Plus we all loved New York. The idea of leaving New York and our social life behind was not appealing in the least."

Jamie had few other options at this point, however. The type of opportunity he was looking for was not available at the other major financial institutions. Citigroup was out for obvious reasons. Bank of America, Wachovia, Wells Fargo were not looking for new leadership. He had nowhere else to turn if he wanted to prove that he could run an operation of that size on his own. While many board members had their concerns about him, Crown remained his biggest fan among the First Chicago executives.

"Jamie brought to the table a wealth of merger-and-acquisition experience because of all the work he had done with Sandy Weill," he said. "We felt we had a good leader who would be able to finish the merger work of the prior decade. While those deals had legally been completed, they weren't functionally complete."

The board remained fairly evenly split, with loyalists from the former Banc One and First Chicago lining up in opposition like the two major U.S. political parties stonewalling each other. Ten members beholden to First Chicago wanted to keep Istock in place as permanent chief honcho. The Banc One people outnumbered them, however, with eleven on their side of the aisle. In the end most of them came around and agreed to present something resembling a united front to the public. They telephoned Jamie with the news while he was skiing with his family in Vail, Colorado, asking him to come to Chicago as soon as possible. Jamie left his wife and daughters in Colorado and flew to Chicago on Sunday, March 26, 2000, thirteen days after he celebrated his forty-fourth birthday. The entire board, which Jamie set eyes on for the first time, was there to greet his arrival. Its collective decision was a foregone conclusion. He had been chosen over a long list of candidates to come aboard as Bank One's new CEO.

"I really appreciate the opportunity, and I'm going to make you proud of the place," Jamie said, shaking everyone's hand. "I believe in eating my own cooking," he added, proving it the next day when the market opened for trading by buying two million shares of the bank's stock at an average price of $28.37 a share, nearly half his net worth at the time.

The company announced his appointment to the media on Monday the 27th, and held a press conference at five in the afternoon at the company's headquarters at 1 Bank One Plaza in Chicago. "Jamie Dimon's business experience, management skills, and strategic thinking will lead our outstanding franchise in the new century," Hall said. "Jamie's fresh perspective and his ability to galvanize employees also set him apart from an exceptional field of candidates from around the country." Jamie performed smoothly, playing it straight.

"I am excited by Bank One's powerful franchise, its dedicated employees and its bright future," he commented. "Together, we can serve our customers exceptionally well and realize our goal of being America's premier financial institution." He remained cool until one reporter tried to dampen his victory by asking him if he thought he could operate without Sandy at his side.

Jamie bristled, glaring at the cheeky journalist. "I couldn't care less," he snapped. "That's not me."

Istock was kept on as president, reporting to Jamie, who now headed the fifth-largest bank in the U.S.—financially wobbly as it was—behind Sandy's Citigroup, Bank of America, Chase, and J.P. Morgan. But there was a lot of fat on the books at Bank One, too much bureaucracy, and Jamie's big challenge would be to take out his cleaver, cut away the flab, and turn Bank One into a lean, competitive, financial machine.

*   *   *

Jamie accepted his new position seventeen days after the Eve of Destruction for the high-tech market. The Nasdaq Composite Index, which is composed about 70 percent of technology stocks, peaked at 5048.62 on March 10, 2000, when the entire sector dove into a breathtaking tailspin, knocking the broad market down with it. Fledgling tech stocks with no earnings and poor prospects found their share prices soaring into the stratosphere, trading at infinite price/multiple earnings. I remember when the portfolio manager for our Sci-Tech Fund caught a lot of flack because his fund was up *only* 100 percent in 1999 while his peers returned an average of 150 percent.

"I'm not chasing all the crap," he said. "I'm sticking to the stable companies in the sector that have track records and good earnings outlooks. I can't play that game."

We loaded his reports with warnings that these returns were not sustainable, and that investors should lighten up on their exposure to tech and diversify their portfolios. Shareholder reports are not the finest literature ever printed, and shareholders by and large give them only scant attention when they appear in their mailboxes or are delivered electronically. But this is shortsighted at best. The three areas of a report that shareholders should read religiously are: first the fund's performance over the longer term; second, the fund's positioning for the future, particularly the stocks and sectors the manager likes and thinks will outperform in coming months; and, perhaps most important, the managers' outlook for the year ahead, whether or not they think share prices are overvalued and how they are likely to do through the next cycle.

Those caveats saved BBF&T a lot of grief when clients heavy in tech stocks threatened to sue the company when the market plunged. We were able to send their lawyers copies of the shareholder reports going back a year and longer, containing warnings about unrealistic performance and advice about minimizing their exposure to technology. Most of those shareholders, who chose to ignore the caveats and took a subsequent beating, were simply never heard from again. A friend of mine was fairly typical. He took a lump sum retirement payment of $250,000 from an oil company he worked for and plunked the entire amount down on the riskiest stocks in the tech sector. Within months he lost the last zero from the value of his portfolio, which tumbled to $25,000.

"You're nuts, Mike!" I told him. "Why did you do it?"

"Greed," he admitted. "I was tired of earning a lousy 20 percent a year when other people were doubling and tripling their money."

Ninety percent of the high-flying tech stocks went out of business entirely, and even the more solid companies in the sector saw their stock values plunge 60 percent to 70 percent. It reminded me of the days when the New York City cabdriver ran up a modest portfolio to $850,000 on gambling companies owned by wise guys, only to see it plummet back to where he started at $35,000. When fear and greed hit the market, it's astounding to see how many speculators will buy stocks at $100 a share when they're going up, but won't touch them at $15 when they still like the business model. Nothing is too expensive when greed rules the day, and nothing is too cheap when fear takes hold. It makes no sense, but it happens every time a bubble builds and then starts to burst.

Jamie faced the same dilemma at the bank he now ran, putting it in good running order and protecting the value of its stock price. After all, he had just invested 50 percent of his own net worth in Bank One stock, and he had no desire to see it evaporate before his eyes. So he had some excess fat to slash away at Bank One. He may not have liked the comparison, but to his credit, he had learned his lessons well as Sandy's chief acolyte. He looked around, took aim, swung his cleaver, and landed it cleanly on Istock's neck. There was room for only one star in the firmament, and Jamie didn't welcome someone else trying to outshine him while he was trying to do his job any more than Sandy did.

Istock didn't know it when they held the press conference announcing Jamie's appointment, but he had only six months left to live in Jamie's orbit before he flamed out like a dying meteor. Next on his list was seizing control of the all-important board of directors, which he accomplished by whittling it down from twenty-one to thirteen members. He assigned that job to Hall and Crown, who operated like a tag team and excised eight existing members off the board over the next twelve months in the face of staunch opposition.

"It's almost as if you're twisting our arms," one board member complained.

"Guilty!" Jamie fired back. "But I'm not doing it for me. I'm doing it for the company." Jamie then proceeded to stack the smaller board with men he could count on, including Charlie Scharf, Bob Lipp, and Steve Burke, his old friend from HBS.

"I had to be careful," Jamie said. "I had a very strict non-compete that I followed to the letter. I couldn't hire you. I couldn't make you an offer. But if you called me I was allowed to say, 'I can't do any of this, but you're free to call Joe.' All these people kept coming, and they came for lesser jobs, lesser pay, to a weaker company."

The bank he now governed was truly gargantuan in size, with $265 billion in assets, eighteen hundred branch offices, fifty-six million Visa credit card customers, and a market capitalization (share price times the number of shares outstanding) of $36 billion. But it couldn't navigate through the choppy financial seas the way it was set up, which is why it needed a new captain at the helm in the first place. To get his ship under control, Jamie spent the next year traveling from branch to branch. He wanted to get to know the main players he had inherited, and for them to become familiar with him and how he operated as well. He visited every office in the country, from the east coast to the west, and pored through the books meticulously, examining compensation packages, contracts, remodeling projects, capitalization expenditures, chains of command—nothing escaped his attention.

"I had to cut it all back," he said. "There were areas where people hardly knew who they were reporting to. They didn't talk, they didn't communicate. All that had to stop. You can't operate efficiently with different cultures warring with each other."

Jamie had no allegiance to any culture but his own, the one he was determined to impose on the sprawling institution and make it function as a unified whole. The problems he encountered afflicted every area of the firm. "Aggressive accounting, a disjointed board, horrible credit problems that could have sunk the company, not enough capital, horrible customer service," he lamented. "We had seven deposit systems, five wire systems, five cash management systems, two capital market systems, multiple complexity." Different branches used a mind-numbing array of computer operating systems—Windows 98 here, Windows 2000 there, Windows NT yonder—plus several word processing applications. None of it made any sense, and Jamie had to fix it all in the midst of a stock market selloff that punished his own company's stock as well as most of the technology companies.

"I believe that Jamie's game plan from the beginning was to get this mess in order and sell the company a few years later," said Bob Gilmartin, who worked with Sandy at Citigroup. "You can't blame him for that, although the old hands at the bank were horrified by the prospect. But the reality was he had no allegiance to the bank. He had his own money at risk. He was hired to do a job, and he was doing it."

Jamie's efforts were facilitated by the hemorrhaging of talent that was taking place at Citigroup, whose stock was hit especially hard by the market selloff that decimated the financial sector as well as the high tech sector. The entire market was affected, as bearish investors took no prisoners on their way out of the exit door. Key personnel, formerly loyal to Sandy, were at risk of watching their careers go under as the great cobbled-together Citi ship began to leak at an alarming rate. They knew Jamie and recognized that he was their main hope of rescue as the seas became more turbulent. Charlie Scharf, Jim Calvano, Bob Lipp, Marge Magner, Heidi Miller, Joe Plumeri, Bob Willumstad, Frank Zarb—one by one they journeyed to Chicago, gutting the ranks of Sandy's top management personnel. The only key player to remain with Citi was Chuck Prince, who functioned as a loaded torpedo that helped sink Sandy's ship a few years later. Finally, Sandy had had enough and called his erstwhile chief apostle.

"You're poaching my people!" Sandy yelled. "You're in violation of our contract."

"I'm not poaching anyone," Jamie responded. "They're coming of their own volition. You should be asking yourself why. If

I were you, I'd be looking inside to see why your people are leaving."

"That never happened to Sandy before," said Dave Dworsky. "In the past, people had always wanted to work *for* Sandy. He took care of those who were loyal to him. This was a completely new experience for him."

It was not just the sagging stock price that prompted the top ranks of Citigroup to abandon ship. Sandy had never concerned himself with reconciling the diverse cultures that existed within his patchwork empire. With Jamie out of the picture now, Sandy reluctantly concluded that Jamie had always tended to those mundane matters. Sandy initiated the deals, but Jamie took care of the details. Aside from its warring cultures, Citigroup had made a series of bad bets repackaging mortgage-backed bonds, which affected the company's profit margins. Sandy's sterling reputation as a Wall Street dynamo suffered as a result, leading to disaffection among his chief lieutenants. Jamie's star, on the other hand, was on the ascendant once again, luring his former colleagues to the Windy City from New York.

"I had to make very quick decisions," Jamie said. "There were people in place who weren't right for their jobs, and I had to identify them and put others in place who could do them better."

"You had to understand what Jamie was doing," said James Crown. "He was cutting out top people at the bank and tearing apart fiefdoms. Most of them were very upset. They didn't know where they stood from one day to the next."

But Jamie knew where he stood— and what he *had* to do to get this behemoth under control. The media were watching his every move closely, waiting for him to mess things up, and he had to focus all his energies on the job at hand, or else go down as the young prince who couldn't make it on his own without King Sandy orchestrating his strategy.

Chapter Sixteen

Getting his arms around Bank One proved to be even more daunting than Jamie anticipated. It was sprawling, it was vast, and it was wildly dysfunctional. Worst of all, the bank's earnings growth was not keeping pace with its major competitors. The company's stock had taken an encouraging 20 percent bounce after the announcement of Jamie's selection as CEO, but it had quickly retreated to pre-Jamie levels under $27 a share. And the media made it clear that they were out for his blood.

"New Bank One President Jamie Dimon had better bring his A-game next month when he reveals plans for the troubled Chicago bank—or he'd better not come at all," read an article in the June 26, 2000, issue of *Fortune.*

Wall Street didn't help Jamie out much at all. Nineteen of the twenty-four analysts who followed Bank One rated the company's stock as a "hold" or a "sell," both of them a kiss of death with savvy investors who translate those ratings as "it's not going anywhere" in the first instance, and "get the hell out of the stock now if you know what's good for you" in the second. The most influential analyst of all, Mike Mayo with Credit Suisse, had put a "sell" on Bank One a year earlier when the stock was hovering around $60 a share, and he refused to upgrade it when Jamie took over.

Business Week chimed in, stating that Jamie was the wrong man for the job, since a "dealmaker is a different personality than a leader."

Jamie was feeling the heat, working seven days a week with his family still living in Manhattan, trying to figure out how he could quickly trim at least $1.5 billion in annual expenditures. "I was pretty much alone that whole year," Jamie said. "It was by far my worst year ever in the business."

The first step was easy, although he was loathe to do it. Bank One was laying out $2 billion a year in dividends to shareholders, and Jamie decided that they needed to be cut in half to $0.21 per share, freeing up $1 billion for operating capital. "We need the capital, we're paying out too much, I'm not confident things are going to get better anytime soon. We're going to cut it. It's the right thing to do." He tried to soften the blow by saying that cutting the dividend was "something that no corporation should ever have to do," but he had to do what was necessary under the circumstances.

It was a tough blow for value investors, who buy stocks paying healthy dividends when the share price has sunk in value. They depend on the income and figure that a good dividend yield served as a cushion for the stock price when the market took a nosedive. Growth investors, on the other hand, didn't worry about dividends since they looked for earnings growth to propel their stocks higher. But Bank One was decidedly not a growth stock, and after Jamie sliced the dividend in half, it wasn't much of a value stock either. It was a sick fish floating in the water, with turkey vultures wheeling overhead waiting for it to expire.

*　　*　　*

Jamie's family followed him to Chicago in the late summer of 2000, in time for their daughters to enroll in the city's prestigious Latin School. They bought a luxurious fifteen-thousand-square-foot

166

spread overlooking Lake Michigan, a twenty-six-room penthouse with eight bedrooms, eleven bathrooms, a gym, a roof garden, and more, for which they paid $4.7 million.

"It was like an embassy, and Jamie and Judy did a lot of entertaining there," said Bob Willumstad.

But, for Judy, New York was still home. She had a difficult time making the adjustment. "I really missed close family and friends," she lamented. "I had a tough time opening up to the welcoming ways of the Midwest." She eventually became active in the community, however, hosting fund-raising parties for Chicago's inner-city schools, working alongside Arne Duncan who went on to greater fame as President Barack Obama's secretary of education nine years later. But Jamie and Judy hung on to their New York apartment, lending credence to the rumors that Jamie's real goal was to fix up Bank One for a sale down the road and then move back to New York. Jamie fumed over the charge.

"If I dropped dead out here after twenty years," he said, "and they shipped my ashes back to New York, they'd say, 'See. He never intended to stay out here in the first place.'" The critics proved right, as it turned out, since selling the company and dashing back to New York was exactly what he did as soon as the opportunity became available.

But first Jamie had a major overhaul to perform on the sputtering investment vehicle he now commanded. The figures were daunting, and the market was not cooperating. After slicing the dividend in half, Jamie turned his attention to rank-and-file employees, eliminating twelve thousand from the company's payrolls. He needed to reconcile the diverse deposit, computer, and operating systems, an expensive job that required more capital than Bank One could easily afford. Virtually everything needed to be fixed, the grandiose along with the mundane. It exasperated him to discover that Bank One's branch offices were open two fewer hours a day than competing bank branch offices.

"How could that be?" he said. "You can't operate a bank properly if you crimp on basic services."

When Judy Dimon noticed that an ATM machine hadn't been functioning properly every time she passed by, Jamie quickly took action by inquiring who was responsible for monitoring it. "One of our vendors," he was informed. Jamie complained, and the vendor dispatched a crew to fix the flickering machine. But it was too late. Jamie fired the vendor. "A problem shouldn't persist for months before they get around to taking care of it," he reasoned.

All these changes, big and small, resulted in a $2.9 billion restructuring charge in the second quarter of 2000 alone, which had a devastating impact on the bank's bottom line, with Bank One posting a mind-numbing loss of $1.27 billion. Jamie hoped to get all the write-downs out of the way in his first full quarter on the job, but he was unable to contain the hemorrhaging that quickly. The charges against earnings continued throughout the year, amounting to $4.4 billion for all of 2000. Some Wall Street analysts praised him for making the tough decisions, but the influential Mike Mayo was not among them. "You have to realize that this is a battleship to turn around and Jamie Dimon is not Hercules," he wrote.

Over and over again, Jamie talked about the importance of creating a fortress balance sheet, a rock-solid asset base capable of supporting a company through economic turbulence, but Bank One's balance sheet looked more like a leaking barge than like anything resembling a fortress.

Jamie was irritated that the restructuring was taking longer than he had anticipated. It sent out the wrong signals to the investment community, which focused more on short-term results. To the average person, long term means a year or longer; the institutional flash-trading community regards anything longer than a microsecond as long term. "Jamie felt that when you don't get everything the first time around, it says that there were more problems than we first realized, and we weren't smart enough to see them," said HBS professor Paul Martin, who conducted a detailed study of Bank One's finances.

Tackling Bank One's internal divisiveness and imposing a one-size-fits-all culture was another of Jamie's top priorities. "He expected everyone to take ownership," said Kathy Schroeder, who was in charge of employee development at the bank. "That was part of the culture change. Everybody at every level of the organization was expected to be fully accountable and to look outside the box for new ways of doing things."

While most employees felt the pressure, Jamie also turned up the heat on the bank's top-tier executives. He cut their perks to the bone, canceling their subsidized memberships to exclusive clubs, limo services, even their newspaper subscriptions. "You're businessmen," he told them at meetings. "Pay for your own goddamn *Wall Street Journal*!" Jamie's New York confederates laughed it off, having grown used to his style through many years with him on the firing line back east. But the buttoned-down hometown boys were aghast, wondering among themselves what kind of Ahab-like dictator they had invited to command their floundering vessel.

Jamie had a clear vision of what he had to do to turn the battleship around, in Mike Mayo's words, but implementing that vision was far more difficult than seeing it in his head. He was impatient to put his ideas in motion, and he resented those who stood in his way, questioning the direction he set his sights on. Stagnation among the bank's old guard executives fired his blood to the boiling point. "If there's one thing that grinds my gut, it is bureaucracy," he said, sounding more like General George Patton than like a financial guru. "All I wanted to do was promote and pay

169

those who are good. If they are bad, they have to go. And that is the hardest management decision."

"These were powerful messages, powerful cultural changes," said Crown. "People started to sort themselves into different groups when they saw what Jamie was up to: those who left on their own or were asked to leave; those who figured things out instantly; and those who adapted more slowly and wanted to stay."

Most disconcerting to many of them was Jamie's habit of showing up unannounced at various meetings, sitting in and taking extensive notes, then leaving everyone in a quandary when he exited without speaking a word. It reached a point where the nervous execs tried to find out beforehand when Jamie would be out of town so they could schedule time together without their boss performing his fly-on-the-wall routine. "Jamie never used the term 'cost-cutting,'" Crown explained. "He preferred to call it 'waste-cutting,' and everyone was on edge wondering if they were among the waste he had in mind or not."

Jamie was equally blunt in a letter he crafted to shareholders at the end of 2000. "Problems don't age well," he wrote. "Denying or hiding them guarantees that they will get worse…Bureaucracy, silos, and politics are the bane of large corporations; they must be combatted vigorously and continually." His words earned him plaudits from Warren Buffett, who was renowned for his own informative and entertaining missives to investors in Berkshire Hathaway. "Jamie writes a great letter," said the Oracle of Omaha. "He writes it like he would write it to me if I owned one hundred percent of the bank. It's a very sensible and literate letter from a manager to his owners. You can't find many like that. You particularly don't find them in financial services."

Jamie had a right to be proud that he had earned his stripes with one of the world's great investors and one of its wealthiest men. He had clearly gotten off on the right foot with Bank One, notwithstanding the hurdles he had to overcome at an institution that was struggling to remain afloat when he took the helm. The question he faced now was just how long he would have to wait before his efforts paid off in concrete results. Longer than he would have preferred, it seemed. The stock price was still languishing in the high-twenties to low-thirties, along with other battered shares in the wake of the dot.com implosion. The company's balance sheet started to look more like the fortress Jamie spoke about, but its bottom line was still a deep shade of crimson.

*　　*　　*

Jamie might be forgiven for experiencing a tinge of schadenfreude—a feeling of "shadow" pleasure in the misfortunes of others—over the plight of his old boss Sandy, who was reeling at the top of the pile at Citigroup. Beginning in 2000, consolidation consumed the industry, as several financial giants gobbled one another up in an attempt to challenge Citi's bloated presence on the landscape. Wachovia bought First Union, and other big bank deals were rumored to be in the works.

The same thing had happened in the entertainment industry fifteen years earlier when Ted Turner told Rupert Murdoch he was going to squish him "like a bug. You ain't got any size, Rupert," the Mouth of the South informed the dour Aussie, who proved Turner wrong in the long run with his successful launch of Fox, thanks largely to Barry Diller's ingenuity. So big whales devouring other large whales was not unprecedented in U.S. corporate history, and now that Glass-Steagall was dead, it was the banks' turn to grow fatter than they already were.

The problem at Citi was an internal affair that Sandy had allowed to metastasize without taking proper action. In fact, Sandy was at the center of a storm that was largely of his own making. Citi had made a big bet on WorldCom, which for a while was the second-largest long-distance telephone company in the U.S. after AT&T. WorldCom's stock had been punctured by the bursting of the high-tech bubble in 2000, but the worst was yet to come. The company's CEO, Bernie Ebbers, was later convicted of conspiracy, perpetrating a massive accounting fraud, and filing false documents with regulators, and he was sentenced to twenty-five years in prison. He took another of his top executives down with him.

Sandy' chief industry analyst was a long-time friend named Jack Grubman, The story emerged that Sandy convinced Grubman to maintain a "buy" rating on WorldCom, despite Grubman's reservations, in return for Sandy's help in getting the analyst's children enrolled in the upscale 92nd Street Y nursery school on the Upper Eastside of Manhattan. Sandy denied his complicity, but the financial media jumped all over him, with the *Wall Street Journal* stating that his interests had "diverged" from Citigroup's and condemning him for "lax oversight." The incident marked the beginning of the end of Sandy's reign as the King of Wall Street.

Sandy actually turned on Grubman and distanced himself as far as possible from the hapless analyst. "Regardless of their real relationship," Sandy wrote, "Jack Grubman now seemed inextricably linked to the two dubious WorldCom executives." Grubman appeared before a House Committee investigating the scandal, and Sandy watched his performance on television. "Grubman never was photogenic, and television now captured his dark features and deep-set eyes in a way that made him look sinister. Worse still, he projected an air of arrogance. The testimony seemed to drag on and focused on how Jack interacted with WorldCom's top executives."

In staking out that position, Sandy cast himself in the role of 1952 presidential candidate Dwight D. Eisenhower reviewing the performance of his "sinister" running mate with "dark features," Richard Nixon, as he weaseled his way out of a budding scandal in his famous "Checkers" speech. But at least Ike decided that Nixon had acquitted himself well enough and kept him on the ticket that year instead of hanging him out to twist in the wind.

"It was basically over for Sandy after that," said Bob Gilmartin, Sandy's PR guy at Citi.

"I was as shocked as anyone when that news came out," said Dave Dworsky. "Sandy was smarter than that."

Smart, yes, but an ultimate dealmaker out to preserve his status as the heaviest hitter on Wall Street—unsuccessfully, as it came to pass, in the aftermath of Citigroup's mounting problems in the industry.

Jamie never gloated openly about his old boss's predicament, but it was clear to everyone that he was in a better position than Sandy as the new decade unfolded.

Chapter Seventeen

It took a disaster in the financial sector to set the stage for the next act in Jamie's leading role at Bank One. The disaster took place at J.P. Morgan, once the gold standard of U.S. banking since its founding during the Civil War after several incarnations. J. Pierpont Morgan had once been so powerful that he announced his arrival at Jekyll Island, one of the Golden Isles off the coast of Georgia, by firing cannons from his yacht as he sailed into the harbor. He and his fellow old-line barons, who owned most of the island, believed it was beneath their dignity to allow the *nouveau riche* Andrew Carnegie to set foot on their hallowed ground, forcing Carnegie to establish his own retreat on Cumberland Island, closer to the Florida border a few miles farther south.

Perhaps it was the ghost of Carnegie that exacted its revenge on Morgan's bank a century later, or maybe it was just sheer greed that pushed J.P. Morgan off course in the 1990s, when it began to founder on the shoals of financial instability. A strange new investment vehicle called derivatives, little understood by the Wall Street players who dabbled in them let alone the average citizen of Main Street America, torpedoed the stately bank as it veered from its main lines of business. Actually, there was nothing new about the concept of derivatives; they had been around for decades in the form of stock options, commodities futures, and other relatively benign and constructive products that allowed investors to hedge their positions or to speculate on the direction of prices.

For example, if you owned stocks and sold calls on them to generate extra income, you were using derivatives in the most conservative manner possible. If you were a farmer who grew wheat and sold futures to lock in a certain price for the wheat rather than

175

take the risk that the price of wheat would tumble in the months ahead, you were using derivatives prudently. When speculators used derivatives to gamble on price movements instead of buying the actual stocks or commodities themselves, they were using derivatives in a riskier but acceptable way, with a full understanding of their risk exposure. So, the problem with the derivatives that were created in the 1990s was not the idea of derivatives as an investment tool, but rather the exotic, incomprehensible nature of the ones that were foisted on an unwary public by institutions that did not fully understand precisely what they had created.

"Derivatives are financial hydrogen bombs built on personal computers by twenty-six-year-olds with MBAs," said Felix Rohatyn, who was referring to the latest generation of derivatives to hit the marketplace.

"Why do Wall Street guys keep inventing new ways for people to lose money? Weren't the old ways good enough?" asked Herb Trazenfeld, who paraphrased a question raised earlier by the former CEO of Wells Fargo. Herb was a Harvard lawyer who started in the business with Sandy back in the old Carter, Berlind, Potoma & Weill days in 1960, and he had been around long enough to recognize a disaster in the making when he saw one.

The latest derivatives were indeed financial hydrogen bombs created by young J.P. Morgan MBAs during a June 1994 meeting in Boca Raton, Florida. "It was in Boca where we started talking seriously about credit derivatives," said Peter Hancock, the leader of the group. "That was where the idea really took off, where we really had a vision of how big it could be." There were about forty extremely well-paid hotshots in attendance in Boca, none of them more than thirty years old. Hancock wasn't exaggerating when he talked about how big this hot new idea could become. A year earlier, J.P. Morgan carried a little more than half a billion dollars in derivatives on its books; by the end of 1994, that number had swollen to $1.7 trillion.

The operative word this time around was *credit* derivatives. Forget stock options and commodities futures; they were so old-fashioned, so Old World. Any fool could lose money on them, and many fools—both young and old—did. But credit derivatives were an entirely new breed, one that first took root in the brains of a couple of Hancock's young minions fresh out of college. Their names were Bill Demchak and Blythe Masters. Demchak functioned as Hancock's chief lieutenant, who admittedly was so drunk in Boca Raton that he said, "Frankly, I cannot remember much of our debate." What he did remember was that his hotel bill included charges for a smashed jet ski and a mountain of cheeseburgers, which his colleagues charged to his account as a joke.

Demchak perfected the concept of credit derivatives, which are basically mortgage loans and other debt obligations packaged as securities and sold to investors. They eventually became known as synthetic securities, since they take their value from the underlying loans. The other financial wizard in attendance was a twenty-five-year old former intern, who was slim, glamorous, and stunningly brilliant. Masters took the idea a step further and gave birth to credit default swaps, which safeguarded the issuers of the loans from the risk of defaults by borrowers who failed to make timely payments. As these new speculative vehicles gained traction and started speeding down the highway of financial ruin, they acquired other names, such as collateralized debt obligations. They fostered a mind-numbing array of acronyms and Wall Street mumbo jumbo that was understood only by the geniuses who created them and some top-level execs who took the time to study what they were all about, including Jamie and a few others with the in-depth financial skills.

"I think these products appealed to me because I had a quantitative background," Masters enthused later. "But they are also so creative." She left out that they were creative, in the beginning at least, for those who built, packaged, and sold them, but not so creative for investors who bought them and tucked them into their portfolios.

By the time Hancock and his team flew back to New York, a bit worse from the wear and tear of nonstop partying and throwing furniture in the pool, they all had their marching orders. These new instruments, these new varieties of financial hydrogen bombs, were to be their number-one priority going forward. "You will have to make at least half your revenues each year from a product which did not exist before," Hancock instructed them. That was a tall order, delivering results of that magnitude from a speculative vehicle that most people in the industry, let alone the investing public, had not the vaguest idea of what was being traded in the marketplace. All they knew was that they were buying *something like a bond*, an instrument that paid them a good rate of return, in exchange for putting a certain amount of money in the game. The word *derivative* with its latest hoary implications never crossed their radar screens.

Credit derivatives got a good jump off the blocks when J.P. Morgan and other banks packaged only high-quality loans with little risk of default. They made it easy for the large institutions that sold them to stay within the confines of the 1988 Basel I Accord, which required the banks to hold capital reserves amounting to at least 8 percent of their outstanding loans—in other words, to have at least $8 in cash on the books for every $100 they lent out. But shortly after J.P. Morgan joined the party in 1994, the young MBAs found even that minimum requirement too restrictive. Top-tier loans were not where the big bucks were made. Riskier loans generated bigger profits, since the banks could charge borrowers higher interest rates for them. The banks considered it a waste of resources to keep so much cash in reserve, which earned so little interest, when that money could be lent out at higher rates to borrowers with poor credit scores. So J.P. Morgan set out to do what all respectable bankers do when regulations crimp their profit margins: they lobbied to change the rules.

"We have to change the way we do business!" Hancock roared repeatedly during meetings with his derivatives team.

"These guys are dinosaurs!" Demchak echoed his boss's rage, earning himself the soubriquet "The Prince of Darkness" from his own underlings.

They found a friend in then Fed Chairman Alan Greenspan. Alan was a true believer in the efficacy of free markets, but what he lost sight of was that banks are not free market institutions. They are, instead, federally subsidized corporate welfare recipients with a safety net below them, provided by U.S. taxpayers, to ensure that when they fall, they do not hit the ground too hard. Alan allowed that perhaps they had a good point after reviewing reams of data submitted by Demchak and Masters. "It is not the role of regulators to stand in the way of free market innovation," said the Oracle of Delphi. In August 1996, the Fed took action by cutting the banks' capital requirements for derivatives in half to 4 percent.

Masters celebrated by extending a $4.8 billion line of credit to Exxon, a long-standing J.P. Morgan client, following the *Valdez* oil tanker spill off the coast of Alaska. She offloaded the risk onto the back of the European Bank for Reconstruction and Development in return for a hefty annual fee, which the EBRD gladly accepted, figuring the chances of Exxon defaulting on the loan were slim to none. The strategy worked, and Masters soon established a reputation as the "Queen of Swaps." With the excitement building at the newest incarnation of J. Pierpont Morgan's old bank, Demchak and Masters grew enamored of the notion of bundling more and more of these high-risk loans together in a single package and selling them to investors.

"Pile them high and sell them cheap!" soon became the mantra of the young J.P. Morgan alumni of the boisterous but pivotal meeting in Boca Raton.

*   *   *

No party lasts forever, and this one was no exception. But it lasted long enough to attract the attention of Jamie as he surveyed the marketplace from his perch in Chicago. He studied the concept of passing mortgage payments from borrowers along to investors as a form of interest payment, and he liked what he saw. Bundling many of these loans together into a single so-called tranche allowed a bank to spread out the risk in the case of individual defaults. There was a lot of money to be made in slicing and dicing and piling them high, and the banks that failed to get in on the action were going to be left behind in the dust. Bank One was not going to be left behind; in fact, Jamie endeavored to advance it to the head of the pack.

Wall Street wizards soon invented their own arcane terminology, as they do with any new vehicle: the highest-quality tranches with minimal risk would be called "senior loans"; those carrying mid-level risk were designated "mezzanine" loans; and the real junk at the bottom, composed largely of no-income-verification mortgages, was euphemistically called "junior" loans. And the juniors were where the real money was to be made. The ratings agencies—Moody's, Standard & Poor's, Fitch—were only too happy to lend credibility to this latest craze by slapping bond ratings on the various tranches, from investment grade such as BBB or higher and high-yield or junk, BB and lower.

"The business opportunities created by credit derivatives, their relevance to clients, the size of the credit markets globally, and the gross in efficiencies in pricing and liquidity that exist are frankly staggering," said Masters, giddy with her early success. "The pace of change in the way that banks manage credit risk has accelerated to a point where we can confidently predict credit risk management will be completely different in two years than it was even two years ago." She had the new lingo down pat, making her creation look like a gift from the gods rather than a time bomb set to explode at some point down the road. Jamie listened closely. He was skeptical at first, somewhat risk averse by nature, but he knew he could not afford to let other banks seize the day while he stood on the sidelines, a mere observer of history in the making.

Jamie was older and wiser than this latest generation of MBAs, who quickly developed a culture of their own, flinging Frisbees and baseballs across the trading floor to see how far they could travel before smashing someone's computer screen. When they weren't busting the company's hardware, they helicoptered down to Atlantic City for a night of drinking and rolling dice before winging it back to New York to gamble on derivatives when the market opened in the morning. Some took to stripping down and mooning their colleagues to "let the air in," creating an atmosphere conducive for marital distress and divorces in several instances. One can imagine the ghost of Carnegie chuckling maniacally as J. Pierpont Morgan spun like a dervish in his grave wondering what kind of special hell had befallen his once-staid bank.

As a sign of just how crazy things had gotten at the bank, Demchak put an unseasoned young woman named Terri Duhon, who knew how to party hardy along with the rest of his team, in charge of a strange new creation he baptized a Broad Index Secured Trust Offering, or BISTRO. What the hell was a BISTRO? Who cared, as long as the exotic package and its indecipherable nomenclature made MONEY for the firm? Demchak's newest protégé, who was now in charge of J.P Morgan's "exotics book"— yes, that's what they called it—had been a Harley-Davidson-riding high school student in Louisiana just ten years earlier. When Terri told her family about her promotion at the bank, they assumed she had moved up to head teller or something of that nature. Little did they know that she was actually managing a derivatives program with tens of billions of dollars at risk.

"It was just an extraordinary, intense experience," she said, somewhat awe-struck by her abrupt change in fortune.

But a strange thing happened on the way to profitability. As popular as credit derivatives and swaps had become, competing banks were earning more from merger-and-acquisition activity, and from the one-stop-shopping financial supermarket model, than J.P Morgan was from its derivatives trades. Credit derivatives had become popular in the span of just a few years, but Hancock and his claque of exuberant MBAs were ahead of the curve. Morgan was earning a return on equity of around 15 percent, while its competitors generated an average ROE of 18 percent. It would take a few years longer for derivatives to really catch on and unleash the widespread mayhem they would inflict on the market in 2008.

The upper echelon executives at J.P. Morgan were understandably disappointed by the results and ushered Hancock & Company off to the sidelines while they refocused on their core businesses like brokerage, insurance, mainstream lending, corporate finance, investment banking, and other more traditional areas of the market. Hancock took the rebuke personally and dug in his heels.

"This is the wave of the future," he said.

"These guys are dinosaurs," Demchak repeated his earlier lament about the rigid mindset of the old fogies at the bank.

"Tim Geithner, when he was at the New York Fed, was oblivious to the oblivious and unsound banking practices under his direct supervision, which led to the subprime mortgage collapse in 2007 and the panic of 2008," said Jim Rickards, the hedge fund manager who consulted with the CIA and NSA about dangerous speculation in the financial world.

"What we're doing is going to be huge," Hancock nevertheless insisted. He made his case before top management about how the bank needed to change the way it did business. "Forget the financial supermarket concept," he pleaded. "We'll eventually make more money turning Morgan into a derivatives boutique. That's where we should concentrate our efforts."

J.P. Morgan a *boutique?* What kind of madness was this? Morgan's CEO Sandy Warner thought Hancock was nuts, and arrogant too. Hancock, Demchak, Masters, and the rest of the derivatives crew believed Warner and his cohorts were "out of touch." When Warner ordered them to stop acting like prima donnas, to attend monthly meetings, and stop isolating themselves from the other departments in the bank, Hancock declared that they were being put under "house arrest." Clearly, they had reached an impasse. Someone had to go, and it wasn't going to be Warner—not immediately.

Hancock descended down the exit ramp in the summer of 2000, a departure cloaked in mystery since J.P. Morgan did not want word to get out that its derivatives business had stalled on the road as it was beginning to build momentum. He was the first in his team to leave without the usual fanfare surrounding the loss of a high-profile employee, but Wall Street's rumor mill picked up on the news in a heartbeat. Why was Hancock leaving? What else was going on at J.P. Morgan that everyone needed to know about? Was the revered bank in trouble? It didn't take long for the media to discover that Warner was scouring the marketplace for a buyer. Why did Warner want to sell? He approached a couple of prospective buyers, including that other Sandy named Weill, but the latter was not interested.

"Morgan reminds me of yogurt," said the CEO of Citigroup. "It's obsessed with its culture. All I ever hear from them is culture, culture, culture."

Aside from its obsession with culture, Morgan had fallen sharply behind its major competitors during the past few years. The

Wall Street Journal sized up Morgan's predicament poignantly when it reported that "Morgan is now on the cusp of the bulge bracket of the world's six top investment banks. Increasingly, however, the biggest profits are not going to a bulge bracket of six banks but to a super-bulge of three firms—Merrill Lynch, Morgan Stanley Dean Witter, and Goldman Sachs."

Warner went on the defensive, contradicting himself when he said "I don't think bigness is a strategy. There needs to be a certain scale." He was the one who told Hancock that bigness mattered and a derivatives boutique was out of the question.

But he knew he had to grow—or risk being squished like a bug in a world more and more dominated by mastodons tromping across the financial landscape, crushing anything smaller that stood in their path.

Chapter Eighteen

Chase Manhattan Bank came to J.P. Morgan's rescue, as the banking mergers continued. In August 2000, shortly after Hancock's departure, Chase CEO William B. Harrison called Warner when he was on vacation in Northern Michigan. Chase and J.P. Morgan had complementary strengths; Chase controlled a mass-market customer base and was paramount in merger-and-acquisition deals, and Morgan harbored a blue-chip client list and a derivatives book, which Harrison believed would blend in nicely with Chase's portfolio. The two companies together would present an impressive balance sheet totaling $660 billion in assets, not far behind Citigroup's $716 billion asset base.

On paper, a deal between the two banks would appear to be a merger of equals, but Harrison was leading from strength while Warner was flopping on the ropes like a battered middleweight contender. Harrison recognized his advantage, which is why he called Warner in the first place. Chase had built itself into a powerhouse throughout the late1990s by financing a host of dot.com companies before the bubble burst, just as Morgan was losing market share by concentrating on credit derivatives. Chase's stock price soared as a result, while Morgan's underperformed the market. Harrison was an imposing figure, a former University of North Carolina basketball star, and he dominated the talks when he met with Warner. They lost little time in erecting the framework of a deal. Chase would buy J.P. Morgan for $30 billion, financed mostly by Chase's still lofty share price. They announced their so-called merger on September 13, 2000, but there was little doubt about who was buying whom.

"How are the mighty fallen!" blared the normally buttoned-down *Economist* magazine in its September 16 issue. "J.P. Morgan, once the dominant financial power in America, and arguably the world, swallowed up by Chase Manhattan, a big, old—but not terribly distinguished rival. Even five years ago, that J.P. Morgan's blue-blooded bank should taint its aristocratic culture by merging with any other institution would have seemed inconceivable."

The combined bank would take on a new name, JPMorgan Chase, putting the more prestigious firm first and dropping a couple of periods or dots, which was somewhat apt in the collapse of the dot.com craze. Harrison and Warner announced that they would reign over their joint roost as co-CEOs, and appoint an equal number of executives from each bank to run the various departments. Others at the bank dubbed it the "Noah's Ark" approach since the bank would be governed "two by two." No one understood better than Jamie that a management structure modeled on Noah's Ark would eventually turn into a leaking vessel. At this stage of his career, he had fought diligently and successfully against that model several times before. His best approach now was to watch and wait. Sooner or later, trouble that he viewed as inevitable at JPMorgan Chase would evolve into a golden opportunity for him.

As it happened, the new bank came unglued a year later. The dot.com meltdown continued to exact its heavy toll in the marketplace, and Chase was particularly vulnerable since its soaring profits during the past five years had come from helping to inflate the bubble before it burst. The dot.com implosion was bad enough in itself, but the bomb-burst that sent the bank's stock swooning back to earth came from energy giant Enron, a company in which Chase had invested heavily. Enron's bankruptcy set the stage for the mother of all acquisitions, the deal that Jamie had been lusting for ever since he assumed command of Bank One in Chicago.

*   *   *

September 11, 2001, is a day permanently etched in the history books, right alongside Pearl Harbor and the assassinations of Presidents Abraham Lincoln and John F. Kennedy, and of civil rights leader Martin Luther King. I was sitting in my office in Charlotte, working on a report with half an eye glancing occasionally at my computer screen when the first plane hit the tower. It was so surreal that I at first dismissed it as a promo for an upcoming movie. But then the headlines began to scroll across the bottom of the screen, leaving no doubt that this was real-time action rather than fiction. Eighteen minutes later, the second plane hit its mark, and suddenly the entire world went mad. How could his be? How could something as horrific as this be taking place on American soil? This was clearly an act of war, and no one knew who the enemy was yet.

Many people in the financial industry who were not in one of the towers that day knew people who were. BBF&T was no exception. The head of our PR department was in 7 World Trade Center, which had not taken a direct hit, with a traumatizing view of the toxic plumes billowing from the wreckage like ash from an urban volcano, and human bodies hurtling through the air on their way to certain death. One of our fund managers was in the first tower that was struck and fortunately managed to inch his way down a stairwell moments before all escape routes became impassable. He made it to ground level and hugged the side of the building as bodies crashed onto the pavement just yards from where he stood. The toxic clouds followed him as he worked his way north, trying to stay clear of the choking gases.

Sandy observed the carnage on television in his third-floor office at 399 Park Avenue in midtown Manhattan, alarmed about the fate of Citi's sixteen thousand employees working in downtown locations—six of whom would be killed that day—including his asset management team located at 7 World Trade Center, an easy walk from the North Tower. He immediately swung into survival mode. His phone started to ring nonstop, with calls coming in without letup from the media and his major executives. He told those who could make it to attend an emergency meeting that afternoon to discuss how quickly they could activate their backup sites and assure ongoing operations. Tom Jones, the head of the asset management team, finally arrived later that day with various colleagues after their long walk north, all of them covered in soot.

"Our company spent a lot of money for Y2K and put in backup sites, and we never knew how they were going to work," Sandy said. They worked fine, as it turned out, since Citi was up and running the next day.

Paramount among Sandy's fears was the fate of his daughter Jessica, who was flying to Chicago for a business meeting that morning. While she was technically out of harm's way, no one knew at the time how many cities would be targeted and how many commercial aircraft had been turned into bombs by suicidal terrorists. Jessica landed safely, a thousand miles away from Ground Zero. Jamie, too, was a distance removed from the attack in the same city as Jessica, but he pitched in by personally donating $1.2 million to the New York City Fire Department, and he arranged for Bank One to pay for ten Chicago firemen to travel to New York to help in the cleanup effort. When they returned to Chicago, one of them gave Jamie the boots he wore at Ground Zero, which Jamie has kept in his office ever since.

Aside from the personal impact the attack had on so many lives, the broader concern was the effect it would have on the financial markets. The mayhem occurred before the markets opened that fateful Tuesday, with everyone anticipating widespread chaos and panic selling. As a result, the New York Stock Exchange and Nasdaq did not open that day and remained shut down until the following Monday, September 17, the longest blackout in trading since 1933. It was enough time to allow the fears to subside a bit and for brokerage and other financial firms to get their systems functioning again.

On the first day of trading after 9/11, the Dow Jones Industrial Average fell 684 points, a 7.1 percent decline, setting a record for the biggest loss in exchange history for one trading day. At the close of trading on Friday, the DJIA was down almost 1,370 points for the week, suffering a loss of more than 14 percent. The S&P 500 Index plummeted 11.6 percent, blasting away roughly $1.4 trillion in total market value over a five-day period. As expected, airlines and insurance stocks were pummeled hardest. United Airlines and American Airlines, whose flights were involved in the attacks, each fell more than 40 percent.

Citi's Travelers unit was among the insurers with significant exposure to the wreckage, more than $500 million in claims plus another $200 million due to an interruption in operations for the parent company. Those with inside knowledge of the attacks— terrorist organizations and their financial networks—profited from the event by shorting the stock market before they committed their unholy crime. Buying put options is one way to short a stock, and an SEC investigation revealed afterward that 4,516 puts on American Airlines, equivalent to 451,600 shares of the company's stock, were bought on September 10, apparently by people with prior knowledge of the event. Fortunately, the selling abated soon afterward, thanks to a hefty infusion of liquidity from the Federal Reserve. Money is the lifeblood of the financial markets, and Fed Chairman Alan Greenspan made sure that enough of it permeated the system to reassure investors that the central bank would keep its credit lines open.

While the market soon stabilized, the recession bit hard, putting a lid on stock prices. Jamie's efforts had begun to reap dividends at Bank One, resulting in a net earnings gain of $2.6

billion for all of 2001, compared with a $511 million loss a year earlier. But the stock price languished along with the rest of the market as the economy slowed to a halt. The media took note, with *Business Week* reporting in its October 29, 2001, issue that Jamie "knows the bank has to expand. And shareholders are becoming increasingly impatient that it hasn't done so." Jamie was also disappointed with the results, despite the profitable year, saying that he wanted to be "on the acquisition trail," but only "in a prudent way." The market, however, was not conducive to prudent growth in the aftermath of the dot.com meltdown and the 9/11 tragedy.

*   *   *

The Enron scandal erupted like a Texas geyser when audits revealed that the company's hefty profits of the past couple of years had been bogus. Enron employed twenty-two thousand people and reported revenues of $101 billion in 2000 alone. *Fortune* magazine dubbed Enron "America's most innovative company" six years in a row. But creative accounting, to put it mildly, had been responsible for inflating the company's impressive financial results, with the knowledge of Enron's own accountants and banks.

Sandy had had his WorldCom scandal to deal with at Citi, but the Enron scandal dwarfed it by comparison—although it sucked Sandy and Citigroup into its vortex as well. When Enron filed for bankruptcy on December 2, 2001, it was the largest such filing in American corporate history. The news sunk the once venerable accounting firm Arthur Andersen, which had been complicit in the fraudulent accounting by doctoring the books, and it inflicted heavy damage on JPMorgan Chase and Citigroup, Enron's two main banks, which had each earned fees of around $200 million to hide the energy company's losses. Both banks had to cough up fines totaling $300 million for their involvement in the mess.

As for Jamie, he was safely removed from it all, one thousand miles away in the American heartland, ruminating over the lessons he had learned from Sandy many years earlier. "When disaster strikes," Sandy had always told him, "it's either the end of the world or a great buying opportunity. I'm betting that it's not the end of the world."

Chapter Nineteen

By 2002, Jamie had turned his ship around to a point where he could focus on the prey swarming in troubled waters before moving in for the kill. In the wake of the Enron wreck, JPMorgan Chase's stock price had been sliced in half, and Wall Street denizens plus the financial media all smelled the blood floating on the water. "It's unnerving how the bad news keeps piling up at JPMorgan," reported *Business Week*. "Name a scandal-plagued US company in the headlines and one bank keeps showing up behind the scenes: JPMorgan Chase," declared London's *Evening Standard*.

Greenspan's Fed cut interest rates furiously to stabilize the economy as the high-tech sector alone shed $5 trillion in market value between March 2000 and October 2002. Extraordinarily low interest rates, with the prime rate down to its lowest level in decades at 1 percent, fueled a boom in housing, which triggered renewed interest in the credit derivatives spawned by Hancock and his madcap crew at Morgan. Other banks rushed to get in on the action, which Jamie observed with growing interest from his penthouse lair in Chicago. One way or another, he had to find a way for Bank One to participate in the excitement if he was going to become a major player.

Bank One had a singular advantage in that it was standing on firmer ground at the end of 2002 than when he took over almost three years earlier. The company was profitable and had weathered the financial storm in better shape than many of its larger rivals. Wall Street analysts began to speculate on just when Jamie was preparing to strike. The timing could not have been better, and Jamie contributed to the rumors that he was on the prowl when he wrote in his annual report, "A weak economy creates opportunities for strong companies. I believe we are in a position to take advantage of emerging opportunities."

But acquiring a big bank at a price Jamie thought was reasonable turned out to be harder than he envisioned. He approached Bear Stearns and came up against James Cayne, the tough-as-nails—some said egomaniacal—CEO who made George Patton look like the wimpiest general to direct combat operations during World War II. Cayne was interested in selling Bear Stearns, but at a price that made Jamie's head spin. He declared that his financial firm, because of its long history as a bulwark of the industry, deserved a premium that was well above its stock price valuation in the market.

"Jimmy, there's no way we would pay a price like that," Jamie told him when Cayne demanded $100 a share for his company, which was selling for less than half that price at the time. It is worth noting that Jamie would eventually pay $10 a share for Bear when it collapsed in 2008.

Jamie walked away from the deal and began casting around for other likely targets that seemed to make sense. His list included Commerce Bancshares, Fifth Third Bancorp, Golden State Bancorp, National City, and others. "We have the capital, we have the management," he said. "At some point, something will come along that makes sense for us."

The media kept pushing him, running articles on what his next acquisition was going to be, but Jamie refused to be rushed. He still had problems at Bank One to tend to, despite the strides he had made since taking over. "We couldn't even run our own business well yet," he said. "We're going to get this thing fixed, and from that strength, if something makes sense we'll do it."

Fixing Bank One, however, was a long step away from being accomplished. Just as he appeared to be steering his ship into calmer waters, he ran into unexpected turbulence as the calendar ticked off the final months of 2002. As the next year unfolded, Jamie's ship of state was nearly blown out of the water from the air, figuratively speaking, when United Airlines filed for bankruptcy. Bank One had extended loans to the nosediving airline, and Jamie was forced to throw good money after bad money by floating an additional $600 million dollars to United—the first time Bank One had ever lent money to a bankrupt company. Jamie was vindicated a short time later when United emerged from Chapter 11 and repaid the money in full. Still, it was an unnerving experience for him, proof that you never know what kind of problems are lurking around the corner just as you think you're out of danger.

"The blueprint for turning around a company is to make an assessment, stabilize it, get rid of excesses, and grow it," wrote Tom McCandless, a banking analyst with Deutsche Bank. "[Dimon] got all the way up to the last step." He criticized Jamie for not following through and finishing the job. Bank One was still underperforming within the industry, growing its revenues just 17 percent from 2000 through 2003 compared with Wells Fargo's 44 percent. Jamie's only solace was the wreckage taking place at Citigroup under Sandy's guidance. Jamie's old boss decided that it was time to slide down the exit ramp and devote his time and fortune to philanthropic activities. He announced plans to step down and turn the reins over to Chuck Prince, the only one of his top executives to stay with him as the rest of the old crew joined Jamie in Chicago. Jamie knew that Sandy had rewarded Prince for his loyalty, a trait Sandy valued in his lieutenants above all others. But he harbored serious doubts about Prince's ability to keep the giant bank from falling over the edge of a cliff.

*   *   *

Mergers within the industry continued at a fevered pace, and Jamie felt the pressure mounting to do a deal of his own. UBS paid $12 billion to swallow PaineWebber, Credit Suisse handed over a similar amount to acquire Donaldson, Lufkin & Jenrette, Bank of America ponied up an astonishing $48 billion to gobble up FleetBoston, and other mergers were looming on the financial horizon. Jamie scoured the landscape for a bank he could buy at a reasonable price, but he continued to find the asking prices too high. Overpaying to acquire an asset was anathema to him. "It's true that when you have a low-premium deal, you have a better platform to build value," he said. "You can build the business instead of slashing and burning simply to save enough to pay for the premium."

The deal of all deals finally emerged, although it was not the one that Jamie nor anyone else on Wall Street had anticipated. In January 2003, Jamie received a call from William B. Harrison, the co-CEO of JPMorgan Chase, who had yet to recover from his own series of high-premium acquisitions over the years. The former North Carolina basketball player more closely resembled a punch-drunk fighter pinned against the ropes after Chase's ill-timed purchase of Morgan. Jamie was in a buying mood, and he was stunned to hear that JPMorgan Chase was interested in buying *his* Chicago-based institution. Some analysts had speculated all along that Jamie's secret game plan was to get Bank One off the sick list as soon as possible and sell it so he could move back to New York. But most were taken by surprise when rumors began to circulate that Harrison thought that JPMorgan Chase was healthy enough to buy Jamie's bank.

When Harrison approached Jamie in January 2003, Harrison was approaching sixty and looking for a successor. He had taken a lot of flak during the past few years and was regarded as a wounded corporate warrior who lacked the energy to salvage the remnants of his long career. His board of directors was less than thrilled by his performance and was putting pressure on him to step down. He and

Jamie had crossed paths before, and Harrison had watched the younger man ascend from his days as Sandy's acolyte in Baltimore to his current reign atop a major Midwestern bank. They met secretly in New York at various locations, including a suite Morgan rented in the Waldorf Astoria, and on weekends in Harrison's house in Greenwich, Connecticut. By July, the two were close to carving out the framework of a deal.

The sticking point was Harrison's reluctance to *overpay* once more and further damage his already tarnished reputation in the industry. But he need not have worried. Jamie was just as eager as Harrison was to wrap up the negotiations, since it presented a golden opportunity for him to step in as the ruler of one of the most coveted empires in the financial world. Harrison's offer was far from generous. He refused to pay more than the market price for Bank One's stock, and he insisted on paying for Jamie's bank with JPMorgan Chase shares instead of cash. It was hardly an attractive offer, but the sweetener for Jamie was Harrison's willingness to step down within the next two years and name Jamie as his replacement. To save face, Jamie got Harrison to pay a 10 percent premium above Bank One's market value in a stock swap amounting to $58 billion, a puny premium compared to what was going on in the rest of the industry.

"It's been without question the most stressed time a CEO can go through when you're negotiating one of these deals, particularly with Jamie," Harrison said when the two men announced the deal on January 14, 2004. "That's why I look older today."

The rest of the Street did not think so. The media criticized Jamie for not shopping his company around to the highest bidder if he wanted to sell it, since other bank mergers were going through at premiums ranging from 30 percent to 40 percent above market price. For Jamie, however, it was not just a question of dollars and cents. The opportunity to sit atop a financial dinosaur that would become the second-largest in the U.S., with $1.1 trillion in assets, just a couple of notches below Citigroup's $1.3 trillion, was paramount.

"We'll give Citi a run for its money!" he told the media upon his triumphant return to New York City. His major regret was that Sandy would not be there for him to overshadow, since Sandy had already passed the reins over to Chuck Prince.

It was a successful deal for Jamie, if not the best one he could have negotiated for the rest of Bank One's shareholders. By swallowing Bank One, the new JPMorgan Chase would become the second-largest credit card issuer, with $123 billion in outstanding loans, and even more important, it presented Jamie with a chance to participate in the increasingly lucrative world of credit derivatives. Most top executives did not yet comprehend the full ramifications of these toxic new vehicles and preferred to leave the details to the fanatical techies they hired. But Jamie was an exception. He had done his homework and understood them as well as anyone. He was champing at the bit to get in on the action.

*   *   *

Notwithstanding Jamie's claim that a low-premium deal eliminates the need to slash and burn, he went through the personnel roster with a chainsaw, cutting executive compensation from 20 percent to 50 percent and eliminating twelve thousand employees— including Harrison. The two men may have appeared before the cameras shaking hands and smiling, but Jamie was too impatient to wait two years before assuming sole command of his gargantuan new vessel. Harrison was out by October 2005, six months ahead of schedule. As humorist and financial columnist Stanley Bing observed in his book *What Would Machiavelli Do?*, cuts of between

10 percent and 15 percent of the workforce appear to be optimal in such situations. But if you trim executive compensation too much, you risk being assassinated by your own board of directors.

"Yond Cassius has a mean and hungry look. Such men are dangerous," observed Sanford C. Bernstein analyst Brad Hintz, quoting Shakespeare in his description of Jamie.

"The board recognized that giving Mr. Dimon the top job would formally acknowledge what had been Wall Street's worst-kept secret for many months: that Mr. Dimon is already running the show," reported the *New York Times*.

Harrison had already admitted as much himself. "Everybody eventually reports to me," Harrison had said before he left. "But Jamie is the president, COO. He is running the retail side of the bank, and he's also running the finance and risk management function."

With or without Harrison, Jamie had his work cut out for him, continuing to tidy up the mess he had inherited at Bank One, unifying the warring cultures, and resolving the financial mismanagement that permeated JPMorgan Chase like a metastasizing malignancy. He had his arms around the financial colossus he had long been dreaming about, but subduing and controlling it was an entirely different problem. Adding insult to injury, analyst Mike Mayo's low opinion of Bank One's stock under Jamie's leadership had turned out to be prescient as Bank One's revenues slipped another 3 percent in 2003. And Mayo correctly scoffed at Jamie's prediction that he could turn his new bank into a $100 stock within a couple of years. Mayo's skepticism proved right once again, when JPMorgan Chase's share price flamed out at $51.83 before crashing to earth in 2008. During the bull market that ensued in spring 2009, it did ascend as high as $68.14.

Jamie was eager to improve Morgan's results sooner rather than later, and after trimming the employment rolls and cutting expenses, he turned his attention to the bank's derivatives operations in his effort to find a reliable profit center. With the housing market continuing to heat up, Jamie was convinced that credit derivatives represented the pot of gold he was looking for.

"Securitization is a priority!" he told his staff, and by *securitization* he meant the packaging of mortgage loans as debt instruments to be sold to yield-starved investors looking for income. Derivatives drill sergeant Peter Hancock had left in a huff, and his hitman Bill Demchak had departed soon afterward, but Jamie still had Blythe Masters and a few others on board who could get the job done.

Chapter Twenty

"They're terrible results!" Jamie fumed. "Terrible results!"

He was referring to third-quarter 2004 earnings growth—or rather, contraction—which was down 13 percent from a year earlier, which was itself a poor quarter. The analysts, not to say investors in Morgan's stock, were stunned, hoping that the numbers were an aberration, a lingering hangover from the bender JPMorgan Chase had been on before Jamie took over. But the fourth quarter turned out to be no better, lowering 2004's full-year earnings to $4.5 billion from $6.7 billion in 2003. The bank's return on equity was a paltry 6.0 percent compared with the industry average of 15.5 percent. Jamie had inherited a behemoth, but so far it appeared to be maimed beyond what he had anticipated. Trading was off, the bank suffered huge losses in its bond operations, and staggered from sluggish results in its currency and commodities trading divisions.

"Jamie Dimon's flock of faithful is certainly being tested," the *Financial Times* reported. "His huge banking merger is not yet delivering what investors had hoped, and the stock price has not bounced back from the disappointing results of last month, in spite of trading conditions that many reckon are more propitious."

Jamie called upon his old friend Steve Black, who had followed him from Citigroup, and an executive who was instrumental in building Morgan's derivatives business, Bill Winters, to pump some life into the mortgage securitization part of the bank. Winters, in particular, knew the derivatives market as well as anyone on Wall Street.

"Bill has been around since the invention of seamless nylon stockings," said Ian Kerr, a freelance financial columnist. "He knows where all the bodies are buried in that monster derivatives portfolio."

Black and Winters, who had a checkered background roaming around the Balkans and working for a beer bottling plant before wandering into the derivatives market, made for an odd couple indeed. Wall Street wags who knew both men wondered out loud how long the two of them could occupy the same room before they traded punches with each other. Black attempted to defuse their potentially volatile relationship by speaking candidly to Winters.

"We're big boys," he said. "We know that everyone is taking bets on which one of us kills the other. Let's show them that we can actually make this partnership work."

Winters agreed to an early truce, as long as neither of them encroached on the other's bailiwick. Winters got London, where he was based, and Black held sway over the derivatives staff in New York. But, once again, in the interests of civility, it was still shaping up to be a Noah's Ark kind of arrangement—management two by two, which had never gone smoothly in Jamie's case let alone among his sword carriers.

They did their best to make their corporate marriage work, but despite their best efforts, Black and Winters could not prevent JPMorgan Chase from slipping behind other banks in the sales of their securitized mortgage loans. It was a perplexing conundrum for both men, and for their boss as well. On paper, the combined resources of Morgan and Chase should have propelled the bank to the top of the heap. They had the talent, they were pioneers in the industry. But the bickering continued, the culture clashes never ceased, notwithstanding the best efforts of both men to force their teams to work together. The rest of the financial world took notice.

"Given the profile of JPMorgan as an institution steeped in structured finance, it really is surprising that the bank has failed to hitch a ride on the great US remortgaging wave," reported a columnist for *EuroWeek*.

Jamie had little choice but to step in himself to stop the hemorrhaging. He flew back and forth from New York to London, only to discover that the warring factions were not communicating with one another. The internal contention drove him into a rage. "Jamie went ballistic," said Roy Apple, one of his top executives in the Chase Home Mortgage department. "It felt like a state of war."

The only way to fix it was to build an assembly line of sorts, Jamie reasoned. He needed a pipeline that passed along Chase's mortgage loans to the investment people, who would then package them into various securities tranches and sell them as bond substitutes to the bank's clients. This less-than-enviable task fell on the shoulders of a fellow named Bill King. "It took us ages to build," he lamented, feeling the intense pressure, "but Jamie insisted we needed to get all the systems in place before doing anything."

The systems were up and running by the middle of 2005, and theoretically they should have functioned like a well-oiled machine considering the substantial resources that Morgan had at its disposal. The housing market was cooperating, with home prices rising more than 80 percent between 1997 and 2005. But therein lay the groundwork for a potential disaster. The mortgage derivatives presented little or no risk as long as the housing trajectory was upward. But how long could the economy sustain such lofty advances before running into stiff headwinds from investors who were being priced out of the market? How many people could realistically afford a $300,000 house that was currently selling for $550,000 or $600,000? What would happen if homeowners suddenly began to gag on their mortgages, pushed into default because their mortgage payments were exorbitantly high? In that event, credit derivatives would become like junk bonds that offered high yields, but suddenly shriveled in value when the issuing corporations filed for bankruptcy.

Jamie, who believed in taking risk only when the odds were skewed in his favor, began to get nervous. What if? What if? That was the question that kept nagging away at the back of his mind. To be sure, the soothing words that poured from the mouths of the nation's leading economists were reassuring. "There is virtually no risk of a national housing price bubble based on the fundamental demand for housing and predictable economic factors," intoned David Lereah, chief economist of the National Realtors Association. "A general slowing in the rate of price growth can be expected, but in many areas inventory shortages will persist and home prices are likely to continue to rise above historic norms."

And no less an expert than Ben Bernanke, Chairman of the President's Council of Economic Advisers who would replace Alan Greenspan as Chairman of the Federal Reserve in January 2006, advised that, "Although speculative activity has increased in some areas, at a national level these price increases largely reflect strong economic fundamentals, including robust growth in jobs and incomes, low mortgage rates, steady rates of household formation, and factors that limit the expansion of housing supply in some areas."

So, it was a damned if you do, damned if you don't situation. You would be damned if you beefed up your derivatives business and the economy subsequently went into a tailspin, and damned if you failed to participate fully in the derivatives boom while your competitors pulled out all the stops and fattened their bottom lines while doing so. For a hesitant CEO, it was a dilemma with no easy resolution.

*   *   *

"This business does not make any sense," Winters told Jamie when he saw the mortgage default rate climb from under 9 percent to more than 12 percent in the span of a few months.

"You don't have to tell me," the increasingly nervous Jamie agreed. "I know about all of this stuff. The main problem is all of this pressure to grow, grow, grow! It's always there. Nobody has the right not to expect the market to turn against them."

In the face of the darkening clouds mounting on the horizon, Morgan's main competitors—Merrill Lynch, Bear Stearns, Citigroup, Morgan Stanley, and others—zoomed ahead, bolstering their profit margins in a what-me-worry disregard for the gathering storm. Chuck Prince, who had replaced Sandy at Citi, made his now famous remark, "As long as the music is playing, you've got to get up and dance." But the music was turning Wagnerian, with hints of *sturm und drang* booming in the percussion section.

Housing prices were beginning to stall in some of the hottest regions of the country, including San Francisco, Las Vegas, and Miami, triggering new waves of defaults on subprime loans. Jamie wanted to pull back on his bank's exposure, but he was reluctant to do so while the competition flew full speed ahead. At that point, he explored the idea of hedging more of the risk by buying credit default swaps from third parties, which would guarantee Morgan's derivatives against losses from borrowers who defaulted on their loans. But insurance is expensive, and the costs cut into your profit margins. Jamie was first and foremost a numbers guy, and his biggest dilemma was striking the right balance between generating profits from an expanding derivatives portfolio and protecting Morgan's bottom line against a worst-case scenario involving a housing bubble.

Early in 2006, Winters unearthed a different kind of problem entirely. During the previous decade, when Hancock and his derivatives team began to structure the Strange New World of credit derivatives, the so-called credit "spreads" that Morgan and other banks earned on their creations were enough to fatten their coffers. The spread determines a bank's return on the products, which represents the difference between what it pays investors to buy them and what it costs the bank to put the loans together. As long as interest rates remain reasonably high, a bank can offer an attractive yield and still make money for itself. But by 2006, with the economy flagging and the Fed lowering rates to perk it up, the spread was narrowing. Credit derivatives that once generated 10 percent a year in cash flow now produced only 5 percent annually. Jamie charged Winters to look into the situation.

"There doesn't seem to be a way to make money on these structures," reported Brian Zeitlin, one of Winter's top analysts. "The problem is the spreads. They're drying up."

So how were Morgan's main competitors making money on the financial hydrogen bombs in the same environment? It came down to volume. While Jamie and his team were hesitant to roll the dice and go for broke, Merrill Lynch, Citi, Bear Stearns, and the others knew no such restraints. They were financial supermarkets after all. Regular supermarkets, whose profit margins are notoriously low in the 1 percent to 2 percent range, depend on sheer volume to keep their heads above water financially. So, as interest rates declined and the spreads contracted for the banks, they had little alternative except to keep pumping out more and more of these waste products if they wanted to remain in the game.

The volume grew to such a level that credit derivative swaps—floated by what were known as monoline insurers against default on the derivatives—could scarcely begin to keep pace with the demand for their warranties, even as the insurance grew increasingly expensive. It reached a point where the monoline insurers were obligated to cover losses equal to one hundred and fifty times the insurers' underlying equity. In the event of a monumental blowup, the monolines themselves would have to default on their obligations.

"To us, that business model seemed nuts!" said Demchak, who had departed to PNC Bank in Pittsburg.

"We didn't really use monolines much," said Winters, "because we figured they wouldn't be there when you really needed them."

The insurers themselves needed to be insured, and no one outside the vast resources of the federal government—which had set this entire fiasco in motion to begin with—and the central banks, with their unlimited borrowing capacity and power to print money, was large enough to perform that Herculean job.

Chapter Twenty-one

By early 2006, there existed in the financial multiverse a grand total of $12 trillion worth of credit derivatives, a staggering sum equal to the entire size of the U.S. economy. Even some of those who were instrumental in patching this monster together were beginning to get cold feet about the beast they had unleashed.

"There is a type of euphoria about getting into structured credit products right now," said Terri Duhon, the woman Demchak had put in charge of the "exotics book" ten years earlier. "And so you have to ask, are we getting into a state of irrational exuberance?"

It would appear that sociopathic recklessness had long since replaced irrational exuberance in the pantheon of concerns roiling the marketplace. Individual investors were not the only ones clamoring for more and more of these products. Government agencies, municipalities, non-profit charities, pension funds, and other institutions that should have been investing in low-risk vehicles could not get enough of these financial time bombs, in an effort to generate unrealistic returns in a low-interest-rate environment. And, in the interests of greater profitability, the big banks were only too eager to satisfy the insatiable demand. So Jamie may have wanted to rein in his bank's derivatives exposure, but by doing so he ran the risk of falling behind his biggest competitors in an increasingly challenging marketplace.

"Banks now face the challenging task of sustaining their success in creating value," Boston Consulting Group concluded in its study of the industry. "Continuing to increase profitability remains important but becomes more and more difficult as profitability has already reached a new level."

One of the worst offenders in the race to foist more and more of these products on the public was Merrill Lynch. No matter how hard Jamie tried to keep Morgan from falling too far behind Merrill and some of the other banks, he was hard-pressed to keep up with the torrid pace set by Merrill under its go-for-broke CEO Stanley O'Neal. Merrill had jumped to the head of the pack, increasing the volume of its derivatives products from $2 billion in 2001 to $52 billion in 2006. JPMorgan Chase was left far back in seventh place, with a derivatives output totaling a mere $22 billion the same year. Jamie and his team were hesitant to pump out more of the toxic derivatives when its primary insurer, AIG, notified Morgan that it could no longer guarantee the bank against default. AIG's CEO Maurice "Hank" Greenberg was growing leery of the shaky subprime mortgage market and worried about AIG's exposure should the whole house of cards implode.

The demand kept rising, and in a frantic effort to keep pace with it, the big banks leveraged their output to staggering heights, circumventing Fed restrictions on how much debt they could carry on their balance sheets. Citi, for example, was limited to maintaining these so-called assets below twenty times the value of the bank's total equity. So it got around the limitations by placing the derivatives in an extensive network of off-balance-sheet vehicles it created. Was it legal? No one knew for sure, since the financial institutions were now operating in an unexplored universe of investment products that were little understood not only by government regulators—who had long ago gone to sleep at the switch—but also by the geniuses who created the products.

One man who understood the intricacies of these instruments better than any CEO in America was Jamie. He had gone to school on Blythe Masters, who had created the whole concept of credit default swaps—laying off part of the risk on third parties. Masters had rocketed up the corporate ladder at JPMorgan Chase, when Jamie appointed her as chief financial officer of the firm's investment bank at the age of thirty-four, positioning her as one of the most senior and most powerful women in the financial world. Now thirty-six years old, some of her colleagues wondered out loud if she would ascend all the way to the top, assuming that Jamie had a succession plan in mind in the first place—something that seemed highly unlikely. Masters was under the gun to make sure that Morgan didn't fall too far behind the rest of the pack, even as Jamie, Winters, and the other top executives grew increasingly nervous about a housing bubble in the making.

Jamie disdained the idea of using outside consultants. "Those consultants are a crock of shit!" was a familiar invective of his when one of his underlings brought up the subject. But Masters felt she had little choice in the current environment except to pick the brain of one of the top consultants in the field. Basically, what Masters wanted to get a handle on was what she referred to as the "gap factor"—what exactly was holding Morgan back relative to its too-big-to-fail competitors. She called in a fellow named Nick Studer, who was reputed to be one of the top analysts in the business, in spring 2006. Studer spent a couple of months poring through Morgan's books, piece by piece, department by department, business by business, and compared his findings with comparable results at Citi, Merrill, Goldman, and the other major players, and his analysis was not encouraging.

He reported back to Masters that JPMorgan Chase was doing relatively well in foreign exchange and interest rate derivatives, but it was falling woefully behind in equities, commodities, and most important of all, in the securitization of mortgage derivatives. To make matters worse, the gap was *widening* not narrowing. The revenues gap between Morgan and its main rivals had accelerated well past a billion dollars.

"More than a billion dollars?" Masters was stunned. It didn't make any sense. How could this be going on?

She presented Studer's findings to Winters, who was also knocked back on his heels. "Jamie will go ballistic," Winters said. "I've got a mandate to close the gap, and here we're falling further behind."

Winters huddled with Black, his counterpart in New York, and the two of them studied the numbers. "There's no sensible way to make this work," they agreed. There could be only one logical explanation: the competition was throwing all caution to the wind in a headlong race for greater and greater profits. It appeared as though the crew at JPMorgan Chase were the only ones concerned about the dire consequences if the bubble finally burst.

Jamie heard them out and, to their relief, he agreed that Morgan should not ramp up the feeding frenzy to stay abreast of the competition. "The reason we didn't go in further was due to the basic risk discipline of Winters and Black," Jamie said later. "They looked at it and just could not work out how to make the business profitable enough for the risks." He recalled advice he had received from Warren Buffett years earlier: when faced with a dilemma, sometimes it's just better to go off to the golf course and do nothing.

*   *   *

"Billy, I really want you to watch out for subprime," Jamie told Bill King, the man he had put in charge of establishing a pipeline for the bank's mortgage derivatives, over a crackling telephone line while the latter was on a special mission in Rwanda in October 2006. "We need to sell a lot of our positions. I've seen it before. This stuff could go up in smoke."

Jamie sounded agitated, and with solid reason. No less a financial media bulwark than *Barron's* had just published an article stating in no uncertain terms that "a housing crisis approaches. The national median price of housing will probably fall by 30 percent in the next three years." *Barron's* based its projections on the tendency of all investments to move toward a "reversion to the mean" at some point. If stocks, for example, have historically ascended at an annual rate of 10 percent over time, they will eventually retreat to lower levels following an extended stretch of outsized gains. The reverse is also true; following a decade of flat performance, such as we experienced through the Bush years in the early 2000s, stocks will likely begin to accelerate in price until they catch up to historical averages. We saw this take place from spring 2009 through 2015.

But a housing decline of *30 percent* in the next three years! The prospect was terrifying to Jamie and other financial bigwigs who had a lot of skin in the game with their derivatives. The disbelievers always maintain that "this time is different." Every generation of geniuses who migrate to Wall Street with their MBAs in hand believe that this time, *their* time, will be different from previous bubbles because they're smarter than the people who came before them. So they charge ahead with abandon, raking in obscene profits with their latest financial inventions, oblivious to the history of the marketplace. But, sooner or later, the most recent bubble bursts, leaving its wreckage strewn across the landscape.

"What's a financial crisis, Daddy?" one of Jamie's daughters had asked him years earlier.

"Something that happens every seven years or so," he had replied.

And the more Jamie crunched the numbers and conferred with his chief lieutenants, the more he began to worry that another such crisis was lurking just around the corner. David Lereah, the National Realtors Association economist, countered the *Barron's* forecast with one of his own, saying that the housing market was in for a "soft landing," which is economic mumbo jumbo meaning that we're heading down, but not necessarily going to hell in a handbasket. Then Toll Brothers' CEO Robert Toll announced that "builders that built speculative homes are trying to move them by offering large incentives and discounts, and some anxious buyers are canceling contracts for homes already being built." Toll Brothers stock plummeted 50 percent for the year by August 2006, a sure harbinger that all was not well on the housing front.

"When even Toll Brothers, the high-end builder, suffers cancelations, you know the housing boom is over," reported *Forbes*.

Toll Brothers' collapse was quickly followed by Kara Homes, another high-end builder of "McMansions," which filed for bankruptcy shortly after it had enjoyed its two most profitable quarters in the company's history. The handwriting was not just on the wall; it was lighting up the sky, blazing with unrelieved intensity. And through it all, the Wall Street derivatives machine kept churning out its toxic waste products without letup. From October 2006 through the end of the year, the big banks floated a record $130 billion worth of mortgage derivatives on the market, double the amount of the same period a year earlier, 40 percent of which was subprime garbage. Jamie reviewed the numbers with mounting alarm and decided to call a meeting with his top executives in January 2007.

"Should we stop selling these products altogether?" Jamie wanted to know. "Should we hedge our risk more? Should we actually short the market and gamble on a housing decline?"

The last alternative was out of the question; Jamie had publicly touted the mortgage derivatives market as a key area for growth, so it would be untenable for JPMorgan Chase to bet against the market that he and his bank had been instrumental in creating. That would put Morgan in the position of a hedge fund gambling its clients' money in a casino-like environment, which would only roil the markets further. No, Jamie's venerable institution was not about to become a hedge fund, although the temptation was strong.

Hedging its risk even more was also not an option, considering that the primary monoline insurers could not take on any additional risk themselves, as AIG had informed Morgan. So what was left? Selling more and more of the bank's existing positions to whomever would buy them, and closing down the assembly line that churned out these products at an alarming rate. There were no other alternatives. Jamie and his team soon learned that some of their major competitors were now actively betting on a housing crash. Deutsche Bank and that other Morgan, Morgan Stanley, which had been two of the biggest offenders in foisting these derivatives on the public, had reversed their positions. They sold a lot of their inventory, much of it at heavy losses, and were betting on a housing collapse by shorting the market. Jamie was incredulous, bordering on furious.

"We are *not* Goldman Sachs!" Jamie told Black, Winters, and Masters. "They're going to accelerate the bloodletting once word gets out."

Jamie opted for a softer approach, increasing his bank's underwriting standards on the new derivatives it brought to the market, and buying more insurance against defaults as the premiums soared. But it was akin to applying a bandage to client who was hemorrhaging. The soft approach was clearly not enough. In the early months of 2007, the default rate on mortgage loans pushed higher. Household Finance, a giant subprime mortgage lender based in Charlotte, North Carolina, and New Century Financial both announced that their bottom-tier loans were tanking.

Jamie and his derivatives team found themselves in a bind. The cost of insurance when you could get it was skyrocketing, and they were loath to sell the market short. But their top competition, including Merrill Lynch and Bear Stearns, kept plowing ahead in the belief that the market was overreacting to reports of rising default rates, which they thought was only a temporary distraction. They upped the ante by churning out more and more of the products, and also by buying some of the derivatives on Morgan's books to sell to their own clientele.

"There were plenty of people on the other side of the trade, which made it easier for us," said Winters, who was only too happy to unload much of Morgan's inventory on eager buyers who evidently believed the punch bowl would never run dry.

The problem was: somebody was right and somebody was wrong about their outlooks for the markets. Either Merrill Lynch, Bear Stearns, Citigroup, and other major players whose profits were soaring were right in their assessment that the market would continue to boom, which meant that JPMorgan Chase, whose profits were languishing, was dead wrong. Or Jamie and his people were correct in their view that the housing bubble would soon burst and take the entire financial world, not to say the global economy, down with it. There was no way to know for sure until events played out on the world stage, and timing exactly when a significant implosion would occur was always a problem. The numbers were ominous, but sometimes the music can keep on playing for longer than anyone anticipates before it comes to a deafening halt.

Those who had been in the market long enough and personally experienced the painful collapses of the past could almost smell the carnage that lay ahead. Studying the markets from my own lair at BBF&T and sensing the atmosphere of anxiety as I walked down the hallway, the unmistakable stench of bear scat was prevalent. Yes, the bear—a great Bear Market of historic proportions—was lurking just around the corner. It reeked worse than the stench that preceded the 2000 dot.com meltdown, and the 20 percent one-day plunge in the days before October 1987.

It was hard to find a bull anywhere; virtually all the fund managers and equity analysts walked in slow motion beneath a dark, lowering cloud of impending doom. Don't try to time the markets, professionals relentlessly tell the investing public. But there are times when you need to take action. I cut my own family's stock exposure to under 30 percent. You always want to keep some skin in the game, but if the market does fall off a cliff, there's comfort in knowing that only 30 percent of what you have will be cut in half, and the other 70 percent can actually do quite well if it's invested in safe-haven harbors like Treasuries and gold-tracking stocks.

Yes, when the stink of the bear begins to permeate the world around you, you know that something unpleasant is about to hit the fan.

Chapter Twenty-two

The explosion in derivatives continued without letup even as the warning signals flashed brighter red on the horizon. Merrill Lynch accelerated its output in the spring of 2007, in the aftermath of a staggering 50 percent gain in earnings for all of 2006. "Investment banks have had no choice but to build their risk-taking capabilities," said Dow Kim, the driving force behind much of Merrill's CDO frenzy. "Clients want more liquidity and capital from their sell-side providers, and that trend will continue. A lot of our risk emanates directly from our client business."

The problem with that analysis is that the patients don't always know what's good for them. Sometimes the doctor—in this case the sell-side provider—needs to cut off the feel-good pharmaceuticals before the patients get addicted to them. Merrill increased its leverage to thirty-two times the value of its loans by spring 2007, and the other big financial drug dealers quickly followed suit. Goldman Sachs, Bear Stearns, Citi, Lehman Brothers, and others ramped up their ratios to around thirty and higher at the same time. *Any* setback at all at those stratospheric altitudes would be enough to trigger a monumental collapse. It was the same as small investors buying $30,000 worth of stock with only $1,000 to back them up. A drop in value to $29,000 would be enough to wipe them out, except that the stakes were much higher when you've got billions of dollars at risk. The regulators knew all this was going on, yet they did nothing to rein it in. It's hard to believe that anyone in Washington fully understood, or cared enough about, the gargantuan power of the monster that had been unleashed on the public by the Treasury Department and the Federal Reserve.

Jamie and his team could not leave the playing field altogether, In fact, they kept selling more of the derivatives, which benefited earnings, but at a more moderate pace. While they had trouble insuring those loans against default with the premiums soaring, they found a more novel way of hedging Morgan's risk by *shorting* the stocks of their main competitors. Shorting a stock means selling shares that you don't own in the hope of buying the shares back later at lower prices. It is the reverse of the usual process of buying stocks first and hoping to sell them in the future at a profit.

Going short is a strategy fraught with risk—if you're wrong and the stocks keep going up, you can lose a pile of money if you have to buy the stocks back at higher prices than you sold them for. But Morgan had a lot more capital at risk in its derivatives portfolio, so taking losses on those stock trades would be minimal, a type of insurance policy that would most likely be cheaper than buying swaps to hedge the mortgage securities. What it comes down to is there is no such thing as a perfect hedge. You can't hedge 100 percent of a portfolio, since you would be net neutral if you did so; you would make as much money with the hedging strategy as you lost with your portfolio, or vice versa, leaving no room for profits. But hedging 10 percent or 15 percent of what you have at risk makes sense if you are nervous about the state of the market. In that case, you would hope to *lose* money on your short positions because you stand to make a lot more with your primary investments.

*   *   *

By the summer of 2007, Jamie and his traders at Morgan had $32 billion at risk in the mortgage derivatives market, and the bank's clients kept demanding more of the products to satisfy their own lust for robust returns. Jamie knew that if Morgan refused to step up and meet the demand, his bank's clients would turn to his competitors to do so, like junkies seeking out new dealers to feed their addiction to the financial crack cocaine that flooded the marketplace. Jamie was boiling with anger and barely contained frustration.

"They can't get enough!" he bellowed to his staff. "The fact is that every five years or so something bad happens. *Nobody* ever has a right to not expect the credit cycle to turn."

Others who had been pioneers in exploring this Brave New World of credit derivatives were reaching the same conclusions. Bill Demchak, who had been plying his trade in Pittsburg with PNC since departing Morgan, told his traders that it was time to start shedding much of his bank's risk. Andrew Feldstein, who observed the markets as the head of his hedge fund Blue-Mountain Capital, had started sounding the alarm as early as 2005—a bit prematurely, as it turned out, since his bearish stance had drained his profits during the past two years. But by 2007, he was more convinced than ever that the markets were about to plummet. He sold off most of his derivatives positions and shorted the stocks of the banks with the most exposure.

"In an ideal world I would like to think that markets are rational and efficient," he said. "And in my own career I have tried to promote that. But until that ideal world arrives, we will continue to trade."

Alan Greenspan, who had passed the chairmanship of the Federal Reserve over to Ben Bernanke in January 2006, went so far as to call the current situation a "conundrum." He apparently was oblivious to the notion that he had been instrumental in creating much of the conundrum by obliterating Glass-Steagall in the previous decade and implementing unrealistically low interest rates through the early years of the new millennium. "Extended periods of low concern about credit risk have invariably been followed by reversal, with an attendant fall in the prices of risky assets," Greenspan stated in his dry, unassuming manner, which for him was equivalent to sounding the alarms and telling everyone it was time to get the hell out of Dodge.

On June 12, 2007, Greenspan's conundrum turned into a full-scale market rout. A hedge fund with the seemingly innocuous name of High-Grade Structured Credit Strategies Enhanced Leveraged Fund, run by a couple of former Bear Stearns traders with close ties to Bear, suddenly took a nosedive when its subprime mortgage derivatives portfolio blew up. It was the first crack in the dam that was soon about to disintegrate. Ralph Cioffi, one of the former Bear Stearns traders, tried to reassure some deep-pocket investors who asked to pull their money out that all was going well, it was just a temporary blip in the market. But privately he was less than convinced himself. "I'm fearful of these markets," Cioffi had emailed a friend a couple of months earlier. "It's either a meltdown or the greatest buying opportunity ever. I'm leaning towards the former." He expressed these sentiments at the same time he was exhorting his clients to leave their money in his fund and stay the course, according to documents seized by the FBI.

Cioffi deserved high marks for his prescience, if not his integrity. The major problem for the rest of the Street was that Cioffi and his partner Matthew Tannin had borrowed heavily from the big banks to finance their reckless purchases. Among the lenders was JPMorgan Chase, which was on the hook for hundreds of millions of dollars in vulnerable loans along with the usual suspects Bear Stearns, Merrill Lynch, Morgan Stanley, and an all-star cast of the nation's most venerable banking institutions.

"We want our money back!" Black demanded as he and his accountants stormed into Bear Stearns' headquarters in June. He demanded that Bear open its books to him so he could get a better idea of the precise nature of Morgan's risk. "Just stick with us, and it will all be fine. These are high-quality instruments," Bear Stearns' executives tried to placate Black. But when Black saw what was on Bear's books, he was nothing short of horrified. "Your funds are essentially bust!" he screamed. They were filled with bankrupt derivatives with no viable market value. His worst fears had been confirmed, he realized, as he headed back to report his findings to Jamie.

Moody's, one of the major ratings agencies, threw more fuel on the fire when it began to cut its ratings on billions of dollars' worth of subprime mortgage loans. What Jamie, Black, and the others feared more than anything else was a stampede out of the products, which would trigger an avalanche of selling at lower and lower prices, pummeling Morgan's hefty securities portfolios. The mortgages "are defaulting at a rate materially higher than original expectations," Moody's reported in an explanation for its downgrades. The other rating agencies quickly followed Moody's lead, with Standard & Poor's slashing its ratings on billions of dollars' worth of the derivatives. The problem, everyone realized, was not just isolated to Bear Stearns. Everyone's portfolio was at risk.

"This could turn nasty," Black told Jamie and the rest of the team at JPMorgan Chase.

The pending implosion threatened to become global. Morgan's trading partners in Germany, Japan, and other developed regions called Black in New York and Winters in London for advice on what to do with their own troubled portfolios. "Sell your assets now!" Winters told them in unequivocal language. "Sell as much of them as you can!"

* * *

Japan had been through it all in the 1990s, when its markets collapsed in the wake of the country's own financial crisis. "I see striking similarities today with the early stages of our own financial crisis more than a decade ago," said Hiroshi Nakaso, a top executive at the Bank of Japan, on August 2, 2007. During the intervening period Japan's stock market had plunged more than 60 percent, a depth from which it had yet to fully recover. But Nakaso's counterparts in the U.S. were reluctant to draw such parallels.

"The subprime problem appears to be contained," intoned U.S. Treasury Secretary Henry "Hank" Paulson to members of Congress. Paulson had cut his fangs at Goldman Sachs during the past three decades before George Bush brought him into his administration. Fed Chairman Ben Bernanke was equally sanguine, "Given the fundamental factors in place that should support the demand for housing, we believe the effect of the troubles in the subprime sector on the broader housing market will likely be limited." Bernanke also stated that the spillover effect on the nation's banks would be minimal.

Such soothing words from the pillars of the U.S. financial system did little to mollify the traders down in the trenches. As the default rate kept rising and many big banks attempted to offload their derivatives portfolio, even Bernanke began to get a bit nervous. Rising delinquencies and foreclosures were beginning to create "personal, economic, and social distress for many homeowners and communities," Bernanke testified to Congress on July 18, and the problems were "likely to get worse before they get better. But the damage would probably be "in the order of $50 billion to $100 billion," a pittance on the scale of the overall banking system. He noted that any comparisons to Japan's earlier meltdown were largely overblown.

A mere three weeks following Bernanke's sanguine assessment of the current financial environment, American Home Mortgage Investment Corporation filed for bankruptcy, claiming that its $400 billion derivatives portfolio was essentially worthless. Countrywide, the nation's largest mortgage lender, was next. Defaults on its subprime loans had climbed to the highest levels in five years, and the toxic loans were piling up on its books with no buyers out there willing to take them on. The Last Fool Theory had taken hold with a vengeance: everyone makes money selling inventory at higher and higher prices until the last fool wakes up one morning only to find that the demand has dried up virtually overnight. Countrywide's stock cratered when the news came out, taking other financial stocks down with it. The exodus was on, out of riskier assets like stocks and junk bonds, and into the traditional safe havens of U.S. Treasury securities, investment-grade corporate bonds, and gold. The Fed pitched in by slashing short-term interest rates in August 2007, and banks attempted to shore up their own balance sheets by putting a lid on their lending operations and hoarding cash.

With the major banks refusing to make loans to their institutional clients, those that needed to borrow turned more and more to the so-called "shadow banking system" for liquidity. The shadow banking system was made up of other sources of credit outside of the official banks, including money market funds, commercial paper, overnight repurchase agreements among investment bankers, mortgage lenders, and other institutions with deep pockets not subject to government oversight as the regulars banks were. By August, the shadow banking system had swollen to well over a trillion dollars. The sheer numbers of these unregulated loans launched a wave of panic that rippled throughout the industry.

The key issue coming "to a head in the next couple of months is that the shadow banking system is going to have to be put on the balance sheet of the real banking system," warned Paul McCulley, a senior official with the gargantuan bond fund PIMCO.

In other words, if the shadow banks started to fail, they would have to be bailed out by the real banks such as Citi, JPMorgan Chase, Morgan Stanley, and others, which were already suffocating under a massive load of their own debt. If the real banks proved unable to rescue not only themselves but the shadow banks as well, it could lead to a systemic collapse of the entire global financial system and the global economy that depended on it for survival.

Chapter Twenty-three

Until now, the Bush administration had been reluctant to involve itself in the developing crisis. "It's not the government's job to bail out speculators or those who made the decision to buy a home they knew they could never afford," President Bush stated in a press conference in September 2007. "America's overall economy will remain strong enough to weather any turbulence." What W left out was the corollary of his statement; it wasn't government's job to *encourage* people to buy homes they couldn't afford, and to subsidize the banks to make those high-risk loans in the first place.

But that's exactly what the government had been doing for the past decade and longer, primarily by giving government-sponsored entities like Fannie Mae and Freddie Mac carte blanche to buy the mortgage loans floated by the banks and add them to their own portfolios. The banks were then encouraged to make more bad loans, knowing that Fannie and Freddie would shift the growing mountain of bad debt from the banks to Fannie and Freddie's books. It was a massive Ponzi scheme of sorts, a shell game, a rigged smoke-and-mirrors system that merely moved these toxic time bombs from one subsidized entity to another.

But in the end it made little difference to the U.S. taxpayer which institutions staggered under the crushing weight of these financial weapons of mass destruction. It made little difference whether Citi, Morgan, and the other banks went under, or if Fannie and Freddie keeled over. In the end, the Fed would have to come to the rescue, which meant that American taxpayers would foot the bill for the excesses of the banks, the reckless policies of the federal government, and the monstrous tsunami of bankruptcies that threatened to inundate the global financial system. Meanwhile, the CEOs and top executives of the too-big-to-fail banks, among them Jamie, Sandy, and a slew of others, continued to fatten their own coffers with obscene compensation packages, even as the system they helped to create threatened to come crashing down like a multi-trillion-dollar house of cards that would wipe out middle- and working-class families across the globe.

*   *   *

"We'll buy the coffee," one of Treasury Secretary Hank Paulson's underlings announced jocularly when he invited the heads of the top banks to a "voluntary" meeting in Washington in September 2007. Behind the seemingly innocuous invitation, however, the bared fangs of the Treasury Department were unmistakably on display. "Show up, or else!" was the unspoken message behind the invitation—or else the Treasury and the Fed would take the punch bowl away and leave you stranded out there to sober up on your own.

Jamie read between the lines and knew he could not afford to ignore the powwow in the nation's capital, but he figured his bank was healthy enough that the Treasury needed JPMorgan Chase more than Morgan needed the shaky hand of government assistance. He decided not to attend the meeting himself, but rather assign the job as emissary to one of his lieutenants, John Kodweis, an expert in the derivatives arena who reported to Winters.

Kodweis entered the large conference room at Treasury, fully expecting that he would be participating in general preliminary talks about the growing crisis with his counterparts from Citigroup,

Bear Stearns, Merrill Lynch, Lehman Brothers, Morgan Stanley, and other key players. What he discovered instead was that they had all been summoned to participate in what amounted to a huge bailout program for Citi, which had not only its own derivatives portfolios at risk, but also seven shadow banks that Citi had created in an extensive network of failing lenders that threatened to bankrupt the entire industry.

Jamie's assessment had been prescient; the government needed JPMorgan's help more than Morgan needed any assistance from Treasury. Representatives from Citi ran the meeting, with Paulson nodding approval in the background, exhorting all the big banks to create a huge rescue pool amounting to hundreds of billions of dollars to keep Citi from going under. Even money market funds were threatened by Citi's excesses. The normally staid vehicles where investors parked their cash, secure in the belief that their principal was safe, were in danger of "breaking the buck," meaning that conservative investors were faced with the prospect of losing money on these historically risk-free investments.

"Absolutely not!" Winters exploded when Kodweis told him about Citi's rescue plan. "Why do we have to take part in this to bail out one of our top rivals?"

At this point, Paulson stepped in and phoned Jamie directly. "We really want you to take part," Paulson told Jamie. "It's not just about Citi. The whole system is at stake, which affects all of us if it implodes."

Jamie felt he had little choice but to get on board with Paulson's program. "We need to do the right thing," he informed his team. "This is about being a good citizen." Citi was hemorrhaging to death and couldn't survive on its own much longer. Chuck Prince's music had finally stopped playing, and he announced in November that he was resigning. Merrill Lynch, Bear Stearns, Lehman Brothers, and others were also writing down billions of dollars in losses on their derivatives portfolios, pushing the entire global financial system perilously close to the edge of the abyss.

"How did this happen?" Jamie asked a friend of his at Citi.

"We're not exactly sure," he replied. "There are still so many clashing cultures around here that I doubt more than a dozen people outside the derivatives team knew what the hell was going on."

Jamie shook his head. One of the first things he did after taking over at Morgan was to break up the so-called silos, the insulated divisions within the sprawling organization that failed to communicate with the other business units. As the patchwork beasts grew larger and more ravenous in the aftermath of the dismantling of Glass-Steagall, it became increasingly more difficult to turn them into efficient, cohesive operating units. Sandy had not bothered himself with that type of micromanagement when he ran Citi, and Chuck Prince concerned himself with little more than raking in profits from the derivatives securities while the party lasted. Jamie was one of the few CEOs who thought it important enough to get his arms around his own sprawling organization.

Merrill Lynch was the next to tumble, driven onto the shoals of financial ruin with its own extravagances, forcing the resignation of its buttoned-down chairman Stanley O'Neal in November 2007. The problems at Citi and Merrill Lynch set off an indiscriminate crash in banking stocks that took no prisoners. All of their share prices melted down, shedding some $240 billion in market value during the last six months of the year. I ran into a top executive at Citi a while later who was on the verge of a nervous breakdown; he had 90 percent of his multi-million-dollar net worth invested in Citi, which evaporated into the ether as Citi plummeted from a high of $55 a share at the end of 2006 to a low of $3 a share by the time the carnage was over. JPMorgan Chase fared a bit better, nosediving from a high of $52 in early 2007 to $22 a share.

By early 2008, the Fed was in a panic. Timothy Geithner, future Treasury Secretary who was then at the New York Fed, realized that the bloodletting was widespread, not just limited to Citi and a few other major banks. He called the CEOs of the top-tier U.S. banks, including Jamie at Morgan, with an undisguised note of alarm in his voice. "You need to find more capital," he told them all. "You need to find it now!"

The scramble was on to raise cash to keep the banks' balance sheets from crumbling—something that was easier said than done. The market for the derivatives had evaporated, and the cost of insuring them against default had skyrocketed, if you could find anyone willing to take on the risk. Demchak and his minions were dumbstruck by the ominous turn in fortunes. "What kind of monster has been created here?" he wondered. "It's like you've known a cute kid who then grew up and committed a horrible crime." Well, who created the monstrous kid in the first place?

Terri Duhon was even more in denial. "When car crashes happen, people don't blame cars or stop driving them," she observed. "They blame the drivers. Derivatives are the same. It's not the tools at fault, but the people who used those tools." That was like saying we only gave the kids in the schoolyard loaded guns to play with. Who knew they would actually start to pull the triggers?

Winters was more matter of fact. "Every four to five years there is a new excess in banking. The problem this time is extraordinary excess in the housing market." True enough. But when you throw more fuel on the fire because everyone else is doing it, you're only adding to the overall conflagration.

*   *   *

By March 2008, the storm clouds on the horizon had grown darker and more foreboding than ever. Bear Stearns announced that it could no longer operate on its own. If Bear went under, in the aftermath of the Merrill Lynch wreckage, the entire global financial system could tumble down with it. Timothy Geithner scoured the landscape and looked around for a credible suitor, until he zeroed in on JPMorgan Chase as the likeliest candidate for the role. He called Jamie to sound him out.

"I can't do that," Jamie said, feeling it would be foolhardy to add Bear Stearns' liabilities to Morgan's own host of shaky assets.

"We need you to get involved," Geithner told Jamie. Geithner offered to sweeten the pot by lending Morgan $30 billion to make the deal happen. But even that offer was not enough to convince Jamie that he should pursue the bailout. He had Winters pore through Bear's books, only to find that the problems were insurmountable. "It just would not be prudent to proceed," Winters informed Jamie.

Geithner was insistent. The Fed could not allow Bear Stearns to go bankrupt, and the central bank did not want to get into the business of directly taking over failing institutions. JPMorgan Chase was the only viable alternative. The Fed was prepared to make Jamie an offer he couldn't refuse. The central bank agreed to cordon off more than $30 billion worth of Bear's troubled assets and limit JPMorgan Chase's liability to $1 billion; the Fed would cover any damages in excess of that amount. Then Geithner threw in the clincher for Jamie. He offered to sell Bear Stearns to Morgan for $2 a share. The price was staggeringly low. Just months earlier, Bear Stearns' stock had been trading as high as $131, and even after the selloff it was going for $18. Buying Bear for $2 was a no-brainer. In his wildest dreams, Jamie never thought he could acquire the failing behemoth for less than $4 a share. Bear Stearns' headquarters on Madison Avenue was worth considerably more than the $250 million price of the deal.

Reading between the lines, the Fed was actually taking over Bear Stearns while avoiding the appearance of doing so. It was lending JPMorgan Chase $30 billion to buy the troubled bank, guaranteeing Morgan's losses at a maximum of $1 billion—pocket lint for a bank of Morgan's size—and then handing Bear over to Morgan at an arbitrary market price of $2 a share. The public perception was that Jamie was doing another masterful deal in acquiring Bear Stearns at a bargain basement price, but the reality was that he was getting the once-proud institution on a silver platter, courtesy of the most powerful central bank on the planet.

"We could probably have raised the money to do this deal simply by asking for donations from our own employees who didn't want to commute downtown anymore," one of Jamie's executives joked to his staff.

Bear Stearns' shareholders were less than thrilled by the news. Just as Citi's top shareholders had gone broke when Citi's stock plummeted below $3 a share, so too did Bear's big guns see their net worth dissolve when their own shares jackknifed off a cliff. "Diversify! Diversify!" is the well-known mantra that Wall Street professionals incessantly hammer their clients with. Yet, most of the Street's top honchos are anything but diversified, with the great bulk of their assets tied up in their employers' common stock, since stock options constitute the lion's share of their overall compensation.

Hence, the need to concentrate on enhancing the value of that stock, even if it means throwing caution to the wind and maximizing profits no matter how reckless the pursuit becomes. It's a strategy that works when the market is cooperating, but when the economy goes into a tailspin, even the biggest swinging dicks on Wall Street are unable to ward off impending financial impotence. When news of the deal was announced in March 2008, Wall Street wags referred to it as "the boy scouts taking over the mob," since Bear's traders had earned a reputation for taking no prisoners and "eating what they killed." But Jamie and his team discovered shortly afterward that integrating the two institutions would prove to be nearly impossible. They learned to their horror that their operating systems were totally incompatible. JPMorgan Chase "acquired" Bear Stearns in name only. In reality, Jamie had lassoed a beast that was capable of rearing its head and eating Jamie and his lieutenants for lunch.

The JPMorgan Chase-Bear Stearns deal calmed the markets, but only for a brief moment. It was the financial equivalent of plugging with one thumb a hole in the dam that was soon about to burst. On September 7, the Fed effectively nationalized Fannie and Freddie by putting them into conservatorship. It amounted to a government takeover of the country's leading buyers of mortgage debt—appearances be damned; there was no other way to describe the action. At the same time, Lehman Brothers, another bulwark of the industry, was entering the final stages of complete collapse. Without life support from the Fed or some healthier institutions— which were increasingly in short supply—Lehman would soon be gagging for air with the rattle of death issuing from its decaying carcass. If Lehman kicked the bucket, its demise would sound the death knell for the entire industry, and the fate of the global economy along with it.

Jamie was particularly exercised about Lehman Brothers' predicament, since JPMorgan Chase was Lehman's primary clearing house. If Lehman Brothers collapsed, Morgan would be exposed to the staggering liabilities on Lehman's derivatives portfolios. Jamie telephoned Paulson and Geithner to set up a meeting of the walking wounded, and then called a meeting of his top executives. "We're going down to Washington to discuss the Lehman situation," he informed them.

At 6:00 pm on Friday September 12, a gaggle of Wall Street's top executives met in the Fed's large conference room in Washington, D.C. Jamie and the others reasonably expected the weekend discussions to center on the problems at Lehman Brothers,

JPMorgan's exposure to the failing bank's derivatives liabilities, and the Fed's plans for dealing with the situation. Geithner cut right to the chase. "Lehman is on the brink of collapse," he said. "We need you guys to figure out a way to come up with $40 billion to rescue the company.

The bigwigs around the table looked around uneasily at one another. None of them had enough cash on hand to even contemplate a bailout of that size.

"What about the Fed?" Jamie asked.

"The government has no appetite to save Lehman with taxpayer dollars," Geithner said.

"We can't talk about Lehman without talking about AIG," said Black. "AIG is the next one to fall."

Geithner was visibly annoyed. He didn't want to deal with more than one crisis at a time. AIG was gagging on billions of dollars' worth of derivatives swaps it had taken on to insure the big banks against default.

"He's right," said Vikram Pandit, who had replaced Prince at Citigroup. "We need to talk about AIG!"

Geithner was about to lose it. "There is no political will for a federal bailout!" he repeated. He stood up, signaling that the meeting was over. "Come back in the morning and be prepared to do something."

Saturday morning arrived and the bankers assembled more divided than ever about their next course of action. Only two banks, Bank of America and British behemoth Barclays, expressed any interest in riding to Lehman's rescue. B of A dropped out immediately, and Barclays dragged its feet without some reassurance from the Fed, saying this was an American problem that should be resolved by American institutions. Geithner explained as patiently as he could that Hank Paulson at Treasury, and the Fed, were already taking considerable heat for arranging the bailout of Bear Stearns and the de facto nationalization of Fannie and Freddie. Geithner was adamant that the private banks would have to act on their own this time around. The great powwow in Washington broke up on Sunday afternoon, with no agreement on the next course of action. That evening Jamie called a meeting of his entire board of directors in New York City.

"Lehman is about to go bankrupt," Jamie announced solemnly. "We think we are going to be fine. But it is going to be very, very ugly for others. Worse than anything any of us have seen in our lives."

When news of Lehman Brothers' collapse hit the wires just before midnight on Sunday, September 14, the financial markets around the globe went haywire, indicating a freefall in U.S. stock prices when the market opened for trading at 9:30 East Coast Time. Stocks had already been declining from a DJIA high of 14,087 on October 1, 2007, to around 11,000 by this time, but it was only a prelude to what would happen when the Lehman Brothers bombshell hit the market. Within the next day and a half, investors abandoned the entire global financial system, blasting away more than $600 billion in equity valuations as they panicked toward the exits. And the carnage had just begun. Stocks would continue to nosedive over the next few months, with no buyers serving as a safety net, until they thudded back to earth in March 2009 with the DJIA crashing to 6,726. As I sat at my own stock terminal, Sandy's famous words rang in my ears.

"This is either the end of the world or a classic buying opportunity." Well, it turned out not to be the end of the world as we know it, but it sure as hell felt like it at the time.

Good friends, seasoned investment professionals for years past, began to throw in the towel, violating the sage advice they had been giving to clients to stay the course when things looked grim. "Get me out at any cost!" they told their traders. "I can't stand any more pain," was the plaintive cry issuing from their throats. It was total capitulation to the reality of the moment. The problem with recovering from a 50 percent loss in equity is that it takes a rise of 100 percent to get even again. If your net worth falls from, say, $100,000 to $50,000, you need prices to double just to get back where you started.

It wasn't just the collapse of Lehman that spooked investors; money market funds with exposure to Lehman's debt threatened to go under. There was no safe place to put one's assets, since there was no way to value anything with markets around the world drying up. The Europeans were incensed, particularly the French.

"What was horrendous is the decision of Henry Paulson to let Lehman Brothers go," said an irate Christine Lagarde, France's economy minister. "This was a genuine error." Possibly, although Fed Chairman Ben Bernanke wrote in a book that was published in 2015 that the Fed did not have the ability to save Lehman, since it would have required an infusion of cash amounting to $200 billion to cover Lehman's liabilities.

Paulson sent Geithner out on the firing line to defend the government's position. And Geithner stood before the cameras looking like nothing less than the proverbial deer caught in the headlights. He squirmed as he announced a complete reversal in the Fed's stance on bailing out the too-big-to-fail institutions that were toppling markets across the globe. Yes, the Fed would nationalize AIG by extending the insurer an $85 billion line of credit in exchange for taking a 79.9 percent stake in the company.

And the Fed's belated largess would not end there. It poured enough money into the system to facilitate Bank of America's

237

takeover of a reeling Merrill Lynch, to insure the safety of money market funds where investors parked their idle cash reserves while waiting for new buying opportunities, and the central bank initiated the first $700 billion stage of its Troubled Asset Relief Program to transfer the derivatives off the books of the big banks onto the Fed's balance sheet. But Geithner was determined not to take all the heat on his own. Once again he summoned Jamie and the other bank CEOs to Washington on October 14, 2008, and subjected them to a tongue-lashing. "We've entered an era of socialist banking," he reluctantly informed them, demanding that they turn over large swaths of their common stock to the Fed in return to hefty multi-billion-dollar cash infusions. The banks had brought this on themselves, Geithner angrily informed them.

Jamie and the others had the option of opting out of the Fed's double-edged offer, but Jamie was not about to turn down what amounted to free money in exchange for a commensurate amount of JPMorgan Chase's stock. But he was not going to walk away with his tail between his legs either. He wanted the last word for himself.

"God knows, some really stupid things were done by American banks and American investment bankers," he allowed. "But it wasn't just the bankers. Where were the regulators in all this?"

Well, we know where the regulators were. They were sitting in a cage, stripped of their claws and fangs by people like Sandy and Jamie, who thought that restraints on the banks' casino-like activities were restricting their abilities to gamble with the financial stability of the entire world.

PART FOUR

THE MONEY MONSTERS' GOSPEL

Chapter Twenty-four

Jamie laughed when he was asked why he had accepted money from the government if his bank didn't really need it. "Why? They asked me to," he said. "When the Secretary of the Treasury, the head of the central bank, the head of the FDIC, and the head of the New York Fed say, 'We want you to do this because we think it's in the best interest of the United States of America,' you know, we're a little like the Japanese. We're a little patriotic that way. We said, 'Yes, sir!'"

The rest of America and most of the world were not quite as fortunate. When the Fed pumped well over a trillion dollars into the economy in the wake of the 2008 tsunami, none of it landed in the bank accounts of the taxpayers who made such generosity possible. It landed in the coffers of the too-big-to-fail banks (and the too-big-to-jail bankers), the insurers, and other major corporations like General Motors and Chrysler, which proceeded to hoard the cash on their balance sheets while middle- and working-class families collapsed under the load of exorbitant debt and vanishing net worth. The government that precipitated the crisis continued to feed the monstrous institutions whose greed brought the world to the brink of total ruin, allowing them to sit on money designed to rejuvenate the economy. Meanwhile, millions of average investors surveyed the wreckage around them, wondering how they were ever going to dig themselves out of the financial graveyard that the world had become.

Jamie tried to dissociate himself and his bank from the scorched earth financial landscape that blighted the globe from horizon to horizon. It was "unfair and unjust," he said, for public officials to blame him and JPMorgan Chase for manufacturing and selling mortgage-backed derivatives during the years that led up to the financial holocaust. In accepting money from the government and bailing out Bear and other weaker institutions, Morgan was just doing what Ben Bernanke, Hank Paulson, and Timothy Geithner had asked him to do. But investigations into the key role played by JPMorgan prior to the crisis proved more damning. In 2009, less than a year after the onset of the Great Recession, the Federal Home Loan Bank of Pittsburgh initiated a lawsuit against Morgan, accusing Jamie's bank of selling it more than $1.7 billion in shaky mortgage derivatives.

"Pittsburgh FHLB believed that it had made a safe investment," the suit alleged, which instead resulted in hundreds of millions of dollars in losses. The lawsuits against JPMorgan Chase continued over the next few years. The Justice Department and several state attorneys general launched their own investigations into JPMorgan Chase's role in the meltdown. Jamie's relentless effort to spin the story his way contradicted the evidence uncovered by Benjamin B. Wagner, the U.S. Attorney for the Eastern District of California, which showed that Morgan was guilty of the same irresponsible behavior perpetrated by the bank's competitors. A tsunami of subpoenaed documents and e-mails revealed that JPMorgan bankers and traders had underwritten billions of dollars' worth of questionable mortgage-backed securities that Jamie had been telling everyone had originated at Bear Stearns and other banks. Worse, the reckless behavior had occurred on Jamie's watch.

Quick to jump on the bandwagon in his pursuit of JPMorgan Chase and the other Leviathan banks was New York State Attorney General Eric Schneiderman, co-chairman of the task force that President Obama created to investigate and prosecute wrongdoing in the mortgage-backed securities market. Schneiderman said, "Since my first day in office, I have insisted that there must be accountability for the misconduct that led to the crash of the housing market and the collapse of the American economy."

Soon after taking office in January 2011, Schneiderman, a former state legislator from Manhattan's Upper West Side and the first to be elected New York attorney general since 1918, interrogated the junior attorney in his office who had been working with other state attorneys general on what became known as the National Mortgage Settlement. In that deal, announced in February 2012, five of the nation's largest banks agreed to pay $25 billion to settle claims related to home foreclosures in the aftermath of the financial crisis. The litigation arose out of the so-called robo-signing scandal, in which banks foreclosed on homes even though they no longer had the original mortgage documentation. JPMorgan Chase coughed up $1.21 billion to the federal and state governments and provided an additional $4.21 billion in various forms of mortgage relief to homeowners. The country's five largest mortgage servicers also admitted they "routinely" signed foreclosure documents "without really knowing whether the facts they contained were correct."

The beleaguered junior attorney, who was on the job before Schneiderman arrived, explained that no documents had been subpoenaed and no witnesses deposed who were involved in the underwriting of mortgage-backed securities. The behavior of the bankers leading up to the financial crisis didn't seem to be on anyone's agenda at the time. Schneiderman was furious. He couldn't understand what was going on. "At first I thought, maybe there's some cabal, like Treasury and the OCC [Office of the Comptroller of the Currency] and these pro-bank people, stopping the aggressive Justice Department folks," he said. Senator Chuck Schumer visited him and warned him that people in Washington were "trying to rewrite history" about the causes of the financial crisis. There didn't seem to be a conspiracy to thwart the prosecution of Wall Street bankers, the senator explained, just timidity and indifference. Schumer, of course, got much of his campaign funds from the Barons of Wall Street, as did that other former New York Senator, Hillary Clinton.

In March 2011, Schneiderman went to Washington and met with Iowa Attorney General Tom Miller, who was heading up negotiations with the banks on the robo-signing settlement. Schneiderman says he asked Miller if anyone was looking into pre-

243

crash wrongdoing. "My conversation with him indicated to me that no one had investigated," he says. "No one was going to investigate." Unknown at the time to Schneiderman, "there were definitely existing DOJ investigations throughout 2011," said Tony West, a Justice Department lawyer. But it makes sense that Schneiderman never knew about them because the Justice Department kept that information under wraps.

Schneiderman and Miller also spoke about the indemnity against additional liability that the banks wanted as part of the settlement. Scheiderman was hardly surprised to hear that the banks wanted to be released from liability regarding the underwriting of mortgage-backed securities prior to the financial crisis, but he was horrified to learn that Miller and the other attorneys general were prepared to give it to them, according to Schneiderman. After speaking with Miller, Schneiderman decided that he would not sign a general release as part of the settlement. "He didn't like it," Schneiderman recalls of Miller's reaction.

Miller had a different take on the situation. There was never the slightest chance that the banks would be released from any claims regarding their manufacture and sale of mortgage-backed securities, he said. "We had certain goals in mind concerning robo-signing, principal reduction, monetary relief, monitors—and we achieved all those goals, and we were never, in a thousand years, going to give them a relief on securities." Another official close to the National Mortgage Settlement negotiations adds, "There is this allegation that has persisted to this day that we were going to give away the farm, that we were going to release everything, and it was only because of Eric Schneiderman [that we didn't]; where he stood firm, and he interceded, and he said, 'You can't do that,' and his bravery stopped that from happening. Totally, 100 percent false."

When Schneiderman returned to New York, he decided that his office would conduct its own investigation into the Wall Street banks' wrongdoing in the years leading up to the financial crisis. Joseph R. Biden III, the Delaware attorney general and son of the vice president, heard about Schneiderman's controversial decision not to sign on to the mortgage settlement and thought he was doing the right thing. The two agreed to work together. "I informed myself quickly about how bad this was," Schneiderman says. "It was even worse than I had realized, because it was so out in the open. It was like a bank robbery without masks or gloves. There had been bad behavior. People knew it was bad behavior. It wasn't too hard to understand. It was unbelievable to me, actually, and I had a hard time even accepting the fact that there weren't investigations going on, because how could you not investigate this?"

Schneiderman firmly stated that he had no intention of signing the National Mortgage Settlement as it then stood. He went to see Thomas Perrelli, who'd preceded Tony West at the Justice Department. He visited the White House. He introduced himself to Housing and Urban Development Secretary Shaun Donovan (who later directed the Office of Management and Budget). At each stop, Schneiderman says, he was told in no uncertain terms that he had to sign the deal. At times the conversations, even among political allies, became quite heated. Schneiderman's comments to the media further angered his colleagues. He told a Rochester, New York, newspaper that he was "stunned" to learn that no documents had been subpoenaed or depositions taken regarding the underwriting of mortgage-backed securities before the financial crisis, and that he would oppose "a quick, cheap settlement." He said the attorneys general negotiating the settlement "had no leverage." He said he would not give the banks a "full release."

As summer turned into fall, the political heat on Schneiderman intensified. As angry as government officials were at Schneiderman's individualistic approach, they also knew that they needed him on board to get a deal done. In early November 2011, Schneiderman received an unexpected call from Shaun Donovan, who proposed that they work together on a joint investigation into the pre-crash conduct of the banks. The two spent some time working out the details, particularly in terms of delaying the announcement of the National Mortgage Settlement until the full-scale probe was announced. Schneiderman was agreeable.

In an effort to make sure he stayed that way, Schneiderman was appointed co-chair of the residential-mortgage-backed securities "working group" of President Obama's Financial Fraud Enforcement Task Force. Then he was asked to be Michelle Obama's guest at the 2012 State of the Union address, when Obama announced that he had asked Holder to begin a new investigation into pre-crash activities on Wall Street. "I did not come down to Washington just because of my charm," Schneiderman said.

Once it became clear that no general release would be part of the National Mortgage Settlement and that the banks could face prosecution for their pre-crisis underwriting of mortgage-backed securities, H. Rodgin Cohen, a senior partner at Sullivan & Cromwell, went to see Schneiderman. Cohen was considered to be one of the deans of the Wall Street bar. "He was just a guy coming in to chat with me about the situation," Schneiderman said, smiling. They agreed that since there was likely to be additional litigation, there could also be "a peace premium" paid by the banks to settle claims with the federal and state authorities. "We connected immediately," Schneiderman recalls. "He was on the other side, but we saw things the same way." In short order, the relationship would prove very useful to both men.

*   *   *

In March 2012, Tony West replaced Thomas Perrelli at the Justice Department, and the real grunt work of the new task force commenced in earnest. Schneiderman quickly grew dissatisfied. The most important thing to keep in mind, he kept hearing from the Justice Department, was to lower expectations. Schneiderman blew up. "I was not about to let that happen to this working group," he said. He wanted the group to have its own office space and a dedicated staff of investigators, and he wanted it to go for the jugular. Finally, Steve Linick, the inspector general of the Federal Housing Finance Agency—the agency that oversees the conservatorship of Fannie Mae and Freddie Mac—offered the working group some office space.

"We raised a big ruckus," Schneiderman said. "I think the White House eventually called up West and said, 'You've got to do something,' and then they hired a bunch of contractors and they started assigning assistant attorneys general in different U.S. Attorneys' offices around the country to actually do some work." West later confirmed that the White House contacted him to figure out what had Schneiderman so peeved.

Subpoenas filled the air like blackbirds in flight in February and March, and the big Wall Street banks manned the trenches for the coming battle. "We have to prove intent, so sometimes we actually have to cross T's and dot I's a little bit more assiduously than might otherwise be the case," said a Justice Department official. "Before we bring a case, we want to make sure that it's a case we can actually go to court and win." Schneiderman and his team were eager to have cases brought after supporting the National Mortgage Settlement. "They felt very exposed during this period and wanted to have something to show for the fact that they had made this deal," said one person involved in the negotiations.

In October 2012, after a separate, independent investigation that lasted more than a year, Schneiderman sued JPMorgan Chase in state court, claiming that Bear Stearns and its mortgage-origination subsidiary, despite legal representations to the contrary, had failed to properly evaluate the quality of mortgages that the firm was securitizing and selling to investors. In the complaint, Schneiderman argued that Bear Stearns—by then owned by JPMorgan Chase—had "systematically failed to fully evaluate the loans, largely ignored the defects that their limited review did uncover, and kept investors in the dark about both the inadequacy of their review procedures and the defects in the underlying loans. Furthermore, even when defendants were made aware of these problems, they failed to reform their practices or to disclose material information to investors." As a result, the loans "included many that had been made to borrowers who were unable to repay, were highly likely to default, and did in fact default in large numbers."

Schneiderman's complaint was comprehensive, and it included a bevy of outrageous e-mails that had made the rounds at

Bear Stearns, whose bankers had referred to one of the derivatives they floated as a "SACK OF SHIT" and "a shit breather." Bear Stearns sold the deal anyway to investors all over the globe. With that evidence in hand, Jamie called him on the day he filed the complaint. It was unfair to blame JPMorgan for the wrongdoing that occurred at Bear Stearns, he argued. Schneiderman cut him off. "Look, just talk to your lawyers," he said.

That same month, Benjamin Wagner and his team in Sacramento issued their own subpoenas to JPMorgan Chase, demanding to know what the bank had done in the years leading up the 2008 financial crisis. They reviewed hundreds of thousands of internal documents, took the sworn depositions of about a dozen JPMorgan Chase bankers, interviewed dozens who had worked with the bank's mortgage-backed securities, and spoke with the mortgage originators who had sold mortgages to Morgan. Wagner claimed that he found "a pretty strong pattern" showing that "the very due-diligence process that was supposed to be identifying bad loans and weeding them out was essentially being subverted or circumvented in the rush to get these to market."

On March 6, 2013, Holder testified before the Senate Judiciary Committee about the so-called "too big to jail" Wall Street banks. Answering a question from Iowa Senator Chuck Grassley, Holder responded, "I am concerned that the size of some of these institutions becomes so large that it does become difficult for us to prosecute them when we are hit with indications that if we do prosecute—if we do bring a criminal charge—it will have a negative impact on the national economy, perhaps even the world economy."

Holder's comment sounded like nothing less than a cover up, and it infuriated many people who believed Wall Street bankers, traders and executives had to be held accountable for their actions leading up to the financial crisis, and that the Justice Department was shirking its responsibility. But his statement was consistent with what he had written in a June 1999 memorandum: "Prosecutors may consider the collateral consequences of a corporate criminal conviction in determining whether to charge the corporation with a criminal offense." In other words, the collateral damage from bringing the giant banks to heel might cause more problems than it was worth. The government had given birth to these financial mastodons, and now they were simply too big to be held accountable for their actions.

Schneiderman was infuriated with Holder for undercutting his own investigation into the causes of the meltdown. His staff encouraged him to resign from the working group and denounce the administration. They believed that too much of his time was being wasted on what appeared to be an unwinnable war. Instead, the pit bull DNA in Schneiderman rebelled. He went back to Capitol Hill and met with senators he hoped were sympathetic to his cause, including Elizabeth Warren, Carl Levin, Jeff Merkley and Sherrod Brown. "I let it be known that I was unhappy with what was going on," he said.

The other co-chairs of the working group were less than titillated by Schneiderman's attempt at a palace coup. "Whenever you have somebody who you're supposed to be working with and sharing information with—sharing sensitive information with—and then they kind of go and start talking to the press and blasting you, then that informs the way you deal with them going forward," one of the team players tried to explain. In a blatant attempt at damage control, a Justice Department spokesman said that Holder's comments to Congress had no bearing on the determination of the Justice Department to prosecute the big banks. "We will investigate wherever the facts lead," the official said. "I mean, as simplistic as it sounds, this is true."

Around the same time, West asked one of his Justice Department colleagues, Geoffrey Graber, to assess the status of various investigations into Wall Street's mortgage-backed securities business. There were ten U.S. Attorneys investigating wrongdoing, and West wanted Graber to analyze which of these cases could be ready to file by the end of the year. Graber flew around the country, meeting with various U.S. Attorneys, and reported back to West and Holder in the early summer. One of the cases that Graber concluded was furthest along was Wagner's complaint against JPMorgan

Chase. The assessment, West said, "helped us to make some hard choices."

After Graber issued his report, things picked up considerably. At that point, Holder started conducting weekly meetings at which, one participant said, "he became very, very engaged in pushing forward the work of the working group." Even Schneiderman was appeased, temporarily at least. "They started feeling a little bit more of the heat, and they started really to move," he said.

On June 26, in Sacramento, Wagner hosted a team of JPMorgan lawyers to hear why the bank believed that the case he was building didn't rise to the level of criminal or civil liability, and also to learn what JPMorgan's likely defenses would be. Wagner was unmoved: "After listening to a day of their discussion and going back and looking up what we had, we felt pretty confident, and we were plowing ahead."

In early August, Jamie offered to settle the litigation for $1 billion in cash plus another $4 billion of mortgage-related relief. Leading the negotiations for the bank with Jamie was Stephen Cutler, the general counsel and a former chief of enforcement at the Securities and Exchange Commission. But the two sides were light years apart. The prosecution wanted $21.8 billion to settle the case, not the mere pittance Jamie and Cutler had offered.

"I thought it was almost a nonstarter," West said, "and other people in the room said, 'You know, at least it's an invitation to talk.' They knew that we had come back to them with a number that indicated our disappointment with their $1 billion. In fact, they said that to me directly. But that's when the real conversation began."

Chapter Twenty-five

In late August 2013, Wagner said, "the effort to put together a global negotiation was floundering." He turned his attention back to the civil complaint he was preparing against JPMorgan Chase. West was trying to see if a deal could be reached after Labor Day. If it couldn't, the next step would be to allow Wagner's complaint to be filed. For his part, Schneiderman believed that the negotiation would either "go forward," or else it was "going to go off the rails."

Wagner's complaint pricked Jamie's sensibilities. "It certainly quickened the pace of discussions," Wagner said. "We were providing it to show that we thought we had a very strong case, and also that it was coming very soon." The potential filing was the catalyst that moved things along, since once it was made public for all the world to scrutinize, there was no chance of putting the genie back in the bottle. The ensuing media firestorm would be enough to fuel a plethora of lawsuits against Morgan by thousands of victimized investors.

Jamie stipulated that he wanted to resolve any potential criminal charges as part of the overall settlement. He was adamant that there be no public statement of facts regarding wrongdoing by his bankers, and he demanded immunity against any future litigation. West replied that Jamie's stipulations were unacceptable. Jamie and Cutler raised their offer to $3 billion in cash and $4 billion in mortgage relief, and the Justice Department lowered its sights to $15 billion in cash, plus unspecified mortgage relief. The two sides had narrowed the gap, but they were still billions of dollars apart.

"We had gotten as close as we could," West said. The Justice Department filed Wagner's complaint on September 24, and Wagner departed to Washington for the press conference and the attendant photo ops.

"It was clear that we had reached an impasse," West told Stacey Friedman, another JPMorgan Chase lawyer, during a heated telephone call on September 23. He had no alternative except to allow Wagner's complaint to be filed. He thought Friedman would urge Jamie to capitulate by increasing Morgan's offer, but Friedman replied that the bank was not prepared to budge unless the Justice Department dropped its threat of a criminal charge. In addition, Morgan would not agree to the release of a statement of facts. Again, West declined and said there was no room left to negotiate.

The next day, Jamie called West himself. "I kind of think it's important, when the stakes are this high, that the principals get to know one another," Jamie said. He wanted to go to Washington to meet with him and Holder and share his side of the story. He was asking for a sit-down between the capi di tutti capi of the rival clans—the de facto leader of the financial world and the top honchos in government. West said he needed to confer with Holder first to see if he could arrange such a showdown. West also told Jamie that a meeting would have to be held as soon as possible since he didn't want to postpone filing Wagner's complaint.

No sooner had West trekked down the hallway into Holder's office, where Holder was sequestered with James Cole, the deputy attorney general, when West's cellphone rang. Jamie was on the other end again. He said he could come down to Washington to meet with all of them on September 26, and he allowed that the meeting would be productive since JPMorgan Chase was prepared to come up with a significantly higher offer this time. West agreed, with Holder's consent, to postpone filing Wagner's complaint until they had a chance to review what Jamie had to say. There was little question that Jamie was determined to keep the sordid details in Wagner's complaint from the prying eyes of the media and the public. "You have so much power," Jamie told West jocularly, perhaps an effort to soften him up before the meeting.

"Well, I'm not a Master of the Universe like you," West retorted.

If Jamie was willing to at least double his previous offer to around $6 billion to $7 billion in cash, plus $4 billion in mortgage relief, it would be enough to buy some time on the Wagner filing, West reasoned, since he thought he could eventually get Jamie to up the cash offer to double digits. West mused, however, that he was antsy to move forward on the filing for the photo op it would present. "I had my nice blue suit on," he chuckled, "and I was ready for the cameras. Being out there in Sacramento, you don't always get the opportunity to step on a national stage, so at a personal level, it was somewhat deflating. But on the other hand, you don't let ego get in the way of these things. You want to do what's right—not only for my case in the Eastern District of California, but for the department and the government generally. I've always been a team player, so it was back to negotiations."

*　　*　　*

On September 26, Dimon arrived in the citadel of American power and ambition with Cutler, Friedman, and Matt Zames, the bank's chief operating officer. There to greet them in Holder's fifth-floor office at the Justice Department were Holder, West, Wagner, and Cole. Jamie presented his case that JPMorgan Chase was being unfairly singled out for its role in the meltdown and proceeded to increase his bank's offer to $7 billion offer, which he submitted as a "global offer"—one designed to resolve all the state and federal cases against Morgan, plus the federal agency claims. Jamie made it clear that his paramount concern was Wagner's case and the adverse publicity that would entail, which would cost the bank dearly in lost credibility.

"Clearly, they had brought the big guns to show that they were serious about wanting to negotiate," said West. At that point, Holder chimed in with his view that any settlement would not eliminate the possibility of future criminal prosecution against the JPMorgan Chase or its executives. "They left with an absolute clear understanding that there was no way they were going to get the criminal case relieved through a settlement," West said, although the point became moot since the Justice Department never did get around to filing a criminal complaint against JPMorgan Chase. Cutler reiterated Jamie's point that the bank would not agree to a settlement that left the door open to criminal charges. If that was the case, "We're not going to do that," Cutler said. "Listen, we may not resolve this thing."

Jamie made it clear that the buck stopped with him as chairman and CEO of the bank, that he was interested in a global settlement, and that he was committed to getting it done. Holder was also anxious to get the deal done and put the issue behind him and the Justice Department. He was less adamant than West and the others on his side of the table. "When the attorney general speaks like that, presumably everybody else in the room on the government side understood where he was coming from," said West. West only implied that Holder's overarching motivation was to terminate the negotiation as quickly as possible to protect the government from collateral embarrassment for not doing its job properly in the first place.

When the meeting ended, West and Cutler went to work hammering out the specifics on a comprehensive deal that both sides could live with. They broke up into three separate working groups: one to draft the releases from future liability, one to reach an agreement on the cash settlement, and the third charged with crafting the statement of facts, which is mandatory in all such negotiations. "There was concern that that was going to be very, very difficult," West said.

"There would be these bursts of energy, and it would look like we were getting right to the end, and then there would be something that tanked the whole deal."

A major issue was the amount of cash the bank would agree to pay. West insisted on $10 billion in cash, hoping he could get $9 billion. Cutler and JPMorgan Chase were stuck at $7.25 billion. In mid-October, Jamie intervened directly with Holder by telephone, offering $9 billion cash plus $4 billion in mortgage relief. Cutler told Justice Department officials that JPMorgan Chase's board had approved the deal on the perverse assumption that the bank would be reimbursed by, you guessed it, U.S. taxpayers in the form of tax credits. Cutler's remarks almost sandbagged the entire deal, but Holder was as anxious to take credit for this "victory" as Jamie was to resolve the issue surrounding Wagner's complaint, which he was determined to keep from seeing the light of day at any cost.

As it turned out, JPMorgan Chase's $13 billion package was, indeed, partially tax deductible, and the rest he charged to the bank's shareholders by cutting the dividend in half. "I could have killed him when he did that," said Brian Rogers, chairman of T. Rowe Price and manager of the firm's Equity Income Fund, a major investor in JPMorgan Chase's stock.

Despite Jamie's effort to keep Wagner's complaint private, it almost exploded into the public realm when the Pittsburgh FHLB, which had launched its own lawsuit in 2009, requested that JPMorgan Chase turn over a copy to the Pittsburgh bank's lawyers. Jamie almost lost it on October 17 when a state judge in Allegheny County ordered JPMorgan to cough up the Wagner complaint by November 1. Jamie went over the judge's head, so to speak, by contacting the Justice Department to get the order quashed. The Justice Department was only too happy to intervene with its full wrath and fury by getting the deadline pushed back to November 15, and finally to never, to keep the negation with Jamie & Company on track. West allowed that the Justice Department was content with Pittsburgh FHLB getting whatever settlement it could from JPMorgan Chase, just not at the expense of potentially screwing up the larger deal. On January 3, JPMorgan Chase reached a confidential settlement with the Pittsburgh FHLB. One of the terms of the agreement was that the Wagner complaint would never see the light of day.

Finally, after a lot of white-knuckle, eleventh-hour phone calls in the following days, the Justice Department and the state attorneys general announced the $13 billion settlement on November 19, which amounted to $9 billion in cash to be paid to various federal and state agencies, and another $4 billion to consumers "harmed by the unlawful conduct of JPMorgan." JPMorgan Chase was pilloried for wrongdoing in the years serving as prologue to the 2008 Great Recession. "What is JPMorgan trying to hide?" the media wanted to know when they learned that a detailed statement of facts would not be forthcoming.

One media pundit asking that question the loudest was Gretchen Morgenson, columnist for the *New York Times*. After reviewing the watered-down statement of facts released with the settlement agreement, she wrote on November 23 that "Much of it was the same-old-same-old, a not-very-lively description of a corrupted Wall Street mortgage factory, based largely on some facts that have been in the public domain for years. In other words, although it took the Justice Department more than five years to pursue a major bank for its role in the mortgage mania, the investigation seems to have unearthed material that, by and large, could have been dug up with a spoon."

* * *

It was the largest financial settlement in history to date, and the agreement allowed Jamie to keep Wagner's damning changes under wraps, hidden from the glaring spotlight of public scrutiny. What the settlement did reveal, however, was that Jamie's claim that his own bankers and traders had done nothing wrong in the years leading up to the financial crisis simply was not true.

"The investigators and the lawyers were uncovering very viable evidence," said West. "I think there was recognition that we had enough evidence there that would support the complaint and would support a robust lawsuit."

Wagner's complaint remains unfiled to this day, fostering speculation that it contains more comprehensive evidence of wrongdoing than are available in a sanitized "statement of facts" that was a required component of the settlement. Unlike the complaint itself, the statement of facts omits the names of the Morgan executives involved and other specific charges. Among the documents Wagner uncovered was one in which an unnamed

JPMorgan employee, who had been involved in purchasing pools of mortgages from third parties, warned two senior executives that "due to their poor quality, the loans should not be purchased and should not be securitized." She expressed her concerns in a letter to a managing director at the bank, who shared it with other managing directors.

"JPMorgan nonetheless securitized many of the loans. None of this was disclosed to investors," Jamie conceded in the settlement agreement. Separately, William D. Cohan, who was fired by Jamie as a managing director in January 2004, brought a losing wrongful dismissal lawsuit of his own against the bank, but he remains in litigation with Morgan as the result of a soured investment he made with the bank in 1999.

Wagner also found that JPMorgan bankers had decided to eliminate a bunch of low-quality loans—mortgages that had been granted without documented proof of the borrower's income—from a pool of mortgages they were going to buy and securitize. When the originator of the mortgages objected to JPMorgan's decision to remove these loans from the pool, a group of JPMorgan managing directors—including bankers, traders and salesmen—met with the originator and decided to buy two of the loan pools anyway, including those with the rancid mortgages. JPMorgan then proceeded to bundle "hundreds of millions of dollars of loans from those pools into one security." Wagner found that between the start of 2006 and the middle of 2007—when the mortgage securitization frenzy was at its peak—JPMorgan packaged and sold securities containing thousands of mortgages that were rated by a third-party evaluator to be of extremely low quality, meeting few of the bank's underwriting standards.

"Nobody would stand up and say Chase qua Chase—just Chase alone—didn't do things wrong," explained one person close to the investigation. "There clearly is some liability." Reflecting on the details contained in Wagner's complaint that were left out of the statement of facts, West says that the statement "may not have all the bells and whistles that you would have in a complaint, but I feel confident that we were able to craft a statement of facts which lays out the concept that this thing was illegal and created liability. So from that standpoint, I think the public knows that JPMorgan engaged in activity that we considered to be fraud."

The magnitude of the settlement, and the likelihood that it would create a model for other settlements with the Wall Street leviathans, had government officials patting themselves on the back, even though they agreed to cover up the most sordid details of Wagner's complaint. "Without a doubt, the conduct uncovered in this investigation helped sow the seeds of the mortgage meltdown," Holder said at the time the settlement was announced. "JPMorgan was not the only financial institution during this period to knowingly bundle toxic loans and sell them to unsuspecting investors, but that is no excuse for the firm's behavior."

Jamie was more guarded in his comments. In a conference call the day the settlement was announced, he remained uncharacteristically mum while Marianne Lake, the firm's CFO, led financial analysts through the details, including how $7 billion of the $13 billion fine would be tax-deductible. That's a nice perk if you can get it, one denied mere earthlings without access to the loftiest realms of government. Jamie occasionally interrupted Lake with a comment of his own, which prompted Mike Mayo, Wall Street's preeminent banking analyst, to ask Jamie about his aggressive efforts to spin the narrative his way. "How is it that JPMorgan got front and center with this issue? That it's the Department of Justice working out an agreement with JPMorgan when JPMorgan performed so well during the crisis, yet here's the one bank that's paying a $13 billion fine?"

Without missing a beat, Jamie replied: "Mike, you've got to ask [the questions], OK?"

"Some well-heeled clients might prefer your competitors over JPMorgan," Mayo said.

"That's why I'm richer than you," Jamie snapped.

Jamie was seething within. At a CEO summit conference sponsored by Microsoft in May the following year, he told a crowd of executives that he "had to control his rage" about the settlement. According to Cohan, the litigious executive dismissed by JPMorgan

258

Chase, Jamie's temper erupts whenever he is confronted by media coverage he is unable to control. In this case, *his* story was overshadowed by the Justice Department, which finally decided that it had to do *something* to appease the wrath of victimized investors, who would never be made whole in the wake of the meltdown and Great Depression ushered in by the massive Wall Street banks. Unfortunately, the settlement with the Justice Department also shows just how far the government is willing to go to avoid naming names, as well as to keep startling evidence of wrongdoing hidden from the view of the American people.

Needless to say, there are many people eager to claim a large dollop of credit for bringing Jamie and JPMorgan to heel, but virtually no one at the bank was willing to speak publicly about how it all happened in the first place. Jamie was chastened but hardly humbled. After all, why should he answer annoying questions when his board of directors responded to the $13 billion settlement by giving him a raise to $20 million in the aftermath of the lawsuit?

Chapter Twenty-six

The 2008 meltdown dwarfed anything I had experienced in four decades in the business. It truly did appear to be the end of the world as we know it, and while the share prices of solid companies had been hammered down to levels that made them screaming buys, it required nerves of steel to step in and buy them when everyone else was racing to get out at any price they could get. Ford, the only U.S. auto maker that said it didn't require any help from the government in order to survive, was languishing at less than $2 per share after trading as high as $32 in earlier years. It was irrational that investors would consider dumping their stocks at such rock bottom prices when they were only too happy to own them at fifteen times the value. Yet Ford was only one example of thousands of publicly traded stocks sporting unrealistically low valuations.

The carnage continued into the spring of 2009, when investors with strong stomachs realized that they were unlikely to see these buying opportunities again in their lifetimes. If the financial system was going to implode and take the global economy along with it, it hardly mattered if you bought a bushel of stocks of companies that were heading into bankruptcy, since we were all ruined anyway. It could be a replay of the riches-to-rags decade of the 1930s, when only the super-wealthy were spared the indignity of scrambling to put food on the table, or else it was a golden opportunity to ride the tide back up and fatten one's coffers over the next few years. Our financial wizards had learned a few things between the time of the Great Depression and the Great Recession of 2008, and they flooded the system with liquidity to keep it afloat. The result was a booming stock market commencing in early 2009, which saw share prices triple during the next half decade.

                    *   *   *

The deal between the government and JPMorgan Chase did not end the trail of woes for Jamie and his minions at the bank. He needed to do some housecleaning, and one of the first heads to roll was that of his long-standing consigliere Steve Black, who correctly assumed that at four years older than Jamie, he would be unlikely to succeed his boss as top dog at the beleaguered bank. The intrigue was hardly Shakespearean, where motives are convoluted and multilayered. It was a simple question of power and ambition. Black's departure was announced only a few months after his promotion to vice chairman, a well-compensated position that carried no real clout. At fifty-eight, Black was champing at the bit to run something of his own before it was too late, and Jamie had no intention of stepping aside—no more than Sandy did when Jamie was lean and hungry under his former boss's rule at the top of the heap.

"This wasn't something [Black] wanted or needed to do forever," said an executive close to both men. "He wants to run something."

Black was loyal to the end, a good soldier taking a bullet for his leader. "When the outside world puts an individual like [Jamie] on a pedestal," Black said, "and thinks that he's the only person at the company who has any ability, sure it can be a little frustrating. But that's not the way Jamie acts. It's not Jamie's fault."

Bill Winters also left a few months earlier, after Jamie replaced him with Jes Staley, an up-and-coming executive closer to Jamie's age.

The handwringing had only just begun as financial geniuses around the world analyzed precisely what had gone wrong and pondered how the global financial system would benefit from a "new paradigm," as they were quick to label it. Whenever analysts look back and agonize about how their boat got swamped in a major storm, they talk about the need for a new paradigm to keep them from getting shipwrecked in the future. They certainly had a lot to contemplate this time around. "We could be looking at a paradigm shift," said Frederic Mishkin, a former Federal Reserve governor. Well, paradigms are always shifting following a tumultuous event, so Mishkin's assessment was not off the mark.

The evolving consensus was that there simply were not enough houses to serve as collateral for all the derivatives that the big banks wanted to manufacture, so they leveraged themselves up to the eyeballs in order to float more debt than the market could bear. Then they used that debt as a kind of collateral to float even greater quantities of collateralized mortgage obligations. The banks also stretched their collateral by requiring smaller down payments on houses, from 20 percent to 5 percent, thereby freeing up large amounts of mortgage debt to back the derivatives—$95,000 on a $100,000 loan instead of a mere $80,000. And it wasn't just real estate that the banks used for collateral. They securitized hundreds of billions of dollars' worth of loans on credit card receivables, student loans, and corporate bonds—debt backed by other debt—in the form of exotic time bombs they called synthetic collateralized debt obligations.

And what was the new paradigm that the gurus were promoting? Why, JPMorgan Chase and the other banks should not be allowed to do it again—at least not to the extent they did in the past.

"The thing that keeps me awake at night is the thought of some rogue trader somewhere in the world doing something that affects the entire company," said Brian Rogers, chairman of T.

263

Rowe Price. The rogue trader never did rear his head at the Baltimore-based company, but a few did on Jamie's watch at JPMorgan Chase after the bloodbath of 2008. In April 2012, a little-known trader named Bruno Iksil in the institution's London office placed a series of wrong-way bets on a synthetic bond portfolio, creating huge losses for the firm. The incident became known as the "London Whale" scandal because of the location of the trader and the size of his losses.

"It's a complete tempest in a teapot," Jamie said, making a comment that would come back to haunt him when reports surfaced that the London Whale's activities had cost the firm more than $6 billion.

"I had been told a whole bunch of stuff that made me *think* it was a tempest in a teapot," Jamie said sheepishly in his latest effort at damage control. It was only after he analysed the positions himself that he realized the extent of the problem. "There was a moment of, I can't believe what we have," he admitted. For Jamie, who had boasted in the past of the bank's risk management and "fortress balance sheet," the blunder was particularly embarrassing. "I saw it all pass in front of my eyes. I saw the headlines, the investigations, the uproar, the breathlessness. 'Dimon Loses Luster,' 'Dimon in the Rough.' I told everyone, 'This is going to be bad, it's going to go on, and we can't get out of it. So put your jerseys on: We're going to wrestle this thing down and fix it.' "

"We made a terrible, egregious mistake," he told David Gregory on *Meet the Press*. Iksil's was the next head to roll, along with those of the people who were supposed to be supervising his trading activities. "We had to review thousands of e-mails, minutes of tapes," Jamie recounted. "We cleaned up the risk. It scared the daylights out of our people. We crossed the T's and dotted the I's and put in new rules, and we're fine." He hoped this would put the issue to rest.

But it didn't. The Senate Banking Committee demanded Jamie's presence in Washington to explain his bank's role in the London Whale scandal. "*That* I did not expect," he told the senators. Despite the negotiation with Holder, Jamie had long enjoyed favored son status in Washington. After his rescue of Bear Stearns in 2008, he was elevated to the level of American hero—or, at least, to the level of "America's Least-Hated Banker," as the *New York Times* put it. But he tested his standing with the federal regulators by objecting strenuously to what he called "regulatory overreach." He expressed particular disdain for portions of the Volcker rule, legislation that sought to limit banks' proprietary trading activities. "Paul Volcker, by his own admission, has said he doesn't understand capital markets," Jamie said. "Honestly, he has proven that to me."

Meanwhile, the media that had lionized Jamie a short while before began to smart at some of his condescending comments toward them. "You don't even make any money," he told one group of reporters, mockingly, reiterating a putdown he had leveled at Mike Mayo, because Mike wasn't as rich as Jamie was. Then again, precious few ink-stained wretches, who are mere mortals after all, are as rich as the reigning king of Wall Street.

In the wake of the London Whale's losses, Jamie's star began to lose its luster in the financial firmament. "The pedestal that [Dimon] so carefully constructed for himself is now vacant," Graydon Carter wrote in *Vanity Fair*. Occupy Wall Streeters attacked him unmercifully, demanding his head on a platter—or at least some jail time to pay for his extravagances at public expense. Representative Barney Frank and Senator Carl Levin went on television and declared that the staggering losses would have been prevented under, you guessed it, the same Volcker Rule that Jamie had denigrated.

"This was perfect for everyone who was pushing for more regulation," Jamie fumed. "We handed it to them on a silver platter. And then I made that stupid comment about a tempest in a teapot."

But he was more upset by the phrasing he used to describe the London Whale fiasco than he was by the incident itself. "It's such a large number," he allowed, "but if you put it in perspective a little bit, if you had a $100 million market-cap bank that made something like $3 million that quarter and lost $3 million, you wouldn't even talk about it. That's what this was. We didn't even lose money this quarter. We earned $5 billion. The analysts estimate us having a record year." That's why he's richer than you are.

"We're still pleading guilty to being stupid and dumb, though," one of Jamie's PR gurus interjected.

"It was the dumbest thing I have ever seen," Dimon conceded. "It was so complex, so large, so illiquid, so stupid. It didn't get the rigor that it should have entailed." He was reluctant to use Ina Drew, the woman who was in charge of Iksil, as his scapegoat—but he proved he was mortal by succumbing to the temptation. She had been with JPMorgan Chase for three decades and should have known better, and Dimon was being encouraged to fire her by others at the bank. "I felt terrible for her," Jamie said. "I said, 'Guys, that could be your mother. You want me to treat your mother that way?'" But Jamie accepted her resignation nonetheless, although it did not stop people from calling for his own.

"Did I ever consider resigning?" Jamie asked. "No!" Why should he go that far when he had just hung Mother Ina out to dry? "People and companies make mistakes. I guarantee we'll make a mistake next quarter. So what? Businesses make mistakes. Hopefully smaller, and fewer."

Jamie's critics sharpened their knives and flashed their teeth. Many blamed the Obama administration and the Justice Department under Holder for allowing the scandals to fester, one after another, without taking decisive action. Litigators Helen Davis Chaitman and Lance Gotthoffer wrote, "If you are a petty thief, you go to prison in a police van. But if you are a big-time crook, you to Greenwich every day in your limousine." The lawyers claimed that the London Whale fiasco was 100 percent the product of Jamie's management. Bruno Iksil, they contended, was "largely a victim of Dimon and the other sharks that swim at the highest water levels in JPMorgan's executive offices. Why didn't someone go to jail for this?" they demanded to know.

It was not as though the government was unaware of the outrageous activities going on at Jamie's bank. A Senate Report concluded that Jamie and others at Morgan made false statements on April 10, April 13, and May 10, 2012, which "misinformed investors, regulators, and the public about the nature, activities, and riskiness of the CIO's credit derivatives during the first quarter of 2012." The result was a paltry $921 million fine that JPMorgan Chase paid to U.S. and UK agencies with their shareholders' money; none of it came out of their own deep, well-tailored pockets. The only ones who were indicted for their roles in the scandal were Bruno Iksil's boss and a junior trader, bottom-feeders swimming way below the high-water-level sharks at JPMorgan Chase. But not even they did any jail time; as Spanish and French nationals, respectively, their countries refused to expedite them to stand trial in the U.S. and UK, a win-win for Jamie whose name would inevitably have been dragged into the mess as an unindicted co-conspirator.

*   *   *

Would that that were the end of the affair, but this hope proved to be wishful thinking. A new scandal was lurking on the periphery of Jamie's kingdom. Jamie no sooner put the London Whale incident partly behind him, when he was forced to disclose that JPMorgan Chase's records had been subpoenaed as part of the wide-ranging investigation into the bank's role in rigging LIBOR rates. LIBOR, the London Interbank Offered Rate, is somewhat akin to the U.S. fed funds rate, which is the rate at which banks lend short-term money to one another. Both rates determine to a great extent the rate that borrowers pay to finance student loans, and to buy cars, homes, and other items.

The banks in this scandal, including JPMorgan Chase, were accused of submitting false data to boost LIBOR and, therefore, the interest they charged to consumers. LIBOR was hardly an issue that Jamie wanted to be dealing with as all the other scandals sprouted like toxic weeds toward the far horizons, but there it was gob-smacking him in the face with the miasma of 2008, Bruno Iksil, and his problems with the government hovering over the landscape.

The rigging of LIBOR had actually occurred several years earlier, but it was only surfacing now as the authorities finally got around to doing their job and delving into the whole range of subversive activities engaged in by the banks. Officials at the British Bankers' Association had suspected as early as 2006 that all was not right about the data the banks were using to rig LIBOR, but they didn't act at the time because they weren't sure about the extent of the problem. It was only after the 2008 meltdown and the other scandals mushroomed throughout the global financial system that they decided to look more deeply into the situation. What they found was a systematic pattern of rate-rigging at dozens of major banks. Internal memos at Jamie's bank revealed that they were all aware that LIBOR was being set too high, but Morgan executives did "not want the BBA to correct this."

"It was implied that it is in the interest of most of the [banks] to set their contributed rates at a few points higher," wrote John

Ewan, the BBA official in charge of LIBOR. "This is because it makes their loan books a bit more profitable."

Chapter Twenty-seven

And then there was Sandy, Jamie's mentor turned rival, who appeared on CNBC's "Squawk Box" in July 2012 and dropped a bombshell that set the hosts, Becky Quick and Joe Kernan, vibrating in their chairs. "What we should probably do is go and split up investment banking from banking," Sandy said, almost impishly. "Have banks do something that's not going to risk the taxpayers' dollars, that's not too big to fail."

Becky was the first one off the blocks. "Did we just hear Sandy Weill advocate breaking up the model that he created?"

"It doesn't work anymore," Sandy said.

"This is breaking news," Becky said. A second later CNBC flashed a running headline across the bottom of the screen saying, "Sandy Weill Advocates Breaking up the Big Banks."

"There is such a feeling among people," Sandy continued nonchalantly, "among regulators, among the political system all over the world, against the banking system, and I don't think that's going to change so soon."

Sandy clearly reveled in his low-key performance, his timing nothing short of impeccable, secure in the knowledge that his incendiary statement would detonate like a drone strike in Jamie's lap, and also in the lap of Citigroup's current CEO Vikram Pandit. As recently as 2010, Sandy displayed a four-foot-wide portrait of himself in his office, etched with the words "The Shatterer of Glass-Steagall." But now that he was out of the business, a full-time philanthropist tending to his investments and favorite charities, his billions secure outside the reach of the prosecutors, he could afford to be magnanimous and beyond the fray. Jamie, however, was not in the least amused.

"There are huge benefits to size," Jamie responded when he was asked to comment on Sandy's broadside. "We bank Caterpillar in like forty countries. We can do a $20 billion bridge loan overnight for a company that's about to do a major acquisition. Size lets us build a $500 million data center that speeds up transactions and invest billions of dollars in products like ATMs and apps that allow your iPhone to deposit checks. We move $2 trillion a day, and you can see it by account, by company. These aren't, like, little things. And they accrue to the customer. That's what capitalism is. The whole world has become crazy. Businesses get attacked every time they do something."

There is no question that Jamie was feeling threatened by Sandy's remarks; the last thing he wanted was a return to Glass-Steagall. Jamie had already received several death threats since the Crash of 2008—as did the CEOs of financial firms that had nothing to do with the crisis, including Brian Rogers at T. Rowe Price—and there was Sandy, the major architect of the too-big-to-fail model, positioning himself as the knight in shining armor leading the charge to clean up the mess.

"Everyone is talking about the culture, the culture, and all that, and it's just not true," said Jamie. "Most bankers are decent, honorable people. We're wrapped up in all this crap right now. We made a mistake. We're sorry. It doesn't detract from all the good things we've done. I am not responsible for the financial crisis. I hate to tell you. We were a port of safety in the storm. I find it unbelievable that that is the general theme—that you have to walk in a room and act like you are responsible for things you are not responsible for."

A port in the storm that Jamie and his geniuses at JPMorgan Chase were largely responsible for creating, he failed to add. Did he have any regrets about what he had done? Apparently not. "I'm an outspoken defender of the truth," he said. "Everyone is afraid of retaliation and retribution. We recently had an event with a hundred small bankers here, and 85 percent of them said they can't challenge the regulation because of the potential retribution. That's a terrible thing. Okay? This is not the Soviet Union. This is the United States of America. That's what I remember. Guess what. "It's a *free. Fucking. Country.*"

Jamie did admit that his oversight could have been better. Congress called him down to Washington several times during an ongoing investigation into the role of the big banks, diminishing his luster and destroying his chance to become President Obama's new Treasury Secretary, which he was being considered for before the London Whale and LIBOR scandals made the headlines.

Through it all, Jamie remained adamant in his defense of his heavily subsidized industry. "I don't buy this thing that our industry is responsible for all the ills of the world," he told a group of college students. "We have great people at JPMorgan Chase. We operate with a lot of rigor. Our clients are happy with us. Sure, we make mistakes, like we have got this Whale thing. Businesses make mistakes. So we've got to clean them up, learn from them, and get better. And I want you to know the London Whale issue is dead. The Whale has been harpooned! Desiccated! Cremated! I am going to bury its ashes all over." No one ever faulted Jamie for a lack of chutzpah.

Nor did Jamie back down in the face of a tongue-lashing he received from Senator Elizabeth Warren of Massachusetts, a consumer advocate who was elected in 2012. During a meeting in her office in 2013. Warren revealed in her book, *A Fighting Chance*, that their meeting became contentious when Jamie complained that the banks, including his, were being overregulated. "I couldn't believe he was complaining about regulatory restraints less than a year after his bank had lost billions in the infamous London Whale high-risk trading episode," she said. "I thought the banks were still taking on too much risk and that they seemed to believe the taxpayers would bail them out, again, if something went wrong."

Jamie started to shout at her, raising his voice to make his point that his bank was being constrained in its operations. "By this point I was furious," Warren said. "Dodd-Frank had created default provisions that would automatically go into effect, and his bank was almost certainly not in compliance with those rules. I told him that if that happened, 'I think you guys are breaking the law.'" She was referring to the the Dodd-Frank Reform Act passed in 2010, which was the most comprehensive financial reform since the Glass-Steagall Act. Dodd-Frank was a bit of a sprawling mess, but it served as an interim measure for those fighting to reinstate a latter-day version of the original 1933 Glass-Steagall restrictions.

When Warren told Jamie that his bank might be breaking the law, he sat back in his chair and grew quiet for a moment. Incredibly, he replied after a long pause, "So hit me with a fine. We can afford it."

Warren was only too happy to do just that. She arranged to have JPMorgan Chase socked again with another fine, paid for naturally enough by the banks' shareholders. At that point, Morgan had already paid $20 billion in legal fees to the government during the years since the crisis, enough to pay the New York Yankees' expenses for the next twenty years. JPMorgan Chase was even drawn into the Bernie Madoff scandal, disgorging $1.7 billion for failing to alert authorities about its former client's decades-long Ponzi scheme. Knowing that Madoff was a fraud, JPMorgan Chase rid itself of its $275 million exposure to Madoff shortly before he was arrested in December 2008, which amounted to insider trading since the news had not yet been made public.

When she was asked whether or not Jamie should be replaced as a result of these ongoing issues, Warren said, "Look, the real question is, do you have somebody who has shown they understand there were problems in the past and that they have a different plan going forward? What JPMorgan Chase and the other large financial institutions have done is they have continued to get bigger and bigger and load up more and more on risk. I'm waiting for him to demonstrate that understanding. And he's had a long, long time."

Many financial executives came to Jamie's defense and argued that he should be allowed to keep both of his titles as chairman and CEO of JPMorgan Chase after such an overall exemplary career. But others outside the industry thought he should step down and be held personally accountable for role in the financial Armageddon of 2008. There was little question that Jamie's reputation as an executive who could do no wrong was seriously tarnished.

In 2014, the federal regulators finally got around to acknowledging that the country's major banks were still too large to fail six years after the crisis, and they informed the banks that if they failed to downsize on their own, the government would do it for them. Daniel Tarullo, the Federal Reserve governor in charge of regulatory policies, imposed capital requirements on the banks as much as 2.5 percentage points higher than the 8 percent to 9.5 percent of assets required by Basel III guidelines. But even this was so much smoke and mirrors, since the restraints would not go into effect until 2018, a full ten years after the last financial crisis. Tarullo rattled his saber with a lot of fanfare and bombastic rhetoric, stating that "policymakers must devote significant attention to the potential threat to financial stability posed by our most systemic financial firms."

The tough talk was little more than that, hardly the kind of sweeping overhaul required to address what Ben Bernanke called "the worst financial crisis in global history, including the Great Depression." There was a lot of talk about the steps being taking to avert a possible new crisis, urging the big banks to start "getting smaller," but the exhortations fell on deaf ears. The major financial institutions were still operating in too many diverse spheres, taking on too much risk, and doing so with impunity since they knew that the federal government was there to back them up again should recent history repeat itself. The banks and their CEOs knew better than anyone else what privatizing profits and socializing losses really meant. The banks reaped the rewards while the taxpayers would continue to cover their losses.

*   *   *

In the summer of 2014, Jamie faced a different crisis entirely when he announced that he had throat cancer and would be treated with radiation and chemotherapy at New York's Memorial Sloan Kettering Hospital. He had been a heavy cigarette smoker when he was younger and had kicked the habit a decade earlier, but the damage had already been done. He said he would curtail his travel but would maintain day-to-day control over operations at JPMorgan Chase. In a memo to the bank's employees, Jamie said he would begin eight weeks of chemotherapy and radiation treatment at Memorial Sloan Kettering Cancer Center.

"The good news is that the prognosis from my doctors is excellent," he wrote, "the cancer was caught quickly, and my condition is curable. Following thorough tests that included a CAT scan, PET scan and a biopsy, the cancer is confined to the original site and the adjacent lymph nodes on the right side of my neck. Importantly, there is no evidence of cancer elsewhere in my body." Jamie's disease was the variety caused by the HPV virus, or the human papillomavirus strain.

"It wouldn't be unusual," said Doctor Eric Genden, chief of head and neck oncology at Mount Sinai. "This is an epidemic." In 2008, the last year for which data are available, the Centers for Disease Control & Prevention estimated that 2,370 women and 9,356 men developed HPV-caused head and neck cancer, about a third of the cases of head and neck cancer that year. However, Genden added that 70 percent to 90 percent of these cases worldwide have been caused by HPV; the American Cancer Society estimated that in 2015, there could be more than forty-two thousand cases of head and neck cancer in the U.S.

Traditionally, those contracting throat cancer have been older men who smoked and drank heavily, as alcohol and tobacco damage the cells in the throat, triggering the disease. But mostly younger men between thirty-five and sixty-five develop the HPV strain. The main point is that younger CEOs at the peak of their careers like Jamie are most susceptible, and their numbers are increasing.

If there is any good news where cancer is concerned, it is that HPV-caused throat cancer is less deadly and more curable than the old type resulting from chronic tobacco use and drinking. When Sandy heard the news, he wished Jamie well and said he would welcome a call from him. You'd think that Jamie would have been the one expecting a call from his former mentor. In the end, neither of them picked up the phone to initiate the contact, and the two of them have not spoken or resolved the differences that separated them in 1999. A year later, Jamie said he was in remission, but he admitted that there was a 30 percent chance the cancer would reoccur. Optimist that he was, the statistics also indicated that there was a 70 percent chance it would not return at all.

Chapter Twenty-eight

While Jamie underwent treatment, the problems continued to mount at the bank. JPMorgan Chase and a consortium of other major institutions, including UBS, Citigroup, HSBC, and the Royal Bank of Scotland, were fined an aggregate of $4.25 billion for manipulating currency rates in November 2014, an amount that was little more than pocket lint for such mammoth banks. It was just the cost of doing business, which in this case constituted rigging currency exchange rates in a way that enabled them to squeeze additional profits out of their trading partners.

Around the same time, JPMorgan Chase came under siege itself from cyber-attackers, who were able to breach the bank's firewalls and compromise the accounts of seventy-six million households and seven million small businesses. It was one of the largest private-sector breaches ever, outside the realm of the IRS and other government agencies, which were totally unequipped to safeguard the most sensitive information about government employees and millions of taxpayers. Target, Home Depot, and a host of other retailers had already been hacked, exposing the credit card information and social security numbers, in some cases, of more than a hundred thousand shoppers. And now the U.S.'s premier bank had also been penetrated on Jamie's watch, an apparently impregnable fortress that proved to be as vulnerable to cyber terrorists as the shaky defenses of the federal government.

Jamie acknowledged the digital threat in a letter to shareholders. "We're making good progress on these and other efforts," he wrote, "but cyberattacks are growing every day in strength and velocity across the globe." The battle is "continual and likely never-ending," he added. BBF&T, where I worked until August 2015, had been doubling down on its own efforts to tighten security, as was the case with virtually every financial institution in the U.S. and abroad. In 2015, the head of the CIA fell victim to

279

cyberattacks on his personal email account by a high school student. And a secret service agent I spoke to told me that his agency's computers were routinely hacked, and worst of all, "no one in the government had the foggiest notion of what to do about it." Before this, banks were considered to be safe from online assaults because of the huge investments they had made in top-level defenses. Most breaches had involved the theft of ID numbers at ATM kiosks, but the Morgan breach chilled investors with the fear that their personal accounts were exposed to anyone with sophisticated computer skills.

"There is probably no database that cybercriminals cannot compromise," said prosecutor Lisa Madigan.

*   *   *

While Jamie was reeling from the aftereffects of the data breach, the government leveled tighter capital requirements against the largest banks, with JPMorgan Chase feeling the tightest pinch of all. Federal Reserve Chairman Stanley Fischer announced that Jamie's bank had to pony up an additional $21 billion to comply with the latest guidelines, which were clearly launched to force the biggest banks to shrink in size. JPMorgan Chase and the other financial behemoths could either raise additional capital to meet the new benchmarks, an expensive proposition, or they could reduce their operations to fit the size of their existing capital on hand.

"This rule would encourage such firms to reduce their systemic footprint and lessen the threat that their failure could pose to overall financial stability," said Fed Chairwoman Janet Yellen.

"Banks are under assault," Jamie declared in January 2015. He resisted calls to break up his bank, when Goldman Sachs analyst Richard Ramsden suggested that JPMorgan Chase would be more efficient if it split itself into four separate entities: consumer banking; business banking; investment banking; and wealth and asset management. The bank was unmanageable, said Ramsden, with a market capitalization of $220 billion, $2.57 trillion in total assets, and operations in more than sixty countries, making it the U.S.'s largest bank.

"A lot of people just look at size, and it scares them," Jamie said. "But that isn't the determinant. The synergies are huge, both expense and revenues. The unscrambling would be extraordinarily complex, in debt, in systems, in technology, and people." In effect, he was telling the investment world to drink more Kool-Aid.

But Jamie was going to get smaller—or at least leaner—whether he liked it or not. "We still want that preeminent position," he said, "and we're not going to give that up for anyone. We're not a conglomerate of unrelated businesses." But he did acknowledge that there was a lot JPMorgan Chase could do to rein in expenses. "It's our job to get them down," he conceded. He agreed to shed the bank of $100 billion in unprofitable deposits and to shut down three hundred branch offices, about 5 percent of the total, by the end of 2016. Of course that meant that many bank tellers would end up on the unemployment lines, but they were gradually being replaced by ATMs and electronic banking operations in any event. Jamie's move to whittle down the bank to some degree would merely accelerate the inevitable. "If the regulators want more, we can do that," Jamie said.

The regulators definitely wanted more. "We have substantially reduced the amount of risk they can take," said former Treasury secretary Timothy Geithner. "We've cut the profitability of banking roughly in half."

Salaries and bonuses would have to be trimmed at Morgan and the other gargantuan banks, but mainly for the lower-level employees. Jamie's compensation package would scarcely be affected. His total take in 2014 came to $27.5 million. Aside from Geithner, other government officials maintained that not enough was being done. Sheila Bair, former Chairwoman of the Federal Deposit Insurance Corporation, said that the big banks were only making changes around the periphery. But at least they were taking a step in the right direction. "It's not a bad thing for the banks to have to deal with that sort of discipline," she said. The main problem was that micromanaging the banks was a risky conundrum, since society can't function without them, and the banks know that better than anyone else.

Meanwhile, the victims of the banks' excesses, average middle-class investors, were still waiting for someone to be held accountable seven years after their portfolios were bled dry, while the mammoth institutions that triggered the wreckage suffered little more than a proverbial slap on the wrist for their crimes. The lawyers got rich from a series of class action lawsuits that netted some investors little more than chicken feed, at the same time that the largest financial institutions in the country collectively pocketed more than $4 trillion to keep them afloat in the aftermath of the great financial tsunami. Not even felony indictments against JPMorgan Chase, Barclays, Citigroup, and the Royal Bank of Scotland, to which they all pled guilty, resulted in punitive action against the top executives at those banks. They paid their fines out of shareholders' equity and continued to complain about the new regulations that stifled their activities.

Mike Mayo, the bumptious, indefatigable banking analyst who had been a constant thorn in Jamie's side, criticized Jamie for berating shareholders who relied on outside advice from hedge funds, some of which advocated the breakup of the biggest banks. "If you do that you are just irresponsible," Jamie said at a news conference. "I am sorry. And you probably aren't a very good investor either. I know some of you here do it because you are lazy."

Mayo said that Jamie's claims were "ludicrous. If anything, these advisory firms aren't tough enough."

Jamie need not have worried about such trivialities though. In June 2015 he added a new title to his name: billionaire. *Bloomberg* estimated his net worth at $1.1 billion, almost half of it in JPMorgan Chase stock. His financial godfather Sandy was the only other mainstream banker to ascend to that exalted rank—and he earned that distinction like most of the other billionaires who populated the financial universe, hedge fund dynamos or the founders of investment firms, like Steve Schwarzman with the Blackstone Group, and Sandy himself with his patchwork colossus. "The odds are much, much lower for a bank CEO becoming a billionaire than a guy going to a hedge fund or private equity," said Professor Roy Smith at the NYU Stern School of Business. "The real lucre in this business has always been on the transactional side. The CEOs of Wall Street have to deal with litigation, regulation, and the relatively short tenures you have at the top of the pile."

*　　*　　*

Jamie's tenure was not about to end anytime soon, as long as his health held up. At the age of fifty-nine, with deep reserves of fire and energy burning in his gut, it would take a resurgence of his throat cancer or some other debilitating ailment to force him out of the game before he was ready to go. Best of all, his perch atop the largest bank in the financial universe earned him the right to pontificate about any subject that crossed his mind, with the expectation that legions of investors out there were likely to perk up their ears and take notice. And the Gospel According to Jamie was not exactly short on quotable quotes.

"America looks pretty damn good," Jamie said in 2015. "The more that employment is growing and companies are growing, you know, rates going up would be OK. It'll be volatile, it'll be a little scary, but it'll be OK. The fundamental economy is growing."

He avowed that health care companies will continue to grow and save lives, including his own. "I'm actually doing fine. I never stopped working, but I'm mostly back to full health, back to working full time."

Leading the nation's largest bank is the best contribution he can make to the country, he avowed. JPMorgan Chase hired eight thousand veterans and provided financial support for Detroit. "If I do a good job here, I can help people with their careers. We help consumers and big businesses. We help countries and banks, central banks, governments, sovereign wealth funds, and we're hugely charitable," he said.

The outlook for U.S. businesses is looking brighter. He cited job growth, a largely balanced housing market, and higher consumer confidence. He said the most significant headwind facing the American economy is coming from overseas, with ongoing struggles in the Eurozone as peripheral members like Greece and a few others struggle for survival.

Regarding cybersecurity, Jamie assured his bank's clients that they are "completely safe." The bank typically spends $250 million a year on cybersecurity, and Jamie promised to easily double that amount during the next two years. In 2015, JP Morgan Chase found itself fending off about three hundred thousand attacks a day on its security systems. "It's incumbent upon all of us, merchants, banks, retailers, everyone, to come up with a better system," he said, noting that banks pay the price for credit-card breaches that occur elsewhere.

Sounding more like a candidate for a job with the next administration than a bank CEO, Jamie offered his thoughts on the pressing public policy issues of the day. Five major concerns needed to be addressed to keep America competitive in the long term, and he said that he discussed all of them in detail with the White House. The first was corporate taxes and tax reform: "Simplify it, broaden out the base, reduce it, and become more competitive globally." Immigration reform: "Most Democrats and Republicans I know support immigration reform. They may differ on pieces of it." That probably came as a bit of a surprise to Republicans who supported Donald Trump during his quixotic run for the presidency in 2015. The third key issue was education: "Think of secondary education the most, where we're failing a lot of kids in inner-city schools." Fourth was infrastructure: "Most people agree that we don't do good infrastructure planning for roads, bridges, tunnels, schools, and hospitals. We need to do that at the city, state, and federal government level." And finally, trade: "Transatlantic and transpacific trade agreements would be a great boon to the American economy and the global economy."

Jamie downplayed expectations that the Republican-controlled Congress will be less hostile toward banks. "There's a lot of hostility toward banks still that comes out of the population, and even some Republicans," Jamie said. "What I always hope for is a kind of collaboration and working together to come up with a better outcome." JP Morgan Chase, of course, was not the cause of the issues that ignited the 2008 financial crisis, he reiterated for the umpteenth time. "JPMorgan is a very good franchise," he noted. "And the way you should look at a franchise, a business, is from the standpoint of the customers. We are among the most successful global investment banks, most successful global asset managers, and, in the United States, one of the most successful retail and commercial bankers. We do a great job for customers. We are serving what you call SMEs—small businesses, private companies. They're not the largest companies in the world, but think of the next, the Fortune 1,000. Again, it's been very steady. It's done nothing but grow for years. We've accommodated the new rules and regulations. We've served our clients and had quite good returns."

And there was more. He reserved his most serious zingers for Dodd-Frank, which he viewed as a precursor for a return to Glass-Steagall. "Dodd-Frank is two thousand pages long. It covers thousands of rules, regulations, interpretations, and things like that. I've always been a believer in good regulation. And good regulation should be conducive to business and to customer protection. I completely agree with the concept that American citizens shouldn't expect that a failure of a bank would cost them money, or that it would hurt the economy. Dodd-Frank and independent actions of banks go a long way in terms of progress on capital, liquidity, transparency. There are parts that I don't agree with. But, in total, it is what it is. It's not going to change at this point. I do believe that some of these regulations made the markets more volatile, and it remains to be seen how bad that can be."

Regarding President Obama, "I know the president. I like him and respect him. That does not mean I agree with all of our government's policies, whether they come from Democrats or Republicans. I think if we had another set of policies for—not the crisis years, but after that—that we might be growing faster. But we didn't. And some of that was the Republicans' fault by the way. We had a lot of gridlock on a lot of issues. But, the American system is pretty resilient. It did correct faster than others. I'm a really big believer that good policy is really important. So I agree with people who say we want more income equality, we want more consumer protection, and we want sounder banks. I agree with all that. Then the question is how do you do it so that it actually works that way? And that takes analysis, and sometimes collaboration between government and business, to understand how that works."

Jamie worked both sides of the aisle, hedging his bets depending on who was elected president in 2016 and which party ruled the legislative branch. "Wall Street gives money to both because they want to be on the good side of whoever becomes president," he admitted. "But again, on Wall Street, there is no 'Wall Street'; there are individuals. So we have a lot of people who are Republicans, a lot of people who are Democrats, and it's not just because of business reasons. I am still a Democrat. The main reason is because I don't like the Republican stance on some social values. Not that I disagree with all of them. I just don't think they have a right to impose it upon other people. I've been public about that. I think the Republicans have really thoughtful financial policies, and I'm more in the middle on taxation. I don't mind paying higher taxes, because I've done quite well and I'm blessed to live in this country. But I do want the tax system to be efficient and be conducive to growth, which it is not."

As 2015 wound to a close, Jamie occupied the catbird seat atop the U.S. financial system, which exercised a great deal of leverage over the global economy. The big question now is what will trigger the next crash. We know one is coming. Jamie himself says it is something that happens every seven years or so. But the handwriting was on the wall as a mini-meltdown plagued the stock market at the beginning of 2016. Neel Kashkari, the President of the Federal Reserve Bank of Minneapolis, hardly someone who could be labeled a bomb-thrower, echoed left-wing Senator Bernie Sanders in his own call for the big banks to be broken up. St. Louis Fed President Jim Bullard backed up Kashkari by stating on CNBC's "Squawk Box" on February 25, 2016, that the nation's megabanks needed to be split up like the old AT&T monopoly in order to foster innovation at the intersection of financial services and information technology.

With powerful forces on both ends of the political spectrum saying the time has come to reintroduce a modern version of Glass-Steagall, it appears to be just a question of time before a breakup occurs. We don't know yet exactly what Jamie's role will be when it comes about. The sad fact is that ordinary people will be hurt by the next crisis far more than the Jamies and Sandys of the world. They always are. That's one truism that's not going to change anytime soon. You can bank on it.

ACKNOWLEDGEMENTS

In retrospect, my forty-year career in the financial services industry served as an extended research project for this book. From the time I started with Merrill Lynch in 1975 and ended with BBF&T, my path crossed those of many of the key players who populate this narrative. Most of them are fine, dedicated professionals, who put the interests of their clients ahead of their own.

But too many players in this industry are interested in enriching themselves and their firms at the expense of the general public. The prime driver in their lives is excessive greed, which they indulge in freely knowing that their losses, when they stumble, will be subsidized by their cronies in government. The federal government has encouraged their outrageous behavior by passing legislation designed to further its own misguided policies, which led to the Great Recession of 2008, and by overturning the Glass-Steagall Act, which limited the operations of our mammoth financial institutions for sixty-six years. The greatest victims of all in this dangerous charade are the American taxpayers who end up footing the bill for wealthy financial executives who take excessive risks that threaten the global economy. Such was the case in the years leading up to the 2008 meltdown, and these conditions persist today despite the efforts of a few policymakers to rein in the destructive risks taken by our largest financial institutions, which undermine the wellbeing of middle class investors. I would like to thank the good people in the industry, with whom I have worked with or covered over the years, for the lessons and insights I picked up while I was learning the business.

I would also like to thank my dedicated research team at Brickwork India, who performed a lot of the legwork for me throughout the course of my writing this book. Several books were also helpful to me in providing valuable background material. They include *Too Big to Fail* by Andrew Ross Sorkin; *King of Capital* by Amy Stone and Mike Brewster; *Last Man Standing* by Duff McDonald; *The House of Dimon* by Patricia Crisafulli; *Fool's Gold* by Gillian Tett; *The Real Deal* by Sandy Weill; *The Death of Money* by James Rickards; *The Greatest Trade Ever* by Gregory Zuckerman; *The Shifts and the Shocks* by Martin Wolf; *The Seven Sins of Wall Street* by Bob Ivry; *All the Presidents' Bankers* by Nomi Prins; *The House of Morgan* by Ron Chernow; *Meltdown* by Thomas E. Woods Jr.; *The Courage to Act* by Ben Bernanke; *House of Cards* by William D. Cohan; *Tearing Down the Walls* by Monica Langley; *Den of Thieves* by James B. Stewart; *Liar's Poker* and *Flash Boys*, both by Michael Lewis.

Many thanks also to my wife, who has put up with my compulsive writing schedule for fifty years. I think she's gotten used to it by now.

ABOUT THE AUTHOR

Paul Marano is the pseudonym for a best-selling American author.